Marketing Mastery Guide

David L. Kurtz
Seattle University

Louis E. Boone
University of Central Florida

The Dryden Press
Hinsdale, Illinois

CONTENTS

PART I

GETTING MORE OUT OF MARKETING*

DEVELOP USEFUL HABITS

If someone mentions "good study habits," what does that mean to you? How would you explain to another student what good study habits are? And, in contrast, how would you describe poor study habits?

Ask several other students to describe good study habits and poor study habits to you. Find out what their attitudes are. Each person will have different views but the discussions will help you clarify your own attitudes.

The idea behind our emphasis on habits is simply this - study habits either help you or handicap you. Those students who get the most out of school generally agree that the benefits you gain from good study habits make it worth the effort to acquire them.

Several centuries ago Benjamin Franklin discovered that developing new habits was the key to improving his life. When he was in his twenties he decided to improve himself by acquiring good qualities of character. But his first efforts at self-improvement failed. He learned that "habit takes advantage of inattention."

So Franklin developed a realistic and practical plan to acquire useful habits. He reasoned that developing one desirable habit at a time was the best approach. He kept a daily record in a notebook to objectively observe his progress. His approach was to work on one habit at a time for one week at a time. The plan worked well. He gradually acquired the habits he knew would benefit him.

* This section is adapted from Al Siebert and Timothy L. Walter, Student Manual to accompany Understanding Human Behavior (New York: Holt, Rinehart & Winston, 1980), pp. 3-28. Reprinted by permission of Holt, Rinehart & Winston.

Throughout Part I we list many study habits which will help you get more out of school. It might take some effort for you to put these suggestions into practice. You may have to change old habits. It isn't easy to develop new habits, but once you become comfortable with these new habits, studying will take less effort. As William James said, "Habit simplifies movements required to achieve a given result, makes them more accurate, and diminishes fatigue." Good study habits will help you learn more and get a better education.

To get the most out of your time in school start thinking about this question...What study habits would I like to have a year from now? Keep this question in the back of your mind as you read through Part I. Then at the end of Part I you will find a "Learning Habits Checklist." The checklist will help you establish a plan to improve your study habits.

CHOOSE SOME GOALS

When you were a child you may have been asked, "What do you want to be when you grow up?" If you said "doctor," "airline pilot," "teacher," or something socially acceptable, then people were pleased. But what you told them was probably just part of a game you had to play.

The fact is that most students do not know what they want to be. Students are waiting to see where life will take them and are curious about how things will turn out. When students declare an area of study such as management or marketing as a major it is often because the school requires them to declare something at registration time. This situation helps to explain why the motivation to study is low in some students. A goal that is forced on you is not as motivating as a goal that is self-chosen.

The key to making it through college and learning something useful is to choose for yourself some goals that motivate you. Anything can be a goal. It may be to understand accounting, to learn about computers, to figure out how electricity works, to become an advertising executive, to understand why marketing is important to business and government, or to find out what causes nations to fight one another.

If you have nothing specific in mind then choose exploring as your purpose. Take a course to find out which subjects and activities appeal to you the most.

One way to choose motivating goals is to think ahead to the time when you will be out of college on your own. What knowledge, skill, or ability can you acquire for which people will pay? What would you enjoy doing that would be of value to others? What interests, hobbies, or talents do you have now that could be turned into a worthwhile occupation?

If you don't have clear goals and can't think of any that

make you feel excited about your future, see what your college's counseling center has to offer. There are tests you can take and trained counselors to help you explore career opportunities.

BE RESPONSIBLE FOR YOURSELF

Your success in school is your responsibility. It is not the responsibility of instructors, parents, friends, classmates, or administrators. Your teachers will present ideas and information, but whether or not you learn anything is mostly up to you.

Many students have been conditioned by magazines, television, and movies to be passive. They expect to be entertained by the textbook or the instructor. The only writings and speakers they pay attention to are those that capture and hold their attention. If an instructor teaches in a boring way, students are turned off. Students seem to expect teachers to compete for their attention as professional entertainers do.

A student who feels responsible for getting something out of classes is active. He or she makes an effort to draw useful ideas from every instructor and is curious about what textbooks have to offer.

Remember that the best investment you will ever make is in yourself. You may lose your job or money, but no one can take your education away from you.

USE PSYCHOLOGY ON YOURSELF

Once you have chosen some goals for yourself and have accepted responsibility for your own learning, you've made a big step forward. You discover you are in charge of your mind, your life, and your future. With this sense of responsibility comes the realization that you can start using psychology on yourself. You can purposefully use psychological principles of cause and effect to influence your own development and learning. For example, if you daydream in class and look around a lot, you can help yourself pay closer attention by sitting in front - just as you would want to do at a concert or a football game. If you are a slow reader, you can take a reading-improvement course (most of them are free). If you waste a lot of time, you can begin associating with better students so that their habits will influence you. If you fall asleep easily, don't study sitting in a soft lounge chair or lying in bed.

MAKING STUDYING EASIER

Studying is not the same as reading Cosmopolitan or the Wall Street Journal, and reading a textbook is not the same as reading a novel. There can be a big difference between reading what interests you and reading an assignment. Most textbooks are not

3

written to entertain you. You can't get away with reading only the parts that interest you. When it comes to studying, you must provide some of the motivation. Studying can be fun, but sometimes it is very hard work - as hard as physical labor.

Some students rely on will power to make themselves study. They grind away at their books week after week. But few students can make it through the school year on will power alone. They run out of energy. They fall into a state of helplessness in which they may spend most of their time watching television or lying around. They feel bewildered. You hear statements like "I know I'm going to flunk if I don't study, but I can't even make myself open a book."

Once this condition develops, it is difficult to cure, so the best approach is to prevent it. And that is what this section is all about: how to study with less effort while learning more.

SET UP YOUR SCHEDULE

One of the greatest aids to any student is a study schedule. Start by purchasing a monthly calendar with blank spaces. Fill in exam dates and dates when papers and projects are due. Marking exam times helps to keep you aware of what your studying is leading to. Next, fill in concerts, shows, meetings, trips, and so on.

Now you are ready to make up a weekly schedule of your classes and the hours you plan to study. A weekly schedule gives you a clear picture of what you are doing with your time. It helps you to spot an extra hour or two during the day for studying so you can have more free evenings to do what you want.

The steps for effective scheduling:

1. Establish a clear and reasonable schedule, one that you can live with.

2. Budget time to prepare for each class and all exams.

3. Study course notes as soon as possible after each class period, rather than waiting until a week before the exam.

4. Give difficult subjects preferred times with the fewest possible interruptions and disturbances.

5. Reserve time for leisure activities.

6. Stick to your schedule, and reward yourself for having achieved your study goals in the alloted time.

WEEKLY STUDY SCHEDULE

	Monday	Tuesday	Wednesday	Thursday	Friday	Saturday	Sunday
7-8							
8-9							
9-10							
10-11							
11-12							
12-1							
1-2							
2-3							
3-4							
4-5							
5-6							
6-7							
7-8							
8-9							
9-10							
10-11							
11-12							

FIGURE 1. Weekly schedule.

A schedule can have a motivating effect. Knowing that you have a hour on Thursday morning reserved for studying, you will be mentally prepared to spend that hour studying.

Warning: Do not allow yourself to study too much. Schedule time for the other things that you want to do, and stick to your schedule. Many students become so involved in their studying when they first start using the principles in this book that they keep right on studying through their scheduled breaks. Don't let yourself do this. When you reach the scheduled time to stop and go get some exercise, then do it! Make yourself stop studying!

The weekly schedule blank has been reproduced in Figure 1 so that you can make copies of it and post them in your room. But don't fill one out right now - we have more to say about study periods. First, we want you to look over your room.

ELIMINATE DISTRACTIONS

VISUAL DISTRACTIONS

Beverly is like most students. She has created a comfy nest for herself in her room. It includes posters, ribbons, signs, photographs, letters, mugs with pencils, an old bottle, hats, high school yearbooks, and several rocks. All these things have special meaning for her.

And that's the trouble. When she is studying, her mind is easily distracted from her textbook. The rock she sees from the corner of her eye reminds her of a weekend at the beach with a special person. The next thing she knows she has spent thirty minutes daydreaming. Posters, mugs, and other items are nice to have around. But if you study at your desk, keep it cleared off. Some students carry this principle too far. Their rooms look like monastic cells with nothing but bare walls and one small light on each desk.

To reduce eyestrain, your room should be well lit, with the main light source off to one side. A light directly behind or in front of you will be reflected from the glossy pages of your text- books. This constant glare tires your eyes more quickly than indirect lighting. If you can't shift the lamp, shift your desk. Place the desk so that no portion of the bulb shines directly into your eyes. A strong light source pulls your eye toward it. The constant strain of trying to avoid looking at the light causes eye fatigue.

If you study at home, arrange a well-lit place free from visual distractions.

AUDITORY DISTRACTIONS

"Quiet hours" rarely work as well as the rule makers hope. Distracting sounds still interrupt studying. Doors slam, phones ring, horns honk, planes fly over, and people move around. In fact, the quieter the study area, the more distracting these sounds become.

Steady background sounds mask distracting noises. Play your radio or stereo softly while you study to create a steady background of "noise" to mask occasional sounds. Experiment with stations or records until you find what works best for you. F.M. radio stations playing instrumental music are usually best. Talk shows and fast-talking disc jockeys are usually worse for concentration than nothing at all. Some women say that turning on their hair dryers helps them to study, and one student reported that he turns his radio to a place where there is no program - the static keeps him from being distrated.

Don't try to study with the television on. If you want to watch a program, then watch it, but don't try to avoid feeling guilty by having your book open to read during commercials. Studying with your television on is academic suicide. Use television time as a reward. After you've completed a successful study period, say to yourself, "I've earned a reward; I'll watch television."

TERRITORIAL DISTRACTIONS

"Mary! Let's go over to the law library to study."
"Good idea, Ann! I might see that guy I met in the student union last week!"
Some students study in the library to escape from their rooms. It's a good idea, even when no library reading must be done, because the library atmosphere lends itself to studying.

Some students, however, use library time for combined advertising and scouting trips. The purpose is not to study but to find a date. There's nothing wrong with this notion; it's just that a student who goes to the library for this reason should not be surprised if little studying is done.

The problem is that, whenever we enter a new territory, our senses are drawn to the environment. We automatically scan new surroundings. We check the walls, floor, and ceiling. We look at the lights, decorations, and furnishings. We look at the people, wonder about certain sounds, and spend time adjusting to the feeling of a new chair. Every time you go to a new place to study, you check out the surroundings before you settle down to work. To improve your studying efficiency, pick one spot and always try to study there. Studying in the same spot will shorten your warm-up time, and allow you to concentrate better.

STUDYING AT HOME

If you live alone, you can control distractions quite well. If you live with others, some special steps may be necessary. Especially for the re-entering student the student who has been away from school and is now coming back.

The family may have many habits and attitudes that interfere with good studying. Someone walks in the door and immediately turns the TV set on. If you ask for quiet the person says, "I'll keep it low."

Another person walks in and wants to talk, or wants dinner cooked, or needs to be driven to a friend's house.

Whatever the interference is, first ask your family for what you want. Think about what is reasonable and possible. Then ask for it. You may be surprised at how understanding and supportive your family can be. Be sure to express your appreciation and let your family share in your progress.

If you have a family member who is not cooperative, develop a plan for yourself so that you can study and do your course work. Avoid feeling victimized. Instead, come up with a creative plan which will let you continue getting the education you want.

ACCEPT YOUR HUMANNESS

CONCENTRATION SPAN

Karen is a junior marketing major. During the summer she decided that when she came back to college she would study three hours every night without interruption. She put a sign on her door:

OFF Limits from
7 to 10 P.M.

KEEP OUT
THIS MEANS YOU!

Is she studying more? Yes and no. She can make her body sit at her desk for several hours at a time, but she has a problem that she hardly knows exists. While her eyes look at her book, her mind takes breaks. She sometimes reads several pages and then realizes that she has no idea of what she has read. She has been daydreaming while reading!

Does Karen need more will power? No. She needs to accept the idea that she is a human being. She needs to accept the idea that there are limitations on what the human mind can be expected to do.

The way to make studying easier is to start with what you can do now and build on that. On the average, how long can you study before your mind slips off to something else? Twenty-five minutes? Ten minutes? Most students can concentrate on a textbook ten to fifteen minutes before starting to daydream.

Let's say that you find that your average concentration span is about twelve minutes. Now the question is <u>What would you like it to be</u>? Thirty minutes? Forty-five minutes?

Whatever goal you set for yourself, make certain you allow for your humanness. Be realistic. Set a goal that you can reach with reasonable effort, and give yourself enough time to reach it. As a rough guideline you might aim for a time span of fifteen minutes by the end of your freshman year, twenty-five minutes in your sophomore year, thirty-five minutes in your junior year, and forty-five minutes in your senior year. Graduate students should be able to study for about an hour without losing their concentration.

MANDATORY BREAKS

Once you determine your concentration span, set up your study schedule so that you take a brief break after each study segment and a long break about once an hour. If you do, you will find that you can start and return to your studies much more easily than before.

In fact, you will find the end of a study segment coming so quickly that you will be tempted to continue. Don't do it. Keep your agreement with yourself. When you promise to take a quick break after twelve minutes, then do so. Do not allow yourself to study more than the allotted time.

A look at the records of most students shows why it is necessary to take these breaks even when you don't want to. With segmented study hours, studying is easier than expected. But after a while the old ways of studying creep back in.

What happens? The critical point comes when you reach the end of a study segment and find yourself so interested in the material that you decide to keep on. If you do, then your mind seems to say: "I can't trust you. You promised me a break after twelve or fourteen minutes, but after I fulfilled my part you kept me working."

When you promise your mind a break after twelve or fourteen minutes, keep your word. No matter how much you want to keep on, make yourself take a short break. Get up and stretch. Walk out to get a drink of water or a breath of fresh air before starting the next study segment.

MIX STUDY SUBJECTS

Mark is carrying a full load in school: accounting, market-

ing, business law, finance, and statistics. He studies three
evenings a week and uses that time for his toughest subjects.
But when he tries to recall what he's covered in an evening,
he has trouble doing so.

If Mark a slow learner? Probably not. His memory problem
is caused by his study schedule. His study schedule looks like
Figure 2. Mark's memory problem exists because he spends about
three hours on one subject. When a person learns one set of
facts and then goes on to learn a similar set of facts, the
second set will interfere with his memory of the first, and the
first will interfere with the second. The more similar material
a person tries to learn at one time, the worse his memory will be.

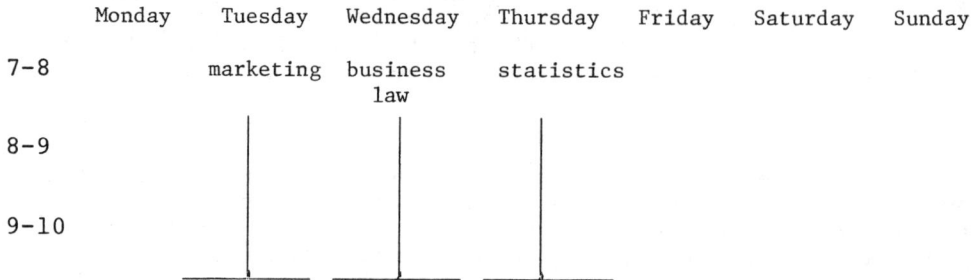

	Monday	Tuesday	Wednesday	Thursday	Friday	Saturday	Sunday
7-8		marketing	business law	statistics			
8-9							
9-10							

FIGURE 2. Mark's evening study schedule - before.

How can you avoid this problem when you have lots of material
to study? The best way is to mix your study hours with dissimilar
material. Do not devote all of one evening to one subject. Switch
subjects every hour or so. Always try to make your new subject
as different as possible from the subject you have just finished.
That way your mind can be assimilating one topic while you are
reading about another. Mark did much better when he revised his
schedule as seen in Figure 3.

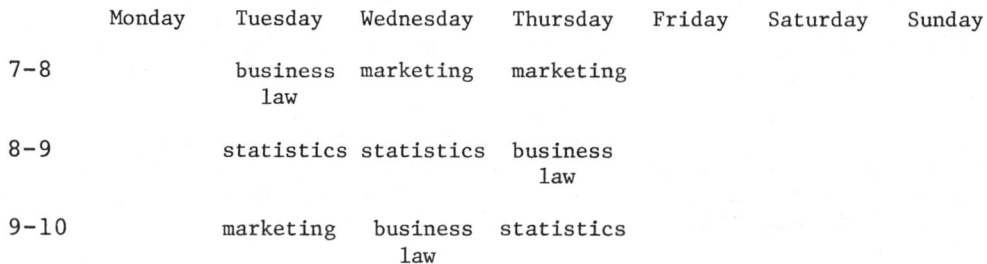

	Monday	Tuesday	Wednesday	Thursday	Friday	Saturday	Sunday
7-8		business law	marketing	marketing			
8-9		statistics	statistics	business law			
9-10		marketing	business law	statistics			

FIGURE 3, Mark's evening study schedule - after.

Although Mark's new schedule shows that he is mixing dissimilar subjects, he could apply another principle of learning. Research shows that material you memorize is retained better if immediately followed by sleep. Insightful learning can occur at any time and is not vulnerable to what follows immediately. This difference means that subjects like statistics and business law tend to be remembered better if studied before bedtime.

BE AN ACTIVE LEARNER

THE FIRST LECTURE

Successful students are active in determining the requirements for each course. They then use their study time to engage in behavior most likely to help them achieve course success. During the first lecture find out the answers to these key questions:

Which chapters in the textbook will be covered?
When will the exams be given?
What material will each exam cover?
What type of questions will be on the exams? Essay? Multiple choice?
What other work will be required?
When will it be due?
How will it be evaluated?
How will grading in the course be determined?
Does the instructor have an outline of the most important terms and concepts
  to be covered?
Should you read the chapter before the lecture each time?
What does the instructor hope each student will understand by the end
  of the course?

These questions are a starting point. Others will occur to you as you go along.

A word of caution: Don't make instructors feel that they are being cross-examined. Be assertive, but be tactful. If an instructor is not prepared to answer all these questions, back off. Try to find out when the information may be available. In general, you will find that instructors enjoy answering questions about what they believe is most valuable in their courses. A few are poorly prepared, however, and may become defensive if pressed too hard.

Some instructors will have the answers to most of these questions on written handouts. If you don't receive a handout, be sure to write everything down in a notebook.

TAKE LECTURE NOTES

By writing down what the instructor says in lectures you are helping yourself to be an active listener. You are also being realistic about the nature of human memory. Human beings quickly forget most of what they hear, no matter how much they would like to be able to remember.

Several days after hearing a lecture, the best that most students can do is to recall about 10 percent of what was said. So, unless you tape-record the lectures or alternate note taking with a friend, you need to take notes at every lecture.

Some students don't take notes. They may be trying an experiment to see whether or not they can get by without note taking, or they may have reasons for wanting everyone to know that they are not involved in the course. At any rate, if you ask a student who doesn't take notes to fill you in on something the instructor said last week, you will quickly learn for yourself how important note taking is for learning.

TIPS ON TAKING NOTES

Use large pages for taking notes. Put the date on each day's notes. Use an outline form as much as possible. Write down complete phrases and statements, rather than single words. Put the notes from each class on separate pages. Keep a different notebook for each course. Write your name, address and phone number in each notebook. On pages 21 - 24 ("Lecture Notes") we give you more explicit tips on note taking.

ACTIVE READING

Reading your textbooks and lecture notes over and over again is an inefficient way to learn course material. Your reading must help you prepare for doing well on tests, meeting course requirements, and developing an understanding of the area you're studying. Successful readers view texts and notes as sources of exam questions. As they read, they look for questions and answers that are likely to appear on their exams. Keep in mind that <u>if you are not reading and studying as if you are preparing to take a test, you are wasting your time</u>!

CHECKLIST FOR SUCCESS

_____ Accept personal responsibility for your success in the course.

_____ Decide to work at developing good study habits.

_____ Outline a weekly study schedule for yourself.

        _____ Avoid studying one subject too long.

        _____ Schedule a brief period each day for reviewing lecture notes.

        _____ Don't schedule too much study time.

_____ Keep your study desk free of mementos.

_____ Mask distracting sounds with soft music or some other steady
background noise.

_____ Arrange good lighting.

_____ Study in the same place each time.

_____ Ask people to be considerate of your need to study.

_____ Determine your concentration span and set up study segments
geared to your current span.

_____ Take short breaks after study segments and a long break each hour.

_____ Learn to distinguish between reading for interest and studying.
Aim studying toward passing tests.

_____ As you read, always look for possible test questions and answers.

_____ Take practice tests to prove to yourself that you've learned a
lot and that you're prepared for your instructors' exams.

BECOMING MORE INTELLIGENT AND SUCCESSFUL IN YOUR CLASSES

We all know that some students are more intelligent than
others. They have better vocabularies, know more, can solve
problems better, understand teachers better, and get higher scores
on tests.

Most of us in academic communities believe that we are intelligent people. A favorite pastime of many students and instructors
is to discuss: "What is intelligence? Is it inborn? Can it be
increased? Is an intelligent person creative? A wise decision
maker? An independent thinker? Is there more than one kind of intelligence? If so, what different kinds are there?"

Our bias is to look for behaviors which are associated with
intelligence. Most psychologists agree that an intelligent person
is an efficient learner. He or she learns and remembers more than
other people. But what behavior leads to this? Asking and answering questions. An intelligent person asks important questions and
searches for the answers.

If we lean back in our chairs and analyze what a successful
student must do, it is clear that such a student must ask and
answer good questions. He or she must do so when writing papers,
reading the text, talking in discussion groups, attending class,
and taking tests.

Think of your textbook. It consists of answers to a lot of
questions. Your instructors spend much of their time developing
questions to ask you in class or on tests. Think of the notes
you take. Are they anything more than answers to questions?
Your instructors have carefully analyzed important books, lectures,

films, and other resources to generate a body of information which they present to you in class. The final task for you is to answer important questions about this information.

ASKING QUESTIONS: KEY TO EFFICIENT LEARNING AND SUCCESS IN CLASSES

Let's look at some simple and highly effective learning techniques. Several thousand students using these techniques found that once they learned to ask and answer intelligent questions they became highly successful in school. They saved hundreds of hours in studying and preparing for courses and were able to spend more time going to movies, watching television, engaging in sports activities, chatting with friends, taking weekend trips, attending concerts, and leading the "good life."

If these things interest you, then let's spend a little more time discussing how you can learn the correct techniques. One thing we promise is that you will achieve your academic goals with a great deal more pleasure and far less pain than you have known in the past. We must sound one word of caution: This goal may require you to change many of your old habits. Such changes are sometimes difficult or painful. Why? Well, when you are used to a standard set of procedures to accomplish your goals, you often become comfortable with them and resist change. Even if you try the new study techniques, you'll have a tendency to go back to your old study behaviors. These old behaviors will help you to accomplish your goals to a degree but with the same pain and tremendous number of hours that you have spent in the past. Once you become accustomed to the new study techniques, a lot of your old superstitious behavior related to studying and becoming educated will fade away. You will begin to get some good feedback from professors, friends, and yourself to indicate that the new methods save time. You will achieve your goals and have time to do things you never had time for in the past. Here we go!

Principle I: Study To Pass Tests

Whenever you are reading from curiosity, allow your mind to go in any direction it wishes. But, when you study, <u>study as if you were practicing to take a test</u>. Practice answering questions! If you don't, you are wasting your time! Remember, it's your time, so why waste it?

Principle II: Ask Intelligent Questions

<u>What is an intelligent question</u>?

First, it is one that you would like answered. Second, it is framed so that in seeking the answer you will learn new and useful things. Third, it might be close to one your instructor asks on a test. Fourth, it can be a way to demonstrate what you already know.

How do you learn to ask intelligent questions?

Practice is the answer. Practice is a useful personal habit to acquire. At first it takes some work, but later the questions arise out of habit.

What will good questions help you to do?

They will help you to determine whether or not you and your instructor are interested in the same thing, focus on the important points while listening and reading, prepare for exams, determine how ready you are to take an exam, discriminate important from unimportant material, determine the important points of lectures and readings, influence your instructor, and save time.

What does a good question look like?

It usually starts with a phrase like

Give several examples of...
Which of these is an example of...
Describe the function of...
What is significant about...
List the important...
Compare and contrast...
Interpret the following...
What is the structure of...
Identify the following...
Why does...

GENERATE INTELLIGENT QUESTIONS

How can I determine what the important questions are?

Pretend that you are the instructor, and generate questions from your texts, lecture notes and old exams. Think of questions before you go to class, and then listen to see whether or not other students ask the same questions or whether or not the instructor supplies answers to those questions.

Write out questions for a lecture or an assignment. Then ask your instructor whether or not he thinks these questions are important and what other questions you should attempt to answer.

Do not be afraid to ask your instructor what he thinks are the important questions!

Most instructors are happy to tell you what they think is important. Give them a chance, and they'll take a mile!

Ask your professor what goals he has for the students in his class. If you want a clear answer, you must learn to ask questions that help him to clarify for himself the questions he would like the class members to answer. You might ask

What should a student be able to do and what important questions should he be able to answer after having completed this chapter (unit, training, program)?

What important questions do you think we should be looking at in this unit (chapter, assignment)?

Can you suggest particular articles or books that highlight the issues we will be discussing in this unit?

What important things should we be looking for in this particular reading (film, case study)?

Such questions should be asked in as positive a manner as possible. Students have a tendency to put insturctors on the defensive. It is your job to ask an instructor in what direction the course is headed and to reward him for telling you. A comment like "Thanks, that really clarifies things for me" is something an instructor responds to well and will increase the likelihood that you won't have to ask next time.

<u>Now that I know what intelligent questions are and how they are determined, where do I begin</u>?

We prefer to start by showing you how you can get a lot more out of your reading by turning it into a question-answering process. We'll then get into note taking, test taking, and a variety of other important study skills, but reading is the more important, so that's where we'll begin!

READING = QUESTION ANSWERING

INCREASING YOUR READING SPEED AND COMPREHENSION IN TEXTBOOKS

One of the fastest ways to spend less time reading assignments is to learn how to figure out the important questions and answers as quickly as possible. First, you should know that a large percentage (perhaps as many as 80 percent) of the words you read are redundant. Most simply link ideas. The ideas are the answers to the questions you wish to answer.

Second, much of what you have to comprehend is already in your head. What you want are the answers to questions that you generate or find in the chapter as you survey and read.

Here are the steps you should go through to increase your reading speed and comprehension:

READING CHAPTER IN TEXTBOOKS

Improved comprehension is the ability to answer more questions from reading assignments. This approach to reading is considered by many experts on study skills and reading improvement to be the most efficient and effective means for getting the most out of reading material in the least time. The primary concern of students using this method will be to ask and answer intelligent questions as they read.

What you should do is described in the following sections.

SURVEY AND QUESTION

The goal of surveying is to determine what important questions are answered in the textbook chapter. First, go to the beginning and end of the chapter and read the chapter objectives, questions, and the chapter summary. This is where you will find the important points the authors wish to stress and the questions students should be able to answer after completing the chapter.

If you can answer the questions and already know what is in the summary and chapter objectives, you probably won't have to read the chapter. But don't decide yet.

How do you survey? The process of surveying involves quickly skimming the chapter to determine what important questions it answers. Look for titles, subtitles, illustrations, pictures, charts, lead sentences in paragraphs, and questions that will give you a basic idea of what the chapter is about.

While surveying it is easy to turn titles, subtitles, and lead sentences into questions. For instance, "Using Humor to Overcome Perceptual Barriers" is a paragraph heading in Marketing. You have simply to turn it into "What is meant by perceptual barriers? How can humor help in overcoming them?"

By generating questions as you survey, you keep yourself alert to the important points in the chapter. Reading becomes an active, goal-oriented process. As you survey, you should formulate questions that, when answered, will give you a good summary of the chapter. The result of your survey will be a list of questions.

To prove your brilliance, you may wish to attempt to answer the questions you have generated in your survey before reading. This attempt serves to tell you how much you already know before spending an exorbitant amount of time reading. Many students are amazed at their ability to answer a large percentage of the questions they have formulated in their survey.

Another helpful technique is to quickly summarize what you already know about the chapter. By talking to yourself about the chapter, you help yourself to focus on the important questions you should be able to answer after having read it.

READ TO ANSWER QUESTIONS

It is now time to read: Read as quickly as you can. Read to find the answers to questions you have generated while surveying the chapter and to find new questions and answers that you haven't predicted while surveying.

Remember: In many instances, your questions and answers will be summarized in titles, subtitles, or lead sentences. Occasionally, you may have to read beyond these headings for more important details. But not with the regularity that caused you to waste a lot of time in the past when you were looking for unimportant details.

When reading to answer questions, you learn to predict important questions before spending a lot of time reading. You learn to read selectively. You read to find answers to questions. When you come to the answer to a question that you hadn't predicted, you simply slow down, formulate the question, and make sure you know the answer. When you come to material you already know, keep on going to find out what you don't know.

RECITE AND WRITE ANSWERS AND SUMMARIES

Now that you have 1) read to answer the questions from your survey and 2) have developed new questions and answers that you hadn't predicted, it is important for you to go one step further.

Recite and write the answers to the questions that you developed while surveying and reading. Equally important, recite and write a short summary of what you have just read. These procedures are excellent means of proving to yourself that you have asked and answered the important questions from each chapter.

Practice talking to yourself (even if people think you're a little crazy) about the answers to your questions. Often students rush on to a new chapter before thoroughly proving to themselves that they are familiar with the contents of the chapter they just read. They say to themselves, "I read it. I know what it's about." DON'T MAKE THAT MISTAKE! Prove to yourself by answering questions and writing chapter summaries that you really do comprehend the chapter.

REVIEW

If you have followed the steps so far, you are in excellent shape to review the chapter at any time. You will have a set of questions and answers representing the contents of the chapter. When preparing for your exam, quiz yourself on these questions until you feel comfortable that you could give accurate answers to them if they were to appear on your exam.

We also suggest summarizing to yourself, orally or in writing, the contents of the chapter and comparing your summary with the one you wrote after having read the chapter.

Taken together, these activities will really give you the feeling that you've mastered the material. When you know you can answer questions correctly and make accurate summaries, you will be more confident that you have mastered the chapter. You will spend less time attempting to re-read chapters and otherwise involving yourself in a variety of superstitious and time-consuming study activities which seldom help you to ask and answer important questions.

THE RESULT

You have now:

1. Surveyed the chapter.
2. Generated questions.
3. Read selectively to answer the questions in greater detail.
4. Found questions and answers that you hadn't predicted.
5. Recited and written answers to questions and chapter summaries.
6. Reviewed the chapter by practicing answering questions and summarizing the chapter.

You should now have a good understanding of the chapter.

ADVANTAGES OF THIS APPROACH

You spend less time memorizing facts that you will soon forget.

You don't waste time reading and looking for things you already know.

Your preparation for tests is a continual process. By the time you take the test you will find that you have answered most of the questions.

You focus on grasping the key concepts. Details are then much easier to remember.

You don't waste time looking for details that are unimportant to you or your instructor.

You learn to take an expert's point of view and to think things out for yourself.

You learn to sit down and generate answers that you didn't think you knew. You then search for additional information, which makes polished answers out of incomplete ones.

You learn to organize and structure your studying. You state your goals as questions, seek answers, achieve your goals, and move on.

DIFFICULTIES OF THIS APPROACH

It is difficult to change old study patterns. You may be accustomed to reading every word, always afraid that you're going to miss something. A new technique such as this may appear reckless and inappropriate to learning. It takes more energy to ask questions and generate summaries than it does to let your eyes passively read printed pages. It is easier just to open a book and start reading.

How can you reconcile these points? There are advantages and disadvantages to everything! This is true for both successful and unsuccessful students. If there were no disadvantages, if it were easy, then everyone would be more successful.

Try the techniques, and look for results like the following:

The quality of your questions and answers will improve with practice.

The amount of time it takes you to generate questions and summaries will decrease.

The amount of time it takes to verify and improve your answers will decrease with practice.

You will be able to cover large amounts of material in far less time.

You will find that you are producing the same questions as your instructors, textbooks, and friends.

With practice, you will find that the summaries you generate come closer to those of the authors.

PREDICTING EXAM QUESTIONS

How do I go about predicting exam questions from sources other than my text?

Once you accept the value of always studying as if you were practicing to take a test, you'll be on the right track. It is important to gear your study behavior to collecting questions and answers that you expect to find on your exams. By using the reading techniques that we have suggested, you will have a good start. Your reading will always be geared to asking and answering important questions.

In addition to this style of reading, there are several other techniques that will help you to collect a good set of exam questions. Note taking, asking friends and instructors, collecting old exams, holding discussion groups, and using textbook and student manual questions are several that we suggest. Let's start with note taking.

SOURCES OF EXAM QUESTIONS

LECTURE NOTES

Think of your lectures as textbook chapters. Each usually has a main theme and makes several important points. If you listen for them, they will be easier to hear.

We encourage you to take lecture notes in outline form. This habit will help you to focus on the main points that can be turned into questions. Your job is to record these questions and to make sure that you know how your instructor would answer them.

Most good instructors answer their questions thoroughly in class, but sometimes they only allude to the answers. Wise students always make sure they know what questions the instructor believes are important. They then go to outside sources if more information is needed than has been supplied in the lecture.

Here are the steps we suggest you follow in taking lecture notes:

1. During the lecture, take notes on the right-hand side of the paper. Leave a large margin on the left.

2. After the lecture, take several minutes to turn your outline into test questions. The main theme and subtopics can be turned into questions. Usually each lecture will supply you with three to seven good exam questions. They should be written in the left-hand margin.

3. At least once a week, review the questions you have asked. Pretend that you are taking a test. Give yourself an oral quiz, or, even better, practice by taking a written quiz. Then compare your answers to those given in your notes or textbook.

Remember: This procedure will help to make something meaningful out of lectures that often leave you in a quandary. Your purpose is to go to lectures looking for questions and their answers. If you come out of each lecture with several questions and answers, you'll be pleased. They're likely to be on your next test!

TEXTBOOKS

Always read the questions that precede the chapter. Such questions are included by our text because we believe that students should be able to answer them after having read the chapter.

Many instructors take their test questions directly from those in the textbook. Surprisingly, many students never look at these questions. They seem to feel that no one could be so stupid as to tell them exactly what they should be able to do after reading the chapter.

Authors usually try to help students, not to trick them! If you are not in the habit of answering chapter questions, we recommend them as the starting point in your effort to organize a good set of questions and answers.

DISCUSSION GROUPS AND FRIENDS

Some of the best sources of test questions, yet often the most overlooked, are friends and fellow students. By talking with other students enrolled in the course or with students who have been enrolled in past terms, you can formulate an excellent perspective of the types of questions and answers you should be looking for. Just as important is finding out what you might avoid.

Many students believe it's difficult to organize formal study groups. Some students simply have a preference for working on their own. This strategy can be self-defeating. By organizing the questions and answers from a variety of sources, you are in an excellent position to compare yours with those of fellow students.

We compare this process with the old pastime of trading cards. You collect as many as you can and simply trade off your extras to build up an even stronger set. Similarly, you find out what questions other students feel are important. You compare your answers to theirs to ensure that you haven't overlooked important information. Everyone comes out stronger than when he entered the game. Everyone is better prepared to ask and answer intelligent questions.

By studying in a group or with one other person, you will help to ensure that you

1. Structure a situation in which other people will encourage you to involve yourself in the study activities we have recommended.

2. Ask and answer questions that you believe are important and are likely to be found on your next exam.

3. Find questions that you yourself hadn't predicted.

4. Refine your answers with additional information supplied by other students.

5. Put together practice tests.

6. Take practice tests.

7. Develop a more efficient and effective process of preparing for exams.

INSTRUCTORS

At the risk of sounding bold, we suggest that your instructor is the best source of information on forthcoming test questions. Many students find it difficult to ask instructors what they think is important. Give them a chance: Ask them!

Ask your instructor: "Could you specify the areas in which we should concentrate our studying?" "Are there particular topics which you feel we should devote more time to than others?"

Whatever you do, don't ask: "Are there any areas you feel are unimportant?" "Which of these chapters should we avoid, considering all that we have to study for this test?" If you ask such questions the instructors may be so peeved they will assign the encyclopedia. Most instructors believe that everything they teach is important. In trying to determine what is likely to be on exams, your goal is simply to persuade instructors to narrow down all the important things they have told you to a precise statement of what your exam will look like. If you are pleasant and thank your instructors for their help, you'll be way ahead of the game. You may even find out the exact format of the exam and which questions are most important!

THE RESULT

Predicting exam questions is the most useful technique we have found in preparing students to learn the important concepts covered in their courses. Equally important, it helps them to pass their exams with much greater ease. If you have followed our suggestions, you will have collected exam questions from

1. Your textbook chapters.
2. Your lecture notes.
3. Lists of questions in your textbooks.
4. Lists of questions in student manuals.
5. Discussion groups and friends.
6. Your instructor.
7. Lists of chapter objectives.

Once you have collected a good set of test questions, you will be better prepared to follow through with the procedures we shall suggest in the next section on tests.

Is the purpose of education to learn how to answer instructors' questions and pass tests?

Yes and no! If you want to understand the experts and even go beyond them it is important to be able to ask and answer the same questions they believe are important. If you're realistic, you know you have to pass the requirements of the course. If you understand what your instructor wants, then you will learn a lot. If your instructor is less than adequate, then it is a matter of meeting his criteria and going on to better courses. There is no need to waste a lot of time in the process.

HOW TO BEGIN?

It is best to begin by practicing predicting and answering exam questions! Each week, count those questions and answers that you have collected from textbook chapters, lecture notes, student manuals, discussion groups, classmates, and your instructors. To monitor how well you are doing, record the number of questions and answers you have for each class.

CHECKLIST FOR SUCCESS

Here is a list of guidelines that will help you to monitor your studying and your success at implementing the learning strategies we've described.

_____ Practice reading to answer questions.

_____ Practice writing answers to questions and chapter summaries.

_____ Generate questions from lectures, textbooks, chapter summaries, student manuals, discussion groups, and chapter objectives.

_____ Ask your instructor what goals he or she has for the students in class.

_____ Keep a weekly record of the number of questions and answers you generate for each class.

DOING WELL ON TESTS

PREPARING FOR TESTS

Now that I have collected a good set of questions and answers, how can I make sure that I'll do well on the tests?

Periodically, go through the questions you have generated to see whether or not you can still answer them. Avoid saying to yourself, "I know the answer to that one." Verbalize or write the answer to prove to yourself how brilliant you have become!

Using the questions you have collected, make up practice tests. Take practice tests under conditions as close as possible to actual test conditions. Then compare your answers with those you have generated from your textbooks, lectures, and so on.

QUIZ YOURSELF

Here are some specific hints about making and taking practice tests, strategies for taking tests, and other useful preparation techniques.

Many students find it helpful to write their questions and answers on 4 x 6-inch cards. As you collect questions from the sources we have suggested, transfer them to the cards. The answers should be placed on the backs of the cards.

This system is similar to the old flash-card system that many of us have used in learning our multiplication tables, spelling, and foreign languages. Most students like this system because it gives them a central filing system of questions and answers. Rather than fumbling through review of notes and textbooks, they go to their stacks of question cards and quiz themselves.

That sounds great for most students, but what about those of us who spend most of our time working problems in accounting and finance? How can this technique help us?

One of the most important insights that students can develop is recognition that success in a particular course is based upon solving specific problems, especially in mathematics, accounting, finance, and statistics.

Review for students in these courses should be no different from review for other students. They must practice working problems as similar as possible to those that will be found on their next exam. By recording sample problems on 4 x 6-inch cards, they will develop files of important problems that they should be able to solve if they wish to advance to more complex mathematical and scientific problem solving.

MAKING AND TAKING PRACTICE TESTS

Practicing the exact behavior you will be required to perform in a test situation not only prepares you to do well, it also helps you to relax and builds your confidence. After successfully passing practice tests, students seldom feel the uneasiness and tension about tests that have accompanied old study routines. They know they have studied the right questions, and they sleep better for knowing they've studied correctly. Here is how to make and take practice tests.

1. Determine the amount of time you'll be given to take your instructor's exam; take practice test over the same length of time. Taking them under realistic time pressure is important. If you force yourself to do so, you'll feel more comfortable when you're actually in the testing situation.

2. Arrange the questions you've been accumulating from chapters, lecture notes, study groups, and other sources into practice tests.

3. Try to put the questions into the same format that the test will offer (multiple choice, short essay, and so on).

4. Take your practice tests under conditions as similar as possible to those under which you'll be tested. The classroom in which you'll be tested is the best place to take practice tests. If it is not available to you, make sure you practice in a room where you won't be bothered.

5. Try to answer your questions without referring to your books or other sources of information.

6. When attempting to answer questions for which you need more information, try to guess and make up things as if you were in a real testing situation, trying to earn at least partial credit. This procedure forces you to take what you already know and to determine what might be the answer, rather than saying, "I just don't know!" Yes, this approach is known as "bulling," and it often makes the difference between an A and a B! Bulling is writing out an answer that makes sense to you, even though you don't remember exactly what was said in the textbook or lecture. You often know more than you think. An imaginative answer can be a good way to demonstrate your comprehension.

7. Once you have completed the test, compare your answers with those that you have in your own set of questions and answers. Use your textbooks and notes to refine your answers.

8. After noting the questions you have answered well and those in need of improvement, design a new test. Follow the same procedure that we have outlined in steps 1-7. Take the new test and continue repeating the steps until you think you have mastered all the questions and answers likely to appear on your instructor's test.

WEEKLY AND FINAL PRACTICE TESTS

When you take weekly practice tests in each subject area, you'll find that exam panic and last-minute cramming are a thing of the past. Before each scheduled test, take a comprehension practice test made up of sample questions from your weekly tests. You'll be pleasantly surprised at how much easier it is to pass your final practice test when you have been taking weekly tests.

This process allows you to master smaller amounts of information each week and then to put everything together in a final practice test just before you take the real thing.

THE ADVANTAGES OF PREPARATION STRATEGIES

But isn't this strategy very time consuming?

It may appear so, but we have found that students who concentrate on collecting test questions and answers, taking weekly practice tests (or quizzes), and taking final practice tests spend far less time on irrelevant and wasteful studying. These students practice exactly what their instructors will require of them, "asking and answering intelligent questions."

TAKING YOUR INSTRUCTORS' TESTS

Now that you know how to prepare for a test, let's make sure that you know how to relax and use your time wisely once you have the real test in your hands.

GENERAL RULES

1. Read the instructions to determine the types of questions you'll be expected to answer. Determine where you'll earn the most points. Don't spend a lot of time reading; just form a basic idea of how the test is set up, and plan your attack.

2. Divide your time to ensure that you schedule enough for all portions of the test. Otherwise, you'll devote too much time to the most difficult parts and wind up "choking" when you find that you won't be able to complete the whole test.

3. Before starting, determine whether or not answering the easier questions will earn you just as many points as answering the more difficult questions. If so, complete the easy ones first. After answering them you'll have more confidence, and you will be able to pass on to the more difficult questions.

4. Make sure you understand what each question is asking. If the directions say, "Give several examples of...," then do exactly that! Give instructors exactly what they ask for. Don't twist questions around into something else.

5. If you don't understand a question or find it extremely difficult, place an x by it, and move on to easier questions. You can come back later. This procedure saves time and prevents anxiety. Most important, you may find the answer hidden in other questions as you move through the test. Don't waste precious time trying to dig it out from the back of your brain. Expect the answer to come to you as you work on other items, just as you do when trying to recall a person's name. Relaxing and expecting the name to come to you in a few moments works better than struggling to remember.

ANSWERING ESSAY QUESTIONS

Outline Answers Outline your answer to an essay question before writing it. In this way you will ensure that you include key ideas for which you will earn points from the grader. The procedure saves time in the long run. You can organize your answer and can be sure to include everything that is important. You will feel more organized when you begin to write and will have fewer uncertainties about whether or not you have included everything that you should.

   Define Terms   Define the terms that you will use in your answer. Be sure to call attention to any uncertainties in your mind about the question asked.   This approach often clarifies for the instructor why you have answered the question in a particular manner.

   Use Subheadings and Examples   As you write, be sure to use subheadings for longer answers.   They help you and the reader feel some organization in your answer.   It is crucial to use examples to support your main points.   There is less opportunity to argue about whether or not you really know what you are talking about if you can present several examples to substantiate your position.

   Polish Answers   Above all, write legibly!   After you have finished writing, pretend that you are the grader.   Ask yourself: "Have I misread or misinterpreted the questions?   What did I leave out?   Have I made any careless mistakes?"   Allot time at the end to polish your answers, add necessary points, and deal with more difficult questions that have puzzled you.

ANSWERING OBJECTIVE QUESTIONS

   Never, never leave an answer blank, unless there is a penalty for guessing.   If there is a penalty, guess only when you can eliminate at least half the possible options, two options where there are four in a multiple-choice question, for example.

   Read objective questions carefully, but answer them quickly. If the answer is not immediately obvious to you check off a tentative answer and come back to it.   Later items in the test often give clues to the answers in earlier items.   Contrary to the popular advice about never changing answers, it can be to your advantage to change answers.   The research evidence shows that when students have prepared well for an examination the number of students who gain by changing answers is significantly greater than the number of students who lose by changing answers.

   Answering Multiple-Choice Questions   As you answer multiple-choice questions, always be sure to eliminate the obviously incorrect answers first.   You will save considerable time and will help to reduce anxiety about choosing the correct answer.

   Read and answer each question quickly.   After you have answered all questions, go back and check to see that you have read them correctly.   If you have time, reread them all.   If not, reread those that you marked with X the first time through because you were unsure of your answers.   Never change an answer when rereading unless you are absolutely certain your new answer is correct.

<u>Answering Matching Questions</u> Check to make sure you have read the directions for matching questions carefully. Sometimes students believe that matches are so obvious that they do exactly the opposite of what is asked. If the instructions say, "Match those that are different" or "Match those that are opposite," you will feel rather foolish if you have spent a lot of time matching those that are similar.

A real time saver is answering the easy ones first. This tactic reduces the chance of guessing incorrectly on more difficult matches.

<u>Answering True-False Questions</u> Never waste a lot of time pondering true-false questions. Many students have been known to waste major portions of test periods attempting to "solve" true-false questions as if they were Chinese puzzles. If an answer isn't immediately apparent, don't become frustrated. Simply move on to the next question. Just one or two questions aren't worth that many points. They don't deserve the precious time that could be devoted to other, more important questions. The points you miss on a true-false question can usually be picked up later in an essay question through some rather shrewd use of your imagination, called "bulling."

As we mentioned before, students who change answers can improve their scores, but only if they have carefully reread a question and thought over the answer before making the change. Avoid guessing at all costs!

QUESTIONS YOU DIDN'T THINK YOU COULD ANSWER

Students are often amazed when we ask them to try answering questions and writing summaries after simply surveying a chapter. They say, "But I haven't read it yet!" They then go ahead, do it, and find that their answers and summaries are fairly accurate, sometimes close to perfect. How do they do it? Stored in their brains they have so much information of which they are unaware. When they force themselves to start talking about what they know, they're often amazed.

We want you to remain humble, but on the same note we want you to be able to pull yourself out of jams by answering questions to which you don't have immediate answers. In a test situation only you can answer the question (unless you wish to risk the chance of being thrown out for cheating).

What can you do when you come to a question that baffles you? Try to remember that in your reading you're likely to have picked up some information that is relevant. If that's all you write, you're likely to earn a few points, which is more than you'll have if you leave it blank. While taking the exam, you're likely to pick up some information related to the answer you need. If you can't figure out the exact answer, you can probably figure out an approximation, especially in math, in which students may often work out problems and come up with incorrect answers. They may not receive complete credit, but partial credit is surely better than a big zero.

Using your imagination takes practice and even a little confidence. It is not the most important study skill that we can recommend, but it can be valuable at times.

YOU CAN WRITE COMMENTS ABOUT THE TEST

If, in spite of all your excellent preparation, you are still quite nervous about the test then try imagining that written across the top of the test is the statement, "Feel free to write comments about the test items."

Wilbert J. McKeachie, known for his research on ways to improve teaching, discovered that, when this statement was printed at the top of tests, many students did better. The students who were helped most were those who had stronger than average fears of failing. And an interesting result was that it didn't matter whether they actually wrote anything about the test or not! Just the presence of the statement was enough to improve the scores of students who had strong fears of failing.

So, when you are taking a test, remember that you should feel free to write comments about the test items! If you believe that a question is poorly worded, then say so. But also go on to explain why and perhaps to suggest a better wording. The whole purpose of the examination is to show that you know something about the subject. Note: If you have doubts about the instructor's allowing comments on the questions, then go ask!

ASK QUESTIONS DURING THE EXAM

Instructors know that their questions are not always clear. Sometimes the wording isn't as accurate as it should be. That's why most instructors will answer questions about test questions during exams.

Take advantage of this willingness. If there are one or two questions that just don't compute, go ask the instructor such questions as "When was this material covered?" "I saw all the films but don't remember the one that this was covered in; can you give me any clues?" "Where was this information presented in the textbook?" "The way this item is worded, there are several possible answers, this one and this one. Which do you want?"

If you are drawing a blank anyway, you have nothing to lose by seeing whether or not the instructor will give you some hints. He will not give you the answer, but a comment like "That item is is from the chart at the end of Chapter 7" may give you the clue you need. Try it. Asking the instructor for clues can be worth several extra points on every exam.

THE ADVANTAGES OF THESE TEST-TAKING STRATEGIES

The strategies described in this chapter can improve your confidence by encouraging you to attack your tests in a reasonable and predictable manner. By using these techniques, you should achieve more points on any given test.

When taking tests, you will find that you don't make those stupid mistakes which make you want to kick yourself and ask, "Why didn't I use my brain?" You will read the questions carefully, plan your time well, determine the value of specific questions, and answer questions in ways likely to earn the maximum number of points. You will engage in test-taking behaviors that we most often observe in students who comprehend their course material and do well on exams. In essence, you will be a more successful student and will still have time for friends!

Again we emphasize that students who use these techniques seldom

1. Misread the test questions and answer them incorrectly.

2. Waste time on questions that stump them.

3. Waste time answering questions with information they know is irrelevant.

4. Run out of time and fail to complete the test.

5. Lose points as a consequence of changing their answers at the last minute.

6. Have difficulty answering questions that require them to "bull" a little.

7. Develop exam panic when a test appears more difficult than they had predicted.

8. Fail tests (they usually receive B or better).

Students who use these techniques report that they

1. Get better grades on tests.

2. Receive more points for answers than they would have predicted.

3. Feel more relaxed and confident while taking tests.

4. Feel confident that they haven't wasted their time while answering complex as well as simple questions.

5. Feel better organized while taking tests.

6. Seldom leave out important information from answers.

7. Are able to complete exams in the allotted time.

8. Get higher grades in their courses.

ONE FINAL TIP

It is not necessary to play the "suffering student" game. Learning can be pleasant. Studying for exams can be efficient if you use the principles we've just discussed. If you prepare well for exams, then the night before each exam you can relax and do one more very helpful thing: <u>Get a good night's sleep!</u>

LEARNING HABITS CHECKLIST

Directions: On each of the items below, rate yourself as you are now and as you would like to be a year from now. Use these numbers:

1 = almost never
2 = sometimes
3 = half the time
4 = usually
5 = always

	NOW	NEXT YEAR
1. Skim newly acquired course books to determine what important questions will be answered in the books.	___	___
2. Begin courses by asking instructors questions about course goals and requirements.	___	___
3. Attend classes.	___	___
4. Take good lecture notes.	___	___
5. Use a study schedule.	___	___
6. Minimize study distractions.	___	___
7. Consciously work at developing good study habits.	___	___
8. Study for short, realistic time spans.	___	___
9. Mix study subjects.	___	___
10. Study by asking and answering questions.	___	___
11. Make up and practice taking tests.	___	___
12. Give your instructors feedback on things they do well.	___	___
13. After studying for limited periods of time, relax and have fun doing what you enjoy.	___	___
14. Enjoy learning and being successful in courses.	___	___

On the other hand, if the foregoing is not for you, then here is a

CHECKLIST OF WAYS GUARANTEED TO MAKE RELATIVES UPSET, FRUSTRATE INSTRUCTORS, AND FORCE ADMINISTRATORS TO REVEAL THEIR TRUE CHARACTER BY PUTTING YOU ON ACADEMIC PROBATION:

_____ Don't look at any textbook until shortly before exam time.

_____ Avoid the library except to read magazines and check out the action.

_____ Never study.

_____ When attending class, do not take notes.

_____ Sit back and wait to see if the instructor can get your attention.

_____ Daydream. Sit and stare out the window wishing you were some place else.

_____ Whisper and pass notes to other students.

_____ Read a magazine in class.

_____ Pretend you are taking notes while writing a letter to someone.

_____ Never ask questions in class.

_____ Find something about the instructor that you don't like... posture, clothing, voice, way of lecturing, etc.

_____ Wait until the last minute to study, decide that it's too late to start now, and go to a movie instead.

_____ After doing all the above, blame the school for being such a miserable place, the instructors for being incompetent and the administration for being _____ (fill in your own favorite term).

PART II.

Chapter Study Units for

MARKETING

This part of the MARKETING Mastery Guide is a study program to be used with MARKETING, the text for your marketing course. Each chapter contains the following:

1. A list of chapter objectives
2. A written summary of the chapter
3. A matching exercise designed to stress the key marketing terms in the chapter.
4. A true-false and multiple choice practice test with answers provided at the end for assessing your performance.
5. A final practice test comprised of true-false and multiple choice questions. This final "dry run" test can serve as your final review prior to a scheduled examination covering this chapter.

Before you begin the study program, you should decide upon your goals for the marketing course and how you will measure your success in reaching them. In the box below, write a brief statement of what you hope to achieve in this course.

MY GOALS

By following the suggestions in Part I and by using the materials in the MARKETING Mastery Guide in a systematic fashion, you can achieve these goals.

PART ONE: THE MARKETING ENVIRONMENT

Chapter 1

INTRODUCTION TO THE MARKETING PROCESS

Chapter Objectives

When you have finished studying this chapter you should
be able to:

Define utility and explain the relationships between each
of the three kinds of utility to production and marketing.

Contrast production orientation and consumer orientation
and explain why production orientations dominated business
philosophy for decades.

Describe the evolution of the marketing concept.

Identify the variables in the marketing mix.

Discuss the three basic reasons for the study of marketing.

Identify the various approaches to the study of marketing.

Chapter Summary

The two primary functions of any organization are production and marketing. Traditionally, industry has emphasized
production efficiency, often at the expense of marketing.
Sometime after World War II, however, the *marketing concept*
became the accepted business philosophy. The change was
caused by the economy shifting from a seller's market to
a buyer's market.

Marketing is the development and efficient distribution of
goods and services for chosen consumer segments. It is
applicable to both profit-oriented and non-profit organizations. Marketing decision making can be classified into
four strategies: (1) product, (2) pricing, (3) distribution, and (4) promotion. These four variables together
form the total marketing mix. Marketing decisions must be
made in a dynamic environment determined by competitive,
legal, economic, and societal functions.

Three basic reasons for studying marketing are (1) marketing
costs may be the largest item in the personal budget; (2)

there is a good chance individual students may become
marketers; and (3) marketing provides an opportunity to
contribute to society as well as to an individual organization.

Six approaches to the study of marketing are commodity,
functional, institutional, managerial, systems, and societal.
This textbook follows an integrated approach in studying
the field.

Directions. Match the marketing term or concept listed below with the appropriate definition chosen from the list to the right, and write the appropriate letter in the space to the left of each term or concept. The correct answers are printed upside-down at the bottom of this assignment.

_____ 1. BROADENING CONCEPT

_____ 2. BUYER'S MARKET

_____ 3. COMMODITY APPROACH

_____ 4. DISTRIBUTION STRATEGY

_____ 5. FUNCTIONAL APPROACH

_____ 6. INSTITUTIONAL APPROACH

_____ 7. MANAGERIAL APPROACH

_____ 8. MARKETING

_____ 9. MARKETING CHANNELS

_____ 10. MARKETING CONCEPT

_____ 11. MARKETING MIX

_____ 12. PRICING STRATEGY

_____ 13. PRODUCTION ORIENTATION

_____ 14. PRODUCT STRATEGY

a. the development and efficient distribution of goods and services for chosen consumer segments.

b. approach to the study of marketing that concentrates upon such marketing institutions as retailing and wholesaling.

c. approach to the study of marketing that views marketing as a functional element of the organization, which is, in turn, a subsystem of the overall system.

d. an organization-wide consumer orientation with the objective of achieving long-run profits.

e. a market characterized by an abundance of goods and services.

f. marketing decisions in the areas of physical distribution of goods and selection of appropriate marketing channels.

g. marketing decisions in the areas of setting profitable and justified prices.

h. marketing decisions in the areas of personal selling, advertising, and sales promotion.

i. the proper blending of the marketing variables of product, distribution, price, and promotion to produce consumer satisfaction.

j. approach to the study of marketing that involves the categorization of all goods and services and the development of efficient distribution systems for each category.

k. the steps a good or service follows from producer to final user.

39

_____ 15. PROMOTIONAL STRATEGY

_____ 16. SELLER'S MARKET

_____ 17. SOCIETAL APPROACH

_____ 18. SYSTEMS APPROACH

_____ 19. UTILITY

l. organizational emphasis on the efficient production of quality products.

m. the want-satisfying power of a product or service.

n. approach that studies marketing from the perspective of the chief decision maker in the organization, the so-called marketing manager.

o. approach to the study of marketing that focuses upon the buying, selling, transporting, storing, grading, financing, entrepreneurial risk taking, and issuing marketing information functions.

p. marketing decisions in the areas of package design, branding, trademarks, warranties, product life cycles, and new-product development.

q. approach to the study of marketing that views the marketing system from a macro viewpoint and explores the various facets of the marketing-societal interface.

r. the expansion of marketing concepts to non-profit organizations.

s. a market characterized by a shortage of goods and services.

The preliminary practice test is designed to help you assess your mastery of text material in this chapter. The test consists of 20 questions focusing upon materials in the chapter and is useful in indicating how well-prepared you are at this stage to take an exam covering this material. The correct answers are printed upside-down at the end of the practice test.

A. MULTIPLE CHOICE. Choose the answer which <u>best</u> answers the question or best completes the sentence.

1. Procter & Gamble's success with Ivory soap clearly illustrates the importance of:

   a) gaining attention through "floating soap" gimmick
   b) coordinated strategy planning in meeting the needs of the dynamic competitive environment
   c) strategic placement of magazine ads
   d) point-of-sale promotion
   e) using manufacturers' agents to obtain channel dominance

2. Economists define <u>utility</u> as:

   a) the want-satisfying power of a a product or service
   b) the need-creating power of a product or service
   c) the principal production function of the firm
   d) all of the above
   e) none of the above

3. Kurtz and Boone define marketing as:

   a) the process of advertising manufactured goods and services
   b) the promotion and sale of consumer goods and services
   c) transporting goods and services to the customer
   d) the development and efficient distribution of goods and services for chosen consumer segments
   e) the creation of a need for a particular product or service on the part of the consumer

4. A production orientation stresses:

   a) consumer research
   b) creation of a quality product
   c) creation of a customer-oriented product
   d) promotion of new products
   e) all of the above

5. The need for a consumer orientation on the part of business can be traced to:

   a) shortages in consumer goods resulting from World War II
   b) intense consumer demand before the war
   c) the advent of a strong buyer's market after World War II
   d) the advent of a strong seller's market during World War II
   e) international competition following World War II

41

6. Marketing decision-making can be classified into four strategies:

   a) product, pricing, distribution and promotion
   b) product, pricing, manufacturing and promotion
   c) promotion, product, pricing and selling
   d) distribution, product, pricing and selling
   e) none of the above

7. To be successful, marketing decisions must take into account the following environments:

   a) competitive and economic
   b) societal and political
   c) legal and societal
   d) a and c above
   e) all of the above

8. What is the basic idea behind the saying, "If you make a better mousetrap, the world will beat a path to your door?"

   a) that research and development are the most important tasks of a firm
   b) that a quality product will sell itself
   c) that price is not an important consideration
   d) a and c, but not b
   e) b and c, but not a

9. The trend toward increased emphasis on the marketing function began:

   a) during World War I
   b) during the Industrial Revolution
   c) during World War II
   d) during the Great Depression of the 1930s
   e) with the advent of television

10. Time utility is best illustrated by which of the following statements?

    a) "Michelon doesn't make a second-best."
    b) "Over 15,000 franchised locations to serve you."
    c) "Our laundry features 60-minute service."
    d) "The quality goes in before the name goes on."
    e) "We're Number 1. We're tough. And we're Glad."

B. TRUE-FALSE. In the space to the left of each statement check the appropriate line to indicate whether the statement is true or false.

True False

_____ _____ 1. The four basic kinds of utility include form, time, and product.

_____ _____ 2. The creation of utility requires that an organization know what consumers want, or can at least approximate buyer opinion.

42

```
True  False
```

✓	___	3. Marketing activities begin with new product concepts and designs developed to meet specific consumer needs.
✓	___	4. In the final analysis, the marketing concept dictates that the customer determines the marketing program.
✓	___	5. A production orientation takes the position that a good product (in terms of physical quality) will sell itself.
___	✓	6. The saying, "if you make a better mousetrap, the world will beat a path to your door." is characteristic of a marketing orientation.
✓	___	7. Inadequate consumer research is a leading cause of marketing failure.
___	✓	8. Marketing was thrust into a more important role with the coming of Henry Ford's mass production line.
✓	✓	9. The decline in consumer goods production during World War II was instrumental in helping to spread the need for a marketing orientation.
✓	___	10. Marketing decision-making involves the four strategies: product, pricing, distribution, and promotion.

FINAL PRACTICE TEST.

This final practice test is designed to provide reinforcement of
the success of your studies and the adequacy of your preparation
for exams covering the material in this chapter. Like the preliminary test, the final practice test consists of 20 questions
focusing materials covered in this chapter. However, the correct
answers are reprinted on the last page of the MARKETING Mastery
Guide.

A. MULTIPLE CHOICE. Choose the answer which <u>best</u> answers the question or best completes the sentence.

1. Production and marketing are the two basic operating functions of:

    a) profit-oriented organizations only
    b) non-profit oriented organizations only
    c) both profit and non-profit oriented organizations
    d) none of the above

2. The 4 basic types of utility include:

    a) form, time, ownership, and use
    b) ownership, place, promotion, and form
    c) form, time, place and content
    d) form, time, ownership and place
    e) none of the above.

3. The four basic types of utility are:

    a) created during the production process
    b) created during the marketing process
    c) created during the selling process
    d) both a and c are correct
    e) created during the marketing and production processes

4. The marketing program is least affected by:

    a) the vice-president in charge of marketing
    b) the retailers
    c) the customer
    d) the president and board of directors of the firm
    e) all of the above affect the choice of effective marketing programs

5. Marketing activity was developed through:

    a) the exchange of production surpluses
    b) primitive, substance-level societies
    c) shortages of goods in modern society and intense consumer demand
    d) improvements in manufacturing techniques
    e) all of the above

6, The marketing concept is:

    a) a company-wide consumer orientation with the objective of achieving immediate profits
    b) a company-wide consumer orientation with the objective of achieving long-run profits
    c) a company-wide consumer orientation with the objective of reducing fixed production costs
    d) a company-wide consumer orientation with the objective of increasing total sales
    e) none of the above

44

7. The term <u>marketing mix</u> refers to:
   a) the total assortment of products a given firm has on the market
   b) the blending of the four strategy elements of marketing decision-making to satisfy chosen consumer segments
   c) the total assortment of advertisements used for any given product
   d) the group of people at whom a promotional campaign is aimed
   e) none of the above

8. Which of the following statements is <u>not</u> listed in the text as one of the basic reasons for studying marketing?

   a) marketing has become the focus of increasing government regulations
   b) marketing costs may be the largest item in the personal budget
   c) there is a good chance that individual students may become marketers
   d) marketing provides an opportunity to contribute to society as well as to a company

9. A leading cause of marketing failure is:

   a) marketing budgets are far too great
   b) inadequate product design and testing
   c) inadequate consumer research
   d) all of the above
   e) none of the above

10. The starting place for effective marketing is:

   a) a creative advertising plan
   b) the consumer
   c) the product manager
   d) the product designer
   e) the president of the firm

B. TRUE-FALSE. In the space to the left of each statement check the appropriate line to indicate whether the statement is true or false.

True False

___✓___ _____ 1. Utility is defined as the want-satisfying power of a product or service.

_____ ___✓___ 2. The creation of form utility is one of the marketing functions of the firm.

_____ ___✓___ 3. Marketing is the sale and efficient distribution of goods and services for all consumers.

_____ ___✓___ 4. Marketing activity should be confined to the areas of an organization developed to deal with it.

_____ ___✓___ 5. Marketing activities have been stressed by American manufacturers throughout the twentieth century.

```
True    False
____    ___✓    6. A firm's ability to produce a quality product almost always
                   guarantees that item's success.

____    ___✓    7. A quality product will always be successful, regardless of
                   price.

✓   ___✗___✓    8. A production surplus is necessary in order for marketing
                   activities to flourish.

____    ___✓    9. A seller's market, one with a shortage of goods and services,
                   is conducive to a marketing orientation.

___✓    ___✗   10. The marketing concept is defined as a company-wide consumer
                   orientation with the objective of achieving long-run profits.
```

Chapter 2

THE ENVIRONMENT FOR MARKETING DECISIONS

Chapter Objectives

When you have finished studying this chapter you should be able to:

Identify the environmental factors that impact the consumer and the marketing mix.

Explain how an organization develops a competitive strategy.

Explain why marketing is a *visible* function of any organization and why it is different from other functions.

Trace the legal framework within which marketing decisions are made.

Explain the relationships between the Sherman Act, Clayton Act, and the Cellar-Kefauver Antimerger Act.

Explain the purpose and functions of the Federal Trade Commission and the three procedures used to carry out the duties of the FTC.

Outline the economic factors that affect marketing strategy.

Explain how the societal environment influences marketing.

Chapter Summary

The four specific environments for marketing decisions are competitive, legal, economic, and societal. These four are important to the study of marketing because they provide a framework within which marketing strategies are formulated. They are among the most dynamic aspects of contemporary business.

The competitive environment is the interactive process that occurs in the marketplace. A firm's marketing decisions influence the market and are, in turn, affected by competitors' strategies. The legal environment attempts to maintain competition as well as regulate specific marketing practices. The economic environment often influences the manner in which consumers will behave toward marketing appeals. The societal environment may become the most important to marketers. The matter of adapting to a changing societal environment has advanced to the forefront of marketing thought.

<u>Directions</u>. Match the marketing term or concept listed below
with the appropriate definition chosen from the list to the right,
and write the appropriate letter in the space to the left of each
term or concept. The correct answers are printed upside-down at
the bottom of this assignment.

_____ 1. CLAYTON ACT (1914)

_____ 2. COMPETITIVE ENVIRONMENT

_____ 3. CELLER-KEFAUVER ANTIMERGER
          ACT (1950)

_____ 4. CONSUMER GOODS PRICING
          ACT

_____ 5. CONSUMER PRODUCT SAFETY
          ACT (1970)

_____ 6. CORRECTIVE ADVERTISING

_____ 7. DEMARKETING

_____ 8. ECONOMIC ENVIRONMENT

_____ 9. ENVIRONMENTAL PROTECTION
          ACT (1970)

_____ 10. EQUAL CREDIT OPPORTUNITY
          ACT

a. Federal legislation prohibiting
    price discrimination that was not
    based on a cost differential. The
    act also outlawed selling at an un-
    reasonably low price in order to
    eliminate competition.

b. In international marketing, a firm's
    maintaining of a separate selling
    operation in a foreign country.

c. Federal statute requiring that the
    name of the animal from which a fur
    garment was derived be identified.

d. The process of cutting consumer de-
    mand for a product to a level that
    can be supplied by the firm.

e. Federal antitrust legislation that
    prohibits restraint of trade and
    monopolization, and subjects vio-
    lators to civil suits as well as
    to criminal prosecution.

f. A marketer's relationship with
    society in general.

g. Federal legislation restricting
    tobacco advertising on radio and
    television.

h. Federal antitrust legislation that
    exempted interstate fair trade con-
    tracts from compliance with anti-
    trust requirements.

i. Federal legislation strengthening
    the Pure Food and Drug Act, to
    prohibit the adulteration and mis-
    branding of food, drugs, and
    cosmetics.

j. Federal legislation establishing
    the Environmental Protection Agency
    and giving it the power to deal
    with pollution issues.

_____ 11. FAIR CREDIT REPORTING
ACT (1970)

_____ 12. FAIR DEBT COLLECTION
PRACTICES ACT (1978)

_____ 13. FAIR PACKAGING AND
LABELING ACT (1967)

_____ 14. FAIR TRADE LAWS

_____ 15. FEDERAL TRADE COMMISSION
ACT (1914)

_____ 16. FLAMMABLE FABRICS ACT
(1953)

_____ 17. FOOD, DRUG, AND
COSMETIC ACT (1938)

_____ 18. FUR PRODUCT LABELING
ACT (1951)

_____ 19. INFLATION

_____ 20. KEFAUVER-HARRIS DRUG
AMENDMENTS (1962)

_____ 21. LEGAL ENVIRONMENT

k. A rising price level that results
in reduced purchasing power for
the consumer.

l. The numerous laws passed by a
multitude of authorities - federal,
state and local.

m. Amendments to the Pure Food and
Drug Act, requiring generic labeling of drugs and a summary of
adverse side effects.

n. A situation in which an economy has
both high unemployment and a rising
price level.

o. Federal legislation requiring disclosure of the annual interest rates
on loans and credit purchases.

p. Federal legislation that halted all
interstate usage of resale price
maintenance agreements.

q. Federal legislation that prohibited
the adulteration and misbranding of
foods and drugs in interstate
commerce.

r. Statutes permitting manufacturers
to stipulate a minimum retail price
for a product.

s. Federal legislation prohibiting the
interstate sale of flammable fabrics.

t. A federal statute that strengthened
anti-trust legislation by restricting practices such as price discrimination, exclusive dealing, tying
contracts, and interlocking boards
of directors.

u. The process of interaction among
competitors that occurs in the
marketplace.

v. A setting of complex and dynamic
business fluctuations that historically tended to follow a four-stage
pattern: 1) recession, 2) depression, 3) recovery, and 4) prosperity.

w. State laws requiring sellers to
maintain minimum prices for comparable merchandise.

_____ 22. MILLER-TYDINGS RESALE PRICE MAINTENANCE ACT (1937)

_____ 23. OVERSEAS MARKETING

_____ 24. PUBLIC HEALTH CIGARETTE SMOKING ACT (1971)

_____ 25. PURE FOOD AND DRUG ACT (1906)

_____ 26. ROBINSON-PATMAN ACT (1936)

_____ 27. SHERMAN ANTITRUST ACT (1890)

_____ 28. SOCIETAL ENVIRONMENT

_____ 29. STAGFLATION

_____ 30. TRUTH-IN-LENDING ACT (1968)

_____ 31. UNFAIR TRADE LAWS

_____ 32. WEBB-POMERENE EXPORT TRADE ACT (1918)

x. Federal legislation requiring that the kind and percentage of each type of wool in a product be identified.

y. Federal legislation that prohibited "unfair methods of competition" and established the Federal Trade Commission (FTC) as an administrative agency to oversee the various laws dealing with business.

z. Federal legislation amending the Clayton Act to include restrictions on the purchase of assets, where such purchase would decrease competition. Previously, only "acquiring the stock" of another firm was prohibited, if it lessened competition.

aa. Federal legislation that excluded voluntary export trade associations from restrictions of the Sherman Act, but only in their foreign dealings.

bb. Federal legislation outlawing harassing, deceptive, or unfair collection practices by debt-collection agencies.

cc. Federal legislation providing for individuals' access to credit reports about them and the opportunity to change information that is incorrect.

dd. Federal legislation banning discrimination in lending practices based on sex, marital status, race, national origin, religion, age, or receipt of payments from a public-assistance program.

ee. A federal statute requiring the disclosure of product identity, the name and address of the manufacturer or distributor, and information concerning the quality of the contents.

ff. A policy of the Federal Trade Commission, under which companies found to have used deceptive promotional messages are required to

_____ 33. WOOL PRODUCT LABELING
ACT (1939)

correct their earlier claims with new messages.

gg. A federal statute that set up the Consumer Product Safety Commission, authorizing it to specify safety standards for most consumer products.

The preliminary practice test is designed to help you assess your mastery of text material in this chapter. The test consists of 20 questions focusing upon materials in the chapter and is useful in indicating how well-prepared you are at this stage to take an exam covering this material. The correct answers are printed upside-down at the end of the practice test.

A. MULTIPLE CHOICE. Choose the answer which <u>best</u> answers the question or best completes the sentence.

1. The first U.S. legislation which prohibited restraint of trade and monopolization is known as:

   a) Webb-Pomerene Act
   b) Sherman Antitrust Act
   c) Clayton Act
   d) FTC Act

2. The traditional pattern followed by business fluctuation has been:

   a) prosperity, depression, recovery, recession
   b) depression, recession, recovery, prosperity
   c) recession, depression, recovery, prosperity
   d) none of the above are correct

3. Corrective advertising is most closely related to:

   a) the Clayton Act
   b) the Truth-in-Lending Law
   c) the Wheeler Lea Act
   d) Consumer Goods Pricing Act

4. Which is not one of the four major marketing mix elements?

   a) promotion
   b) pricing
   c) distribution
   d) competition
   e) product

5. The Miller-Tydings Resale Price Maintenance Act focused upon:

   a) fair trade contracts
   b) unfair trade laws
   c) corrective advertising
   d) the F.T.C.

6. "Creeping" inflation is characterized by:

   a) modest increases in the general price level that go largely unnoticed
   b) loss of jobs
   c) poor marketing practices
   d) a surge in the economy

7. The struggle among companies in the same industry or among substitutable products is known as:

 a) traditional economics
 b) competition
 c) marketing
 d) two of the above
 e) all of the above

8. State laws requiring sellers to maintain minimum prices for comparable merchandise are known as:

 a) retail laws
 b) antiprice laws
 c) anti competition legislation
 d) unfair trade laws

9. Consumer price consciousness can lead to:

 a) "buy now" behavior in the belief that prices will rise in the future
 b) reallocating purchasing patterns
 c) postponing purchases
 d) two of the above are correct
 e) all of the above are correct

10. Which environment is expected to become relatively more important to marketers in the future?

 a) competitive
 b) legal
 c) societal
 d) economic

B. TRUE-FALSE. In the space to the left of each statement check the appropriate line to indicate whether the statement is true or false.

True False

____ ____ 1. The success or failure of a product can be determined by the competitive environment.

____ ____ 2. The Clayton Act called for the establishing of an administrative agency to oversee the various laws dealing with business.

____ ____ 3. Since people are basically the same, marketers should approach everyone in the same manner.

____ ____ 4. Pricing and promotion are the most highly regulated areas of marketing.

____ ____ 5. Unfair trade laws are national laws requiring sellers to maintain minimum prices for different merchandise.

____ ____ 6. The Truth-in-Lending Law enables individuals to have access to their credit reports.

____ ____ 7. Societal variables seldom change.

True False

____ ____   8. The legal environment attempts to maintain competition as
                  well as regulate specific marketing practices.

____ ____   9. Any increase in price results in a decrease in demand.

____ ____   10. The legal environment has a negative effect on marketing
                  activities.

FINAL PRACTICE TEST.

This final practice test is designed to provide reinforcement of
the success of your studies and the adequacy of your preparation
for exams covering the material in this chapter. Like the preliminary test, the final practice test consists of 20 questions
focusing materials covered in this chapter. However, the correct
answers are reprinted on the last page of the MARKETING Mastery
Guide.

A. MULTIPLE CHOICE. Choose the answer which best answers the
                     question or best completes the sentence.

1. The competitive environment can be defined as:

    a) a major marketing mix variable in the marketing process
    b) an outside factor that influences marketing strategy
    c) a factor which can be controlled by a marketing manager
    d) the interactive process that occurs in the marketplace
    e) both b and d are correct

2. Another name for the depression-era legislation referred to
    as the Anti A&P Act was the:

    a) Robinson-Patman Act
    b) Clayton Act
    c) Wheeler-Lea Act
    d) Webb-Pomerene Act

3. Which of the following is not one of the four marketing environments:

    a) competitive
    b) commercial
    c) legal
    d) economic
    e) societal

4. Shell Oil is publicizing gas saving tips through a series of advertisements and brochures. This is an example of:

    a) corrective advertising
    b) demarketing
    c) institutional advertising
    d) both a and b

5. As a result of advertisements, both AMF and STP were recently ordered by the Federal Trade Commission to:

    a) use corrective advertising
    b) correct earlier claims with new promotional messages
    c) pay a fine
    d) a, b and c are correct
    e) a and b are correct

6. Future marketing legislation will probably come from:

    a) state and local governments
    b) court decisions
    c) Federal Trade Commission
    d) Food and Drug Administration
    e) all of the above

7. Which of the following terms describes an economy characterized by high unemployment and a rising price level at the same time?

    a) depression
    b) inflation
    c) stagflation
    d) recession

8. Which of the following is a procedure used by the Federal Trade Commission?

    a) conferences
    b) consent method
    c) formal legal action
    d) two of the above
    e) all of the above

9. The first legislation dealing with a specific marketing practice was:

    a) Food, Drug and Cosmetic Act
    b) Pure Food and Drug Act
    c) Kefauver-Harris Drug Amendments
    d) Flammable Fabrics Act
    e) none of the above are correct

10. Shortages can be caused by:

    a) brisk demand which exceeds manufacturing capacity
    b) lack of raw materials
    c) high prices
    d) both a and b are correct
    e) none of the above

B.   TRUE-FALSE.   In the space to the left of each statement check the appropriate line to indicate whether the statement is true or false.

True   False

____ ____ 1. The four interacting environments for marketing decisions are key marketing mix variables in the marketing process.

____ ____ 2. Marketing is the most visible of all business functions.

____ ____ 3. Inflation only occurs during recessionary periods.

____ ____ 4. Marketing activity is different in each stage of the business cycle.

____ ____ 5. The Celler-Kefauver Antimerger Act amended the Clayton Act.

____ ____ 6. The Pure Food and Drug Act was the first activist legislation dealing with a specific marketing practice.

____ ____ 7. Marketing has little relationship with economics.

____ ____ 8. A deteriorating economic environment means increased sales for some firms.

____ ____ 9. Inflation increases the consumer's purchasing.

____ ____ 10. It is best to reduce marketing activities during economic declines.

Chapter 3

CONSUMER BEHAVIOR: BASIC CONCEPTS

Chapter Objectives

When you have finished studying this chapter you should be able to:

Explain the self-concept and its components.

Identify the individual factors influencing consumer behavior.

List and explain the levels of the needs hierarchy.

Identify the components of an attitude.

Briefly explain the components of the learning process.

Chapter Summary

Understanding consumer behavior is the first step in formulating a marketing strategy. Consumer behavior is viewed as a problem-solving approach by which the consumer makes decisions and takes actions in order to satisfy felt needs.

Consumer behavior results from both individual and environmental influences. This chapter focuses on the individual determinants of consumer needs, motives, perception, and attitudes. Another vital subject in the study of consumer behavior is learning--the changes in behavior that result from past experience. The components of the learning process are drive, cues, response, and reinforcement.

After studying the individual factors in consumer behavior, the next subjects are the environmental factors affecting behavior. These outside influences are the subject of the next chapter.

Directions. Match the marketing term or concept listed below with the appropriate definition chosen from the list to the right, and write the appropriate letter in the space to the left of each term or concept. The correct answers are printed upside-down at the bottom of this assignment.

_____ 1. AFFECTIVE COMPONENT

_____ 2. ATTITUDE

_____ 3. BEHAVIORAL COMPONENT

_____ 4. COGNITIVE COMPONENT

_____ 5. CONSUMER BEHAVIOR

_____ 6. CUE

_____ 7. DRIVE

_____ 8. ESTEEM NEEDS

_____ 9. IDEAL SELF

_____ 10. LEARNING

_____ 11. LOOKING-GLASS SELF

_____ 12. MOTIVE

_____ 13. NEED

_____ 14. PERCEPTION

a. The individual's reaction to the cues and drive.

b. A subconscious level of awareness.

c. Any object existing in the environment that determines the nature of the response to a drive.

d. Attitude-scaling device that utilizes a number of bipolar adjectives on a seven-point scale.

e. The desire to be accepted by members of the family and other individuals and groups.

f. Any strong stimulus that impels action; the first component of the learning process.

g. The idea that consumers are consciously aware of only those incoming stimuli they wish to perceive.

h. The way individuals think others see them.

i. An objective view of the total person.

j. The acts of an individual in obtaining and using goods or services, including the decision processes that precede and determine these acts.

k. The component of an attitude referring to tendencies to act or behave in a certain manner.

l. The relationship between the actual physical stimulus and the corresponding sensation produced in the individual.

m. The component of an attitude referring to the individual's information and knowledge about an object or concept.

_____ 15. PHYSIOLOGICAL NEEDS

_____ 16. PSYCHOPHYSICS

_____ 17. REAL-SELF

_____ 18. REINFORCEMENT

_____ 19. RESPONSE

_____ 20. SAFETY NEEDS

_____ 21. SELECTIVE PERCEPTION

_____ 22. SELF-ACTUALIZATION NEEDS

_____ 23. SELF-CONCEPT

_____ 24. SELF-IMAGE

_____ 25. SEMANTIC DIFFERENTIAL

_____ 26. SOCIAL NEEDS

_____ 27. SUBLIMINAL PERCEPTION

_____ 28. WEBER'S LAW

n. Need to feel a sense of accomplishment, achievement, and respect from others.

o. Self-image to which the individual aspires.

p. The way individuals view themselves.

q. The manner in which an individual interprets a stimulus; the often highly subjective meaning that one attributes to an incoming stimulus or message.

r. The reduction in drive that results from a proper response.

s. The primary needs for food, shelter, and clothing that are present in all humans and must be satisfied before the individual considers higher-order needs.

t. Any changes in behavior, immediate or expected, that occur because of experience.

u. The component of an attitude referring to feelings or emotional reactions.

v. An inner state that directs people toward the goal of satisfying a felt need.

w. The lack of something useful; a discrepancy between a desired state and the actual state.

x. One's enduring favorable or unfavorable evaluations, emotional feelings, or pro or con action tendencies.

y. A mental conception of oneself, comprised of four components: real self, self-image, looking-glass self, and ideal self.

z. Need for fulfillment, for realizing one's own potential, for using one's talents and capabilities totally.

aa. The proposition that the higher the initial intensity of a stimulus, the greater the amount of the change in the intensity that is needed for a difference to be perceived.

bb. Need for security, protection
from physical harm, and avoidance
of the unexpected.

The preliminary practice test is designed to help you assess
your mastery of text material in this chapter. The test consists of 20 questions focusing upon materials in the chapter
and is useful in indicating how well-prepared you are at this
stage to take an exam covering this material. The correct
answers are printed upside-down at the end of the practice test.

A. MULTIPLE CHOICE.   Choose the answer which _best_ answers the
                      question or best completes the sentence.

1. When purchasing goods and services, people tend to choose
    products which will:

    a) reinforce their self-image
    b) conform to their image of how others see them
    c) help them move closer to their ideal self-image
    d) all of the above
    e) none of the above

2. Consumer behavior results from:

    a) pressures exerted upon the individual from his or her social peers
    b) influences from within the individual's self
    c) educational influences
    d) all of the above
    e) none of the above

3. A major difference in the purchasing behavior of indus-
    trial consumers and ultimate consumers is that:

    a) industrial consumers are subject to fewer outside influences
       than ultimate consumers
    b) industrial consumers are more objective than ultimate consumers
    c) ultimate consumers have more outside influences acting upon their
       decisions than industrial consumers
    d) there are no major differences between industrial and ultimate
       consumers
    e) additional influences from within the organization may be exerted
       on the industrial purchasing agent

4. The most basic need in Maslow's hierarchy is:

    a) safety need
    b) social need
    c) physiological need
    d) need to excel
    e) all of the above are of equal importance

5. The self-actualization need is most prevalent:

    a) in third-world countries where people tend to lack an identity
    b) in communist countries where pressure to conform causes identity
       crises
    c) in highly religious cultures

d) in developed countries where a sufficiently high income allows most other needs to be satisfied

e) in all cultures; the need for self-actualization is universally important

6. The perception of an object or event is the result of the interaction of two types of factors. These are:

a) stimulus factors and individual factors
b) stimulus factors and response factors
c) individual and group factors
d) response factors and individual factors
e) rational factors and irrational factors

7. The term psychophysics refers to:

a) the state of an individual's inclination to purchase an item
b) the relative orientation of various socio-economic groups' attitudes toward advertising
c) the progressive deterioration of the individual's ability to perceive all incoming stimuli
d) the increase in governmental regulation of advertising
e) the relationship between actual physical stimulus and the corresponding sensation produced in the individual

8. Which of the following statements is <u>not</u> one of the reasons subliminal advertising cannot induce purchasing?

a) strong stimulus factors are required just to gain perception
b) stimulus must be consciously understood to induce purchasing
c) only a very short message can be transmitted
d) individuals vary greatly in their thresholds of consciousness.
e) a subliminal message may not be perceived the same way by different individuals.

9. The components of an attitude include:

a) cognitive and behavioral
b) affective and informational
c) institutional and cognitive
d) environmental and behavioral
e) none of the above

10. Which of the following is not a component of the learning process?

a) drive
b) cues
c) responses
d) reinforcement
e) innovation

B. TRUE-FALSE. In the space to the left of each statement check the appropriate line to indicate whether the statement is true or false.

True	False		
____	____	1.	The looking-glass self is the way individuals see themselves.
____	____	2.	People tend to choose products which will move them closer to their ideal self-image.
____	____	3.	Basic determinants of consumer behavior include motives, perceptions, and attitudes.
____	____	4.	Motives are inner states that direct people toward the goal of satisfying a felt need.
____	____	5.	The needs for security, protection from physical harm, and avoidance of the unexpected are all primary needs in Maslow's hierarchy.
____	____	6.	The need for esteem is more prevalent in developed countries.
____	____	7.	Selective perception refers to the idea that people are consciously aware of only those incoming stimuli they wish to perceive.
____	____	8.	Stimulus factors are the characteristics of the physical object such as color and shape.
____	____	9.	Weber's law refers to the inverse relationship between the sound level in a television ad and the number of people who tune it out.
____	____	10.	Attitudes are formed over a period of time by the individual and are highly resistant to change.

This final practice test is designed to provide reinforcement of the success of your studies and the adequacy of your preparation for exams covering the material in this chapter. Like the preliminary test, the final practice test consists of 20 questions focusing materials covered in this chapter. However, the correct answers are reprinted on the last page of the MARKETING Mastery Guide.

A.   MULTIPLE CHOICE.   Choose the answer which best answers the question or best completes the sentence.

1.   Marketing research studies are useful in determining the following concerning the buying habits of consumers:

 a) if a given product does what it is supposed to do
 b) who the consumers are and when and where they buy
 c) what and how consumers buy
 d) b and c, but not a
 e) none of the above

2.   Which of the following is not a component of the self:

 a) imagined self
 b) real self
 c) self-image
 d) looking-glass self
 e) ideal self

3.   Which of the following is not a basic determinant of consumer behavior?

 a) aspirations
 b) motives
 c) attitudes
 d) perceptions
 e) needs

4.   Maslow's need hierarchy is based upon certain important assumptions. Which of the following is not one of these assumptions?

 a) Man's needs are arranged in a hierarchy of importance.
 b) Man's primary motivation is economic.
 c) As soon as one need is at least partially satisfied, another emerges and demands satisfaction.
 d) Only the needs which have not been satisfied can influence behavior.
 e) Man is a wanting animal whose needs depend upon what he already possesses.

5.   The following are all physiological needs except:

 a) safety
 b) food

c) shelter

d) clothing

6. Perception has an important influence on individual behavior because:

a) how individuals are perceived by others affects their self esteem

b) individual behavior resulting from motivation is affected by how stimuli are perceived

c) individuals who are less perceptive are not accepted by their peer group

d) all of the above

e) none of the above

7. The following are all stimulus factors except:

a) size

b) image

c) color

d) weight

e) shape

8. Weber's law refers to:

a) the first federal statute regulating false advertising

b) the relationship between initial intensity of stimulus and the amount of change in the intensity necessary for a difference to be noticed

c) the relationship between the number of advertisements an individual is exposed to, and the point at which he tunes them out

d) the relationship between the amount of money in the advertising budget for a new product, and the direct returns which result

9. Which of the following statements about attitudes is not true?

a) Attitudes frequently change within short time spans.

b) Attitudes are formed through individual experience.

c) Attitudes are highly resistant to change.

d) Attitudes are formed over a period of time.

e) Attitudes are a person's favorable or unfavorable evaluations, emotional feelings, or pro or con action tendencies.

10. The semantic differential refers to:

a) differences in speech patterns in different parts of the country

b) the various educational levels advertisers attempt to reach

c) an attitude-scaling device used to determine customer feelings toward a product

d) a and b, but not c

e) none of the above

B   TRUE-FALSE.   In the space to the left of each statement check the appropriate line to indicate whether the statement is true or false.

True   False

____   ____   1. The self-image is the way individuals think others see
                   them.

____   ____   2. The ideal self is the image to which the individual
                   aspires.

____   ____   3. Consumer behavior results primarily from environmental
                   influences.

____   ____   4. A need must be sufficiently aroused before it can serve
                   as a motive to buy something.

____   ____   5. Maslow's needs for security, protection from physical
                   harm, and avoidance of the unexpected are all physi-
                   ological needs.

____   ____   6. The desire to be accepted by family and other indivi-
                   duals and groups is known as the social need.

____   ____   7. The most basic human needs is for self-actualization.

____   ____   8. The perception of an object or event is the sole result
                   of individual factors.

____   ____   9. The relationship between physical stimulus and the
                   corresponding sensation produced in a person is called
                   psychophysics.

____   ____ 10. Subliminal perception has been proven to induce pur-
                   chasing in individuals who would otherwise strongly
                   resist purchasing.

Chapter 4

CONSUMER BEHAVIOR: ENVIRONMENTAL INFLUENCES AND
THE CONSUMER DECISION PROCESS

Chapter Objectives

When you have finished studying this chapter you should
be able to:

Identify the environmental influences on consumer behavior.

Explain the determinants of reference-group influence on
the individual.

Evaluate the two-step flow of communication concept.

Identify the major alternative role categories in household decision making.

Distinguish between culture and subculture.

Outline the steps in the consumer decision process.

Explain the factors involved in determining whether cognitive dissonance is likely to occur.

Chapter Summary

Consumer behavior may be defined as the acts of individuals in obtaining and using goods and services,
including the decision processes that precede and determine these acts. Consumer decisions result from both
individual and environmental influences. Chapter 3
focused on the individual factors of needs, motives,
perception, and attitudes, and described the process by
which individuals learn. This chapter's prime concerns
are the environmental factors affecting behavior.

Environmental influences include such outside forces as
the influences resulting from membership in social groups,
aspirations for membership in other groups that serve as
points of reference, family ties, and the broader attitudes and life styles resulting from being a part of a
particular culture and/or subculture. The simplified
model of the consumer decision process allows us to see
the interactions of the basic determinants and the influences of forces from the individual's environment in
shaping consumer behavior.

Market analysis based on physical characteristics is insufficient. It is also necessary to consider the consumer as an individual with basic motivations, attitudes, and life styles. This difficult task must be attempted if the marketing concept is truly applied.

Key Terms and Concepts

Directions. Match the marketing term or concept listed below with the appropriate definition chosen from the list to the right, and write the appropriate letter in the space to the left of each term or concept. The correct answers are printed upside-down at the bottom of this assignment.

_____ 1. ASCH PHENOMENON

_____ 2. AUTONOMIC HOUSEHOLD DECISION MAKING

_____ 3. COGNITIVE DISSONANCE

_____ 4. CULTURE

_____ 5. EVALUATIVE CRITERIA

_____ 6. EVOKED SET

_____ 7. EXTERNAL SEARCH

_____ 8. INTERNAL SEARCH

_____ 9. OPINION LEADER

_____ 10. PROBLEM RECOGNITION

_____ 11. REFERENCE GROUP

_____ 12. ROLE

_____ 13. SEARCH

_____ 14. SOCIAL CLASSES

a. The complex of values, ideas, attitudes, and other meaningful symbols created by people to shape human behavior and the artifacts of that behavior as they are transmitted from one generation to the next.

b. A separate and distinct segment of the prevailing culture.

c. The rights and duties expected by other members of the group or the individual in a certain position in the group.

d. Those features the consumer considers in making a choice among alternatives.

e. Postpurchase anxiety that occurs as a result of an imbalance existing between a person's congnitions (knowledge, beliefs, and attitudes).

f. The second stage in the decision process, during which the individual gathers information related to the attainment of a desired state of affairs.

g. Households characterized by an equal number of decisions being made by each spouse.

h. The relative position in the group of any individual member.

i. The relatively permanent divisions in a society into which individuals or households are categorized based on prestige and community status.

j. The individual in any group who is the trend-setter; who is respected, often sought out for advice, and who served as an information source about new products.

70

_____15. STATUS

_____16. SUBCULTURE

_____17. SYNCRATIC HOUSEHOLD
DECISION MAKING

_____18. TWO-STEP PROCESS OF
COMMUNICATION

k. Those groups to which a person identifies and orients his or her behavior patterns.

l. The number of brands that a consumer actually considers in making a purchase decision.

m. Depiction of the degree of conformity that groups and group norms can exhibit on individual behavior.

n. Mental review of stored information relevant to the problem situation.

o. The first stage in the decision process during which the consumer becomes aware of a discrepancy between the existing state of affairs and a desired state of affairs of sufficient magnitude to take action.

p. Households characterized by a majority of decisions being made jointly by both spouses.

q. The gathering of information from outside sources by the consumer who is involved in the search process.

r. The Katz & Lazarsfeld proposition that communications flow from mass media to opinion leaders and then to the masses of the population.

ANSWERS: 1. (M); 2. (G); 3. (E); 4. (A); 5. (D); 6. (L); 7. (J); 8. (N); 9. (Q); 10. (O); 11. (K); 12. (C); 13. (F); 14. (I); 15. (H); 16. (B); 17. (P); 18. (R).

The preliminary practice test is designed to help you assess your mastery of text material in this chapter. The test consists of 20 questions focusing upon materials in the chapter and is useful in indicating how well-prepared you are at this stage to take an exam covering this material. The correct answers are printed upside-down at the end of the practice test.

A. MULTIPLE CHOICE.   Chooose the answer which <u>best</u> answers the question or best completes the sentence.

1. Reference group influence is <u>strongest</u> when which of the following products is being considered?

    a) soap
    b) furniture
    c) clothing
    d) air conditioners
    e) cars

2. Warner's class rankings are determined by all of the following <u>except:</u>

    a) occupation
    b) education
    c) family background
    d) dwelling area
    e) amount of income

3. The following categories are applicable to household decision-making:

    a) autonomic
    b) syncratic
    c) symbiotic
    d) a and b
    e) none of the above

4. A household decision-making situation where most decisions are jointly made by the male and female partners is termed:

    a) syncratic
    b) male dominant
    c) autonomic
    d) symbiotic
    e) none of the above

5. The consumer decision process applies to which of the following purchase situations:

    a) first time purchase of a needed product
    b) purchase of a high-priced, long-lived article
    c) routine purchase handled in a habitual manner
    d) all of the above
    e) none of the above

6. The number of brands that a consumer actually considers in making a purchase decision is known as:

    a) the internal set
    b) the evoked set
    c) the external set
    d) the intrinsic set
    e) none of the above

7. The phenomenon closely associated with postpurchase evaluation is:

    a) cognitive dissonance
    b) cognitive anxiety
    c) postpurchase inadequacy
    d) a and b above
    e) none of the above

8. All of the following are examples of an internal search for information except:

    a) actual personal experiences
    b) personal observations
    c) store displays
    d) memories of exposures to persuasive marketing efforts
    e) informaton stored in memory dealing with similar products

9. Which of the following is not an environmental determinant of consumer behavior?

    a) social influences
    b) family influences
    c) cultural influences
    d) subcultural influences
    e) consumer perceptions

10. Subcultures

    a) are found within cultures
    b) have their own distinguishing modes of behavior
    c) can be expected to be found in a heterogeneous culture such as the U.S.
    d) all of the above
    e) a and b only

B. TRUE-FALSE. In the space to the left of each statement check the appropriate line to indicate whether the statement is true or false.

True False

____ ____   1. Status is the relative position in the group of any individual members.

____ ____   2. Both formal and informal groups supply each member with both status and roles.

True False

_____ _____ 3. It is essential that an individual be a member of a particular reference group for that group to be, in fact, a reference group.

_____ _____ 4. Group influence is negligible in the purchase of such goods as canned peaches and laundry soap, since these are typically products whose purchase is unknown to others.

_____ _____ 5. Income is a primary determinant of Warner's class rankings.

_____ _____ 6. Opinion leaders are individuals who are likely to purchase new products before others do and to serve as information sources for the group.

_____ _____ 7. The opinion leader is found in all three types of communication flows discussed in Chapter 4.

_____ _____ 8. Historically, the wife has been responsible for the majority of the family purchases.

_____ _____ 9. Studies of family decision-making have shown that working wives tend to exert more influence in decision-making than non-working wives.

_____ _____ 10. A marketing program that has proven successful in the U.S. may automatically be successfully applied directly in international markets.

ANSWERS: Multiple Choice. 1. (E); 2. (E); 3. (D); 4. (A); 5. (D); 6. (B); 7. (A); 8. (C); 9. (E); 10. (D). True-False. 1. (T); 2. (T); 3. (F); 4. (T); 5. (F); 6. (T); 7. (T); 8. (T); 9. (T); 10. (F).

FINAL PRACTICE TEST.

This final practice test is designed to provide reinforcement of the success of your studies and the adequacy of your preparation for exams covering the material in this chapter. Like the preliminary test, the final practice test consists of 20 questions focusing on materials covered in this chapter. However, the correct answers are reprinted on the last page of the MARKETING Mastery Guide.

A. MULTIPLE CHOICE. Choose the answer which <u>best</u> answers the question or best completes the sentence.

1. Which of the following represents the most important influence in consumer purchase actions?

   a) self-images
   b) family
   c) reference groups
   d) cultural environment
   e) all of the above are important factors in purchase behavior

2. For the influence of a reference group to be great, the following factor(s) must be present:

   a) the item must be one that can be seen and identified by others
   b) the item must be conspicuous
   c) the item must be a brand or product that not everyone owns.
   d) all of the above
   e) a and b only

3. Opinion leaders

   a) tend to be generalized in scope of product influence
   b) are characterized by considerable knowledge and interest in a particular product or service
   c) are found within all segments of the population
   d) b and c
   e) none of the above

4. The change in the female's role as sole purchasing agent for most household items is due to:

   a) a shorter work week
   b) the large number of women in the work force
   c) smaller-sized households
   d) all of the above
   e) a and b above

5. The consumer decision process involves the following stages, <u>in order</u>:

   a) problem recognition, evaluation of alternatives, purchase decision, post purchase evaluation, search, purchase act
   b) problem recognition, search, purchase decision, evaluation of alternatives, purchase act, post purchase evaluation
   c) evaluation of alternatives, problem recognition, search, purchase decision, purchase act, postpurchase evaluation
   d) problem recognition, search, evaluation of alternatives, purchase decision, purchase act, postpurchase evaluation

6. The first step in the consumer decision process, problem recognition, occurs due to:

   a) routine depletion of the individual's stock of products
   b) an inadequate assortment of products

c) dissatisfaction with the consumer's present brand or product type

d) changed financial status

e) all of the above

7. Which of the following is an example of subjective evaluative criteria?

a) E.P.A. ratings of fuel efficiency

b) Federal government comparison of retail prices

c) the sophisticated image of Calvin Klein sportswear

d) a and b above

c) none of the above

8. Dissonance is likely to increase:

a) as the dollar value of the purchase decreases

b) as the dollar value of the purchase increases

c) when the rejected alternatives have undersirable features

d) when the rejected alternatives have desirable features

e) b and d above

9. Which of the following explain why some brands are eliminated from the evoked set?

a) consumer unawareness of certain brands

b) high cost of certain brands

c) dissatisfaction due to previous use

d) unfavorable word-of-mouth

e) all of the above

10. The Asch phenomenon is applicable in which of the following marketing situations:

a) the choice of an automobile model

b) choice of a residential location

c) the decision to purchase an item at a Tupperware party

d) all of the above

e) none of the above

B.   TRUE-FALSE.   In the space to the left of each statement check the appropriate line to indicate whether the statement is true or false.

True False

_____ _____   1. Consumer behavior and, more specifically, purchase actions are dictated solely by the individual's makeup.

_____ _____   2. Roles are what other group members expect of individuals outside the group.

_____ _____   3. Reference groups are those groups to which an individual "refers" for his or her standards of behavior, but not for goals and personal values.

True False

    ____ ____   4. Since most persons view themselves as individuals, groups are rarely influential in purchase situations.

    ____ ____   5, There is no well-structured class system in the U.S., the "land of equality."

    ____ ____   6. Members of the upper-lower class (ordinary working class) tend to enjoy life and live day to day; whereas members of the upper-middle class tend to be more status conscious and more child and home centered.

    ____ ____   7. Individuals rarely tend to be opinion leaders for specific products and services; generalized innovators seem to be the norm.

    ____ ____   8. In a two-step process of communication, there are two sets of intermediaries between the mass media and the market target.

    ____ ____   9. In an autonomic household decision-making situation, an equal number of decisions is made by each partner.

    ____ ____   10. Culture is the complex of values, ideas, attitudes, and other meaningful symbols created by people to shape behavior and the artifacts of that behavior.

PART THREE

PLANNING THE MARKETING EFFORT

Chapter 5

MARKETING PLANNING AND FORECASTING

Chapter Objectives

When you have finished studying this chapter you should be able to:

Outline the strategic planning process.

Differentiate among planning, strategic planning, and marketing planning.

Explain the strategic planning/marketing strategy interface.

Identify the five positioning strategies that can be employed by marketers.

Explain the various influences on marketing strategy.

Explain the steps involved in the forecasting process.

Chapter Summary

Planning is the basis for all strategy decisions. Planning is the process of anticipating the future and determining the courses of action to achieve company objectives. Strategic planning refers to strategy-oriented planning. Marketing planning is the implementation of planning activity as it relates to the achievement of marketing objectives. The planning process begins with a recognition of problems and opportunities. Subsequent steps are the development of alternative courses of action, the evaluation of alternatives, the selection and implementation of chosen alternatives, and the following up to determine the effectiveness of the decisions.

This chapter describes the evaluation of the strategic planning process as well as General Electric's special contribution to the development of this activity. Effective strategic planning is now regarded as a prerequisite to survival. It should be viewed as an organization-wide responsibility involving chief executive officers, heads of operating units, and corporate strategic planning personnel.

Five alternative positioning strategies can be identified:
(1) balancing strategy, (2) market retention strategy,
(3) market development strategy, (4) growth strategy, and
(5) new venture strategy. Three primary variables influencing strategy formulation are the corporate environment, company resources, and management values. Potential
future influences on the planning/strategy interface are
the marketing system itself, public and legal pressures,
marketing changes, and technological changes.

Sales forecasting is an important component of both planning and controlling marketing programs. Forecasting
techniques may be categorized as quantitative or
qualitative (or subjective). The most common approach to
sales forecasting is to begin with a forecast of the
national economy and use it to develop an industry sales
forecast. That forecast is then used to develop a company
and product forecast.

Directions. Match the marketing term or concept listed below with the appropriate definition chosen from the list to the right, and write the appropriate letter in the space to the left of each term or concept. The correct answers are printed upside-down at the bottom of this assignment.

_____ 1. CONCENTRIC DIVERSIFICATION

_____ 2. CONGLOMERATE

_____ 3. GE BUSINESS SCREEN

_____ 4. INPUT-OUTPUT MODEL

_____ 5. LINE EXTENSION

_____ 6. MARKETING PLANNING

_____ 7. MARKETING STRATEGY

_____ 8. PLANNING

_____ 9. PROGRAM EVALUATION REVIEW TECHNIQUE (PERT)

_____ 10. SALES FORECASTING

_____ 11. STRATEGIC BUSINESS UNITS (SBU)

_____ 12. STRATEGIC PLANNING

_____ 13. TACTICAL PLANNING

a. Planning tool used in minimizing project completion time by determining the most efficient sequence for work to be performed.

b. The process of anticipating the future and determining the courses of action to achieve company objectives.

c. Type of planning in which the focus is upon implementation of those activities specified in a strategic plan.

d. A new product that is closely related to existing product lines.

e. A conceptual matrix designed to help marketers determine appropriate marketing strategy for a firm by matching the strengths of the business against those of the industry involved.

f. An estimate of company sales for a specified future period.

g. Related product groupings or classifications within a conglomerate, so structured for optimal planning purposes.

h. The implementation of planning activity as it relates to the achievement of marketing objectives.

i. A conglomerate's act of adding only those new businesses that are easily integrated into the company's existing technological and/or marketing framework.

j. The process of determining **an** organization's primary objectives, and allocating funds and proceed-

80

ing on a course of action to achieve those objectives.

k. The overall company program for selecting a particular market segment and then satisfying consumers in that segment through the elements of the marketing mix.

Sophisticated models of an economy which reflect the impact on supplier industries of increased production in a given industry.

m. A firm with unrelated multiple businesses.

ANSWERS: 1. (I); 2. (M); 3. (E); 4. (L); 5. (D); 6. (H); 7. (K); 8. (B); 9. (A); 10. (F); 11. (G); 12. (J); 13. (C).

Preliminary Practice Test

The preliminary practice test is designed to help you assess your mastery of text material in this chapter. The test consists of 20 questions focusing upon materials in the chapter and is useful in indicating how well-prepared you are at this stage to take an exam covering this material. The correct answers are printed upside-down at the end of the practice test.

A. MULTIPLE CHOICE. Choose the answer which <u>best</u> answers the question or best completes the sentence.

1. Plans which are broad and long-range, focusing on major organizational objectives, with major impact on the organization for five or more years are called:

   a) primary plans
   b) organizational plans
   c) strategic plans
   d) functional plans
   e) operational plans

2. The following are all true about planning except:

   a) planning is a major responsibility for all managers
   b) types of planning activities vary at different levels
   c) the amount of time spent on planning is uniform at all levels
   d) top management spends a greater proportion of its time on planning activities than does lower-level management
   e) top management tends to concentrate on long-range planning

3. Middle managers spend relatively more time developing:

   a) fundamental strategies
   b) objectives of organization
   c) departmental policies and procedures
   d) unit budgets
   e) weekly plans

4. Which of the following is not a step in the planning process described in the text?

   a) obtaining funds to carry out completed plans
   b) recognition of problems and opportunities in a given situation
   c) alternative courses of action are developed
   d) evaluation of alternatives
   e) feedback mechanism to assess the effectiveness of the plan

5. In the decade of the 1970s, strategic planning emphasis:

   a) remained the same as in the sixties
   b) became diffused throughout the conglomerates
   c) declined due to increased uncertainty about the future
   d) was on internal business opportunities
   e) none of the above

6. Concentric diversification pertains to:

   a) acquiring widely varying areas of business
   b) expanding into foreign markets
   c) adding new products which are synergistic with existing products
   d) acquiring firms which can be easily integrated
   e) c and d, but not a and b

7. Which of the following is not accomplished by G.E.'s business screen?

   a) compares the strengths of various businesses
   b) suggests growth opportunities for additional investment

82

c) indicates the strengths of a given industry
d) shows probable actions of competitors

8. PERT stands for:

a) progressive evaluation and review technique
b) program evaluation and review technigue
c) program evolution and review technique
d) program evaluation and response technique
e) promotion evaluation and revision technique

9. Which of the following is <u>not</u> one of the four components of the Bostom Consulting Group's strategic planning matrix?

a) goats
b) cash cows
c) stars
d) dogs
e) question marks

10. Which of the following is <u>not</u> true in regard to the balancing strategy?

a) used for mature products in established markets
b) use when the competition is well-known
c) company attempts to balance revenues and costs
d) emphasizes planning over control
e) marketing program is seldom revised

B. TRUE-FALSE. In the space to the left of each statement check the appropriate line to indicate whether the statement is true or false.

True False

____ ____ 1. The market development strategy emphasizes new markets and product requirements.

____ ____ 2. A growth strategy is less risky than a market development strategy.

____ ____ 3. Public and legal pressurses are expected to have an impact on future marketing decisions.

____ ____ 4. The top-down method of forecasting begins with an evaluation of the strength of the competition.

____ ____ 5. Quantitative forecasting techniques tend to be more subjective in nature than qualitative techniques.

____ ____ 6. The time spent by managers in planning activities tends to be the same, regardless of their rank in the firm.

____ ____ 7. Middle managers' planning processes include daily and weekly plans.

____ ____ 8. Conglomerates are defined as firms with highly integrated multiple businesses.

True False

_____ ___/___ 9. In the 1970s, conglomerates dominated the private
business sector.

_____ ___/___ 10. Strategic planning is the exclusive domain of top
management.

FINAL PRACTICE TEST

This final practice test is designed to provide reinforcement
of the success of your studies and the adequacy of your preparation for exams covering the material in this chapter. Like
the preliminary test, the final practice test consists of 20
questions focusing on materials covered in this chapter. However,
the correct answers are reprinted on the last page of the
MARKETING Mastery Guide.

A. MULTIPLE CHOICE.   Choose the answer which best answers the
question or best completes the sentence.

1. Which of the following does not result from marketing
planning?

   a) marketing strategies
   b) product lines
   c) pricing decisions
   d) selection of distribution channels
   e) none of the above; they all result from planning

2. Tactical plans are:

   a) devised and executed in times of emergency
   b) short term and focused on short-term activities
   c) extremely broad in scope, affecting the toal organization
   d) long-lasting in nature
   e) focused on long-term activities

3. Supervisory-level mangers tend to develop:

    a) daily and weekly plans
    b) unit budgets
    c) annual and five-year plans
    d) a and c, but not b
    e) a and b, but not c

4. Top managers develop plans dealing with:

    a) unit budgets
    b) fundamental strategies
    c) daily and weekly plans
    d) subdivision of budgets
    e) all of the above

5. Which type of planning dominated the 1960s?

    a) crisis planning
    b) disvestiture planning
    c) acquisitions planning
    d) liquidation planning
    e) a and b, but not c and d

6. The strategic planning of the 1980s:

    a) is characterized by increased interest in growth through
       acquisitions of widely diversified firms
    b) is emphasizing integrated growth
    c) will be de-emphasized due to concentration of tactical planning
    d) d and c, but not a
    e) will be concerned with liquidation of common stock

7. Which of the following is not a major contribution by
    General Electric to the concept of strategic planning?

    a) incorporating service into the sales function
    b) grouping activities into strategic business units
    c) separating planning and policy-oriented activities
    d) development of the G.E. Business Screen
    e) forcing personnel to focus on customer needs instead of internal
       divisions

8. Which of the following are components of an overall
    marketing strategy?

    a) advertising
    b) product planning
    c) promotion
    d) pricing
    e) all of the above

9. The purpose of PERT is to:

    a) illustrate the most profitable direction for the firm
    b) reduce program costs
    c) establish the most efficient sequence for work to be performed

d) a and b, but not c
e) a and c, but not b

10. Which of the following accurately describes the question mark component of the BCG matrix?

   a) low market share, low growth
   b) low market share, high growth
   c) high market share, high growth
   d) high market share, moderate growth
   e) high market share, low growth

B.   TRUE-FALSE.   In the space to the left of each statement check the appropriate line to indicate whether the statement is true or false.

True False

____ ____   1. In a new venture strategy, competition is usually fierce.

____ ____   2. Market retention strategy differs sharply from balancing strategy in the decisions which result.

____ ____   3. Risks tend to be high in a new venture strategy.

____ ____   4. The sale forecast's impact is limited to marketing planning, and doesn't really affect other areas in the firm.

____ ____   5. The most common measure of aggregate economic output is the gross national product.

____ ____   6. Tactical planning tends to focus upon long-range plans and objectives.

____ ____   7. Top management's plans tend to focus upon organization objectives and fundamental strategies.

____ ____   8. Supervisory managers' planning focuses upon quarterly and semi-annual plans.

____ ____   9. Concentric diversification pertains to a company adding new products with a high degree of synergy with the existing product line.

____ ____   10. General Electric's Strategic Business Units force the firm's personnel to focus on customer needs instead of internal divisions.

Chapter 6

MARKET SEGMENTATION

Chapter Objectives

When you have finished studying this chapter you should be able to:

Identify the criteria needed for a marekt to exist.

Distinguish between the consumer goods market and the industrial goods market.

Identify the major recent population shifts.

Describe the age groups that will grow fastest during the 1980s.

Explain the use of the family life cycle in analyzing markets.

Identify Engel's laws and explain their relationship to consumer income and expenditure patterns.

Chapter Summary

Markets are people with purchasing power and the authority to make purchase decisions. The total market can be divided into consumer and industrial markets. The ultimate consumer makes purchases for his or her own use, while the industrial purchaser buys products for use in making other products for resale.

Marketing managers must isolate and evaluate potential market targets that can be profitably served by their firms. This step permits managers to gather pertinent information about a market target for use in accomplishing a second task--developing and implementing an effective marketing mix designed to satsify the selected market target.

This chapter examines a number of physical characteristics of the U. S. and international marketplace. Important subjects treated in the chapter include population size and mobility; the urban-suburban concentration of population; age groups; the family life cycle; household size; income and expenditure patterns; and the use of Engel's laws in predicting spending patterns that develop with increases in income. The topics in this chapter serve as the foundations for market segmentation. They form the basis for the approaches to segmentation discussed in the next chapter.

Key Terms and Concepts

Directions. Match the marketing term or concept listed below with the appropriate definition chosen from the list to the right, and write the appropriate letter in the space to the left of each term or concept. The correct answers are printed upside-down at the bottom of this assignment.

_____1.   CONSUMER GOODS

_____2.   ENGEL'S LAWS

_____3.   FAMILY LIFE CYCLE

_____4.   INDUSTRIAL GOODS

_____5.   MARKET

_____6.   MARKET SEGMENTATION

_____7.   MEGALOPOLIS

_____8.   SSWDs

_____9.   STANDARD CONSOLIDATED STATISTICAL AREA (SCSA)

_____10. STANDARD METROPOLITAN STATISTICAL AREA (SMSA)

_____11. ZERO POPULATION GROWTH (ZPG)

a. A group of people who possess purchasing power and the authority and willingness to purchase.

b. Statements on spending behavior, comprised of three generalizations: as family income increases, 1) a smaller percentage of income goes for food; 2) the percentage spent on household operations, housing, and clothing remains constant; and 3) the percentage spent on other items increases.

c. An integrated economic and social unit containing a Standard Metropolitan Statistical Area (SMSA) with a population of at least 1 million, and one or more adjoining SMSAs related to it by high-density population centers and intermetropolitan commuting of workers.

d. Products purchased by the ultimate consumer for personal use.

e. Products purchased for use either directly or indirectly in the production of other goods for resale.

f. The point at which live births equal the current death rate.

g. Acronym applied to single-person households, an emerging market segment.

h. An integrated economic and social unit containing one city of 50,000 inhabitants, or "twin cities" with a combined population of at least 50,000.

i. An extensive contiguous strip of urban-suburban population.

89

j. The process of family formation and dissolution. The cycle includes many subcategories and five major stages: 1) young single people, 2) young married people without children, 3) other young people, 4) middle-aged people, and 5) older people.

k. The process of dividing a total market into smaller, more homogeneous groups with similar product interests.

Preliminary Practice Test

The preliminary practice test is designed to help you assess your mastery of text material in this chapter. The test consists of 20 questions focusing upon materials in the chapter and is useful in indicating how well-prepared you are at this stage to take an exam covering this material. The correct answers are printed upside-down at the end of the practice test.

A. MULTIPLE CHOICE.   Choose the answer which best answers the question or best completes the sentence.

1. All of the following represent industrial goods <u>except</u>:

   a) raw cotton purchased by Burlington Industries
   b) a set of tires purchased by a neighbor for his car
   c) tires purchased by American Motors for use on the jeep "four wheel drive" line
   d) raw rubber purchased by the Firestone Tire Company
   e) all of the above are industrial goods

2. Although zero population growth was achieved for several years during the 1970s, the U.S. population continued to grow due to:

   a) increased life expectancies
   b) immigration
   c) increases in the number of women of childbearing age
   d) all of the above
   e) a and b only

3. SMSA:

   a) stands for Standard Metropolitan Statistical Area
   b) stands for Stratefied Metropolitan Statistical Area
   c) is an integrated economic and social unit containing one city of 50,000 inhabitants
   d) may contain "twin cities" with a combined population of no more than 50,000 inhabitants
   e) a and c are correct

4. All of the following are part of the five-stage family life cycle <u>except</u>:

   a) young singles
   b) young marrieds without children
   c) other young people
   d) other middle-aged people
   e) middle-aged people
   f) older people

5. The single-person household

   a) has not yet emerged as an important market segment
   b) has a special title, SSWD
   c) buys 26% of all passenger cars, but 50% of specialty cars
   d) accounts for 45 percent of the adult population
   e) b and c only

6. When Engel's laws were tested for validity, the following statements were found to be true:

   a) a steady decline in the percentage of total income spent for food does occur from low to high incomes
   b) percentage expenditures for housing and household operations remain relatively unchanged in all but the very lowest income group
   c) percentage spent on clothing decreases with increased income
   d) all of the above
   e) a and b only

7. Young singles

   a) have a large number of financial burdens
   b) tend to be early purchasers of new fashion items
   c) are not recreation oriented
   d) all of the above
   e) none of the above

8. Which of the following statements is <u>not</u> true of the senior adult market?

   a) At present, one out of nine people is 65 or older.
   b) It does not present the marketing manager with a potentially profitable market segment.
   c) At age 65, this year's retiree average life expectancy is at least another 16 years.
   d) The growth in this market segment means an increased demand for medical care, apartments, and retirement homes.

9. Which of the following statements about U.S. population mobility is correct?

   a) The U.S. population ranks with the population of Australia and Canada as the most mobile in the world.
   b) In an average year, approximately 40 million people in the U.S. change their home address at least once.
   c) The average person moves 12 times in a lifetime in the U.S.
   d) a and c are correct
   e) a, b, and c are correct

10. Which of the following statements apply to the marketing concept?

   a) Marketers must identify, evaluate, and ultimately select a market target.
   b) Marketers must develop and implement a marketing mix designed to satisfy the chosen target group.
   c) The choice of a market target results from the recognition of differences in consumers within a heterogeneous market.
   d) Market segmentation is the process of dividing a total market into a smaller, more homogeneous groups with similar product interests.
   e) all of the above

B. TRUE-FALSE. In the space to the left of each statement check the appropriate line to indicate whether the statement is true or false.

True False

____ ____   1. The choice of a market target results from recognition of similarities in consumers and organizations within a homogeneous market.

____ ____   2. A market requires only people and willingness to buy.

92

True False

  ____ ____   3. The choice of a successful market target requires income as well as people.

  ____ ____   4. Zero population growth is the point at which live births equal the current death rate.

  ____ ____   5. The boundaries of an SMSA cannot cross state lines.

  ____ ____   6. U. S. population is expected to increase by 10% between 1980 and 1990, but this growth will be concentrated in only one age group - young to middle-age adults between thirty and forty-five.

  ____ ____   7. Analysis of life cycle stages often gives better results than does reliance on only individual variables such as age.

  ____ ____   8. A common method of segmenting consumer markets is on the basis of income.

  ____ ____   9. According to Engel's laws, although families spend a greater absolute amount of food purchases, their purchases represent a smaller percentage of their total expenditures as income increases.

  ____ ____   10. SSWDs have not yet emerged as an important market segment.

FINAL PRACTICE TEST

This final practice test is designed to provide reinforcement of the success of your studies and the adequacy of your preparation for exams covering the material in this chapter. Like the preliminary test, the final practice test consists of 20 questions focusing on materials covered in this chapter. However, the correct answers are reprinted on the last page of the MARKETING Mastery Guide.

A. MULTIPLE CHOICE.   Choose the answer which <u>best</u> answers the
                        question or best completes the sentence.

1. Of the following listed below, which physical character-
    istics of the marketplace serve as bases for market
    segmentation?

    a) geographic location
    b) population size and mobility
    c) urban-suburban concentrations
    d) age groups
    e) all of the above

2. Population data indicate which of the following popula-
    tion shifts as being predominant:

    a) shifts to the "Sunbelt" states of the Southeast and Southwest
    b) continuing shifts from interior states to seacoast states
    c) shifts to the west
    d) shifts to the east
    e) a, b, and c above

3. The shift to the suburbs:

    a) has been made primarily by middle-income families
    b) has resulted in radical changes in the cities' traditional
       pattern of retailing
    c) has reinforced traditional city boundaries
    d) has led to the integration of downtown shopping areas of many
       U.S. cities
    e) a and b above

4. An SCSA:

    a) contains an SMSA with a population of no more than one million
    b) contains an SMSA with a population of at least one million
    c) contains one or more adjoining SMSAs that are related to it by
       high density population centers and intermetropolitan commuting
       of workers
    d) both b and c are correct
    e) none of the above

5. Several reasons cited by the U.S. Department of Commerce
    for the trend toward smaller households are:

    a) lower fertility rates, and a tendency for young people to post-
       pone marriage
    b) an increasing desire among younger couples to limit family size
    c) ease and frequency of divorce
    d) all of the above
    e) a and c are correct

6. According to Engel's laws, as family income increases:

    a) a smaller percentage of expenditures goes for food, with the per-
       centage spent on housing and household operations and clothing
       increasing

94

b) a larger percentage of expenditures goes for food, with the percentage spent on housing and household operations and clothing decreasing
c) the percentage of expenditures for food remains constant, with the percentage spent on housing and household operations and clothing increasing
d) a smaller percentage of expenditures goes for food, with the percentage spent on housing and household operations and clothing remaining constant
e) the percentage of expenditures for food remains constant, with the percentage spent on housing and household operations and clothing decreasing

7. Household expenditures can be divided into the following categories:

a) basic purchases of essential household needs
b) other purchases that can be made at the discretion of the household member before the necessities have been purchased
c) other purchases that can be made at the discretion of the household members once the necessities have been purchased
d) a and c above only
e) all of the above

8. Young marrieds with young children at home

a) tend to be heavy purchasers of homes
b) tend to have relatively low liquid assets
c) are less likely to watch television than do young singles or young marrieds without children
d) a and b only
e) none of the above

9. Which one of the statements below is true regarding the population of the U.S. between 1980 and 1990:

a) U.S. population is expected to increase by 20%
b) U.S. population is expected to decrease by 20%
c) the population growth will be concentrated in one group only - persons 65 or older
d) the population growth will be concentrated in two age groups - young to middle-age adults between 30 and 45, and persons aged 65 or older

10. The key to proper classification of goods (consumer vs industrial) is:

a) the determination of the purchaser
b) the reasons for the purchase
c) the form of the good being considered
d) all of the above
e) a and b only

B. **TRUE-FALSE.** In the space to the left of each statement check the appropriate line to indicate whether the statement is true or false.

True False

_____ _____ 1. A fundamental task necessary in applying the marketing concept is that of identifying, evaluating, and ultimately selecting a market target.

_____ _____ 2. Changes in the marketplace typically necessitate adjustments in marketing programs.

_____ _____ 3. Consumer goods are products purchased by the ultimate consumer for personal use, while industrial goods are products purchased for use only directly in the production of other goods for resale.

_____ _____ 4. Although it has only a very small percentage of the world population, the United States possesses a third of the world's income.

_____ _____ 5. The shift from rural to urban areas has been accompanied during recent times by a shift to the suburbs.

_____ _____ 6. The thirteen Standard Consolidated Statistical Areas account for one-third of the population of the U.S.

_____ _____ 7. In the older middle-aged group, (45-64), incomes tend to be highest and spending per person heaviest on items such as children's college education, travel, leisure, luxury goods, and services.

_____ _____ 8. The trend is toward smaller households, with slightly more than half the households in the U.S. being comprised of only one or two persons.

_____ _____ 9. Income distribution in most countries is shaped like an inverted pyramid, with the majority of the families having high incomes, and only a small percentage in the low-income bracket.

_____ _____ 10. Higher incomes for the typical household should mean more discretionary spending power.

Chapter 7

MARKET SEGMENTATION STRATEGY

Chapter Objectives

When you have finished studying this chapter you should be able to:

Explain the importance and role of market segmentation.

Identify the bases of market segmentation

Differentiate among the alternative product-market matching strategies.

Explain the use of market target decision analysis.

Outline the steps in the market segmentation process.

Chapter Summary

The subject of market segmentation was introduced in the previous chapter by analyzing the physical characteristics of the marketplace. These and other determinants are utilized in this chapter to divide the total market into several homogeneous groups.

Potential markets may be segmented on a number of bases. Geographic segmentation employs such variables as city size, climate variations, population density, region, and urban/suburban/rural residential locations. Demographic segmentation, the most widely utilized segmentation base, employs such variables as age, sex, marital status, race/ethnic group, income, education, home ownership, religion, and family life cycle stage. Since demographic variables are easy to identify and to measure, and are associated with the sale of many products, they are frequently used as segmentation bases. In addition, demographic characteristics typically can be easily matched with the audiences of advertising media in reaching potential market targets.

Psychographic segmentation, the third approach to market segmentation, employs life-style analysis to develop profiles of different consumers. Such an approach focuses on the activities, interests, and opinions of product users.

A fourth possible basis for market segmentation is the evaluation of such product attributes as varying usage rates and the benefits desired by product purchasers. Heavy users of the product often represent a sizable share of the overall market.

Marketing managers have three alternatives in matching their product offerings with the needs of their chosen market target. They can 1) employ undifferentiated marketing and attempt to reach an aggregated market with a single marketing strategy; 2) practice differentiated marketing and design unique marketing strategies for each segment of the total market; or 3) choose to satsify one segment of the total market through a strategy of concentrated marketing. In order to select an appropriate product-market matching strategy, marketing planners must carefully analyze such factors as company resources, degree of product homogeneity, degree of product newness, and strategies employed by competitors.

Market target decision analysis allows marketing managers to isolate and evaluate potential market targets that can be profitably served by their organizations. The five-stage decision process listed below provides a systematic approach to implementing a market segmentation program:

1. Identify dimensions for segmenting markets
2. Develop profiles of relevant market segments
3. Forecast the total market potential for each segment
4. Forecast probable market share by analyzing competitors' positions in target segments and the specific marketing strategy that would be utilized in the segment
5. Determine whether expected benefits of competing in a particular segment achieve organizational objectives.

Directions. Match the marketing term or concept listed below with the appropriate definition chosen from the list to the right, and write the appropriate letter in the space to the left of each term or concept. The correct answers are printed upside-down at the bottom of this assignment.

_____ 1. AIO STATEMENTS

_____ 2. BENEFIT SEGMENTATION

_____ 3. CONCENTRATED MARKETING

_____ 4. DEMOGRAPHIC SEGMENTATION

_____ 5. DIFFERENTIATED MARKETING

_____ 6. GEOGRAPHIC SEGMENTATION

_____ 7. LIFE-STYLE

_____ 8. MARKET SEGMENTATION

_____ 9. MARKET TARGET DECISION ANALYSIS

_____ 10. PSYCHOGRAPHICS

_____ 11. UNDIFFERENTIATED MARKETING

a. Dividing a population into homogeneous groups based on the benefits the consumer expect to derive from the product.

b. Dividing a population into homogeneous groups on the basis of location.

c. Dividing a population into homogeneous groups based on characteristics such as age, sex, and income level.

d. Market segmentation technique in which homogeneous segments are isolated through the use of cross-classifications of the total market based upon characteristics utilized as segmentation bases.

e. The process of dividing the total market into smaller, more homogeneous groups with similar product interests, based on any number of characteristics.

f. The directing of all of a firm's marketing resources into a small segment of the total market.

g. A practice employed by a firm that produces numerous products with different marketing mixes designed to satisfy smaller market segments.

h. A collection of statements contained in a psychographic study to reflect activities, interests, and opinions of the respondents.

i. Behavioral profiles developed from analyses of activities, opinions, interests, and life-styles that may be used to segment consumer markets.

j. The mode of living of consumers.

k. A practice employed by a firm
    that produces only one product
    and markets it to all customers
    using a single marketing mix.

Preliminary Practice Test

The preliminary practice test is designed to help you assess
your mastery of text material in this chapter. The test
consists of 20 questions focusing upon materials in the chapter and is useful in indicating how well-prepared you are at
this stage to take an exam covering this material. The
correct answers are printed upside-down at the end of the
practice test.

A. MULTIPLE CHOICE. Choose the answer which best answers the
                     question or best completes the sentence.

1. The following statements about marketing segments are all
    true except:

    a) Functional products such as toothpaste do not need to be aimed at
       a specific segment.
    b) It is difficult for any one marketing mix to satisfy everyone.
    c) A marketing segment is a homogeneous subset of customers.
    d) Some products and services, such as an unbranded detergent, are
       aimed at the mass market.
    e) An enormous number of variables are involved in aiming a product
       at a market target.

100

2. Which of the following statements is <u>not</u> true about geographic segments of the market?

   a) Regional variations in taste often exist.
   b) Geographic segmentation is often the only segmentation necessary for a marketer.
   c) Climate is an important factor.
   d) Residence location within a geographic area is an important geographic variable.
   e) Geography was one of the earliest bases for segmentation.

3. Psychographic segmentation consists of:

   a) life-style analysis
   b) age groupings
   c) income segments
   d) a and b, but not c
   e) none of the above

4. AIO statements referred to in the text consist of:

   a) Attitudes, Interests, and Opinions
   b) Actions, Intellect, and Opinions
   c) Activities, Interests, and Options
   d) Activities, Interests, and Opinions
   e) Achievements, Interests, and Opinions

5. Of the following, which is <u>not</u> one of the available product/market matching strategies?

   a) concentrated marketing
   b) differentiated marketing
   c) undifferentiated marketing
   d) diffused marketing

6. In undifferentiated marketing:

   a) Firms produce only one product and market it to all customers with a single marketing mix.
   b) Firms produce numerous products with different marketing mixes which satisfy smaller market segments.
   c) Firms concentrate all marketing resources on a small segment of the total market.
   d) Firms produce numerous products and market them with a single marketing mix.
   e) Firms produce a limited number of products and market them all with a single marketing mix.

7. Which of the following is <u>not</u> a result of using undifferentiated marketing?

   a) efficiency resulting from longer production runs
   b) minimal inventories
   c) problems with foreign markets
   d) increased threat of competition
   e) maximized inventories

8. Which of the following is <u>not</u> true about concentrated marketing?

   a) A firm chooses to focus its <u>entire</u> effort on satisfying a small market target.
   b) Concentration often allows a firm to maintain a profitable operation.
   c) A change in the size of the segment may result in severe financial problems.
   d) A change in customers' buying patterns results in severe financial problems.
   e) None of the above. They are all true statements.

9. Which of the following is <u>not</u> a basic determinant of a product/market strategy?

   a) company resources
   b) product homogeneity
   c) stage in product life cycle
   d) competitive strategies
   e) state of the economy

10. Which of the following is <u>not</u> one of the five stages in the decision process framework for use in market segmentation?

   a) identifying dimensions for segmenting markets
   b) identify stage of product in product life cycle
   c) forecast total market potential for each segment
   d) decision on selection of target market segments
   e) forecast cost/benefit for each segment

B. TRUE-FALSE. In the space to the left of each statement check the appropriate line to indicate whether the statement is true or false.

True False

____ ____ 1. An attempt to satisfy everyone will always doom a marketer to failure.

____ ____ 2. Four bases for market segmentation include segmentation by product attributes and demographics.

____ ____ 3. Residence location within a geographic area is irrelevant in market segmentation.

____ ____ 4. One reason for using demographics is that they are easy to identify and measure.

____ ____ 5. Geographic and demographic data are all a marketer needs to develop segments.

____ ____ 6. AIO statements consist of Activities, Interests, and Opinions.

True False

____ ____ 7. Undifferentiated marketing refers to firms which produce numerous products to satisfy smaller market segments.

____ ____ 8. Firms that produce only one product and market it to all segments with one mix practice undifferentiated marketing.

____ ____ 9. Efficiency resulting from longer production runs are one benefit of concentrated marketing.

____ ____ 10. Undifferentiated marketing strategies tend to maximize inventory costs.

ANSWERS: Multiple Choice. 1. (A); 2. (B); 3. (A); 4. (D); 5. (D); 6. (A); 7. (E); 8. (C); 9. (E); 10. (B).
True-False. 1. (F); 2. (T); 3. (F); 4. (T); 5. (F); 6. (T); 7. (F); 8. (T); 9. (F); 10. (F).

FINAL PRACTICE TEST

This final practice test is designed to provide reinforcement of the success of your studies and the adequacy of your preparation for exams covering the material in this chapter. Like the preliminary test, the final practice test consists of 20 questions focusing on materials covered in this chapter. However, the correct answers are reprinted on the last page of the MARKETING Mastery Guide.

A. MULTIPLE CHOICE. Choose the answer which best answers the question or best completes the sentence.

1. According to the text, a primary factor in the existence of the market segment which purchases Calvin Klein jeans is:

   a) the fact that the recession has caused people to consider jeans a necessity
   b) the fact that this segment has discretionary income and is willing to pay high prices for a new product

c) the fact that people are searching for their identity through purchasing status label clothing

d) all of the above

e) none of the above

2. Which of the following is <u>not</u> one of the four commonly used bases for marketing segmentation as described in the text?

a) demographic segmentation

b) geographic segmentation

c) psychographic segmentation

d) past buying behavior

e) segmentation by product attributes

3. Which of the following is true about demographic segmentation:

a) Demographic data is difficult to obtain.

b) Climate is a critically important demographic variable.

c) Demographics are associated with the sale of many products and services.

d) Demographics are often referred to in describing the audiences of advertising media.

e) Both c and d are correct

4. Life-style dimensions include all of the following except:

a) activities

b) opinions

c) interests

d) peer group acceptance

e) demographics

5. Psychographic segmentation is important to marketing because:

a) Psychographic data is easy to obtain.

b) Psychographic data combined with demographic/geographic variables presents an overall profile of a particular target market.

c) Psychographic data provides a richer description of a potential market segment than demographic data.

d) Both a and b are correct.

e) Both b and c are correct.

6. In differentiated marketing:

a) Marketers rely upon the uniqueness of their product to attract buyers.

b) Marketers produce numerous products with unique marketing mixes designed to satisfy smaller market segments.

c) Marketers produce one product and market it to all segments with a single marketing mix.

d) Marketers concentrate <u>all</u> marketing resources on a small segment of the total market.

e) none of the above

7. Which of the following is true about undifferentiated marketing?

a) The policy of undifferentiated marketing is becoming more and more popular.
b) Undifferentiated marketing results in lowered efficiency because of numerous production runs required.
c) Undifferentiated marketing tends to maximize inventories.
d) Firms using undifferentiated marketing face a threat from competition.
e) Undifferentiated marketing was more popular in the past than it is today.

8. Which of the following is true about differentiated marketing?

a) Companies using differentiated marketing are not attempting to satisfy a large part of the total market.
b) Firms using differentiated marketing produce only one product with several marketing programs.
c) Firms using differentiated marketing still attempt to satisfy a large part of the total market.
d) Both a and b are correct
e) None of the above

9. Which of the following situations would cause a concentrated marketing strategy to be necessary?

a) a firm with limited resources
b) a firm producing products perceived as relatively homogeneous
c) a firm producing many diverse products
d) a firm producing a product which appeals to many different segments
e) all of the above

10. Segmentation bases should be selected so that:

a) each segment is composed of customers who will react to marketing mix alternatives in a variety of ways
b) customers in different segments will respond the same way to marketing mix alternatives
c) customer could fit into a wide variety of segments
d) each segment comprises customers who will react to a specific mix alternative in the same way
e) Both a and c are correct.

B. TRUE-FALSE. In the space to the left of each statement check the appropriate line to indicate whether the statement is true or false.

True False

____ ____   1. A marketing mix can be found to satisfy everyone.

105

True False

  ____ ____   2. The process of dividing the total market into several homogeneous groups is called market segmentation.

  ____ ____   3. Geographic segmentation is one of the newest bases for segmenting overall markets.

  ____ ____   4. The most common approach to market segmentation is to divide consumer groups according to demographics.

  ____ ____   5. Demographic data are difficult to obtain.

  ____ ____   6. Life-style dimensions do not include demographic variables.

  ____ ____   7. Benefit segmentation cannot be readily applied to a general product such as toothpaste.

  ____ ____   8. Concentrated marketing refers to firms which concentrate all marketing resources on a small segment.

  ____ ____   9. The policy of undifferentiated marketing was more common in the past than it is today.

  ____ ____ 10. Undifferentiated marketing is especially useful in foreign markets.

Chapter 8

COLLECTING MARKETING INFORMATION:

THE ROLE OF MARKETING RESEARCH

Chapter Objectives

When you have finished studying this chapter you should be able to:

Identify the different forms of marketing information.

Explain the origins of marketing research and how it assists the decision maker.

List the steps in the marketing research process.

Explain the types of primary data.

Identify the methods of collecting survey data.

Distinguish between marketing research and marketing information systems.

Explain the steps involved in constructing a marketing information system.

Chapter Summary

Information is vital for marketing decision making. No firm can operate without detailed information of its market. Information may take several forms: one-time marketing research studies, secondary data, internal sales and marketing cost analyses, and subscriptions to commercial information sources.

Marketing research, an important source of decision information, is defined as the systematic gathering, recording, and analyzing of data about marketing problems and opportunities. It involves the specific delineation of problems, research design, collection of secondary and primary data, interpretation of research findings, and presentation of results for use by management in decision making.

The scope of marketing information has broadened as an increasing number of firms have installed planned marketing information systems. Properly designed, the MIS will generate an orderly flow of decision-oriented information as the marketing executive needs it. The number of firms with planned information systems will grow during the 1980s as more managers recognize their contribution to dealing with the information explosion.

Key Terms and Concepts

Directions. Match the marketing term or concept listed below with the appropriate definition chosen from the list to the right, and write the appropriate letter in the space to the left of each term or concept. The correct answers are printed upside-down at the bottom of this assignment.

_c_ 1. DATA

_h_ 2. EXPLORATORY RESEARCH

_____ 3. EXTERNAL DATA

_e_ 4. FOCUS GROUP INTERVIEW

_b_ 5. INTERNAL SECONDARY DATA

_i_ 6. HYPOTHESIS

_l_ 7. INFORMATION

_f_ 8. MARKETING INFORMATION SYSTEM (MIS)

_l_ 9. MARKETING RESEARCH

_k_ 10. PRIMARY DATA

_d_ 11. RESEARCH DESIGN

_a_ 12. SECONDARY DATA

_g_ 13. TEST MARKETING

a. Previously published data in a marketing research study.

b. In marketing research, the type of information that is found in records of sales, product performances, sales force activities, and marketing costs.

c. Statistics, opinions, facts, or predictions categorized on some basis for storage and retrieval.

d. A series of advanced decisions that, when taken together, comprise a master plan or a model for conducting marketing research.

e. A marketing research information-gathering procedure that typically brings eight to twelve individuals together in one location to discuss a given subject.

f. A set of procedures and methods designed to generate an orderly flow of pertinent information for use in making decisions, providing management with the current and future states of the market, and indicating market responses to company and competitor actions.

g. The process of selecting a specific city or television-coverage area considered reasonably typical of the total market and introducing the product with a total marketing campaign in this area.

h. Discussing a marketing problem with informed sources within a firm and with wholesalers, retailers, customers, and others outside the firm and examining secondary sources of information.

109

i. The systematic gathering, recording, and analysis of data about problems relating to the marketing of goods and services.

j. A tentative explanation about some specific event, containing a statement about the relationship between variables.

k. Information or statistics being collected for the first time during a marketing research study.

l. Data relevant to the marketing manager in making decisions.

Preliminary Practice Test

The preliminary practice test is designed to help you assess your mastery of text material in this chapter. The test consists of 20 questions focusing upon materials in the chapter and is useful in indicating how well-prepared you are at this stage to take an exam covering this material. The correct answers are printed upside-down at the end of the practice test.

A. MULTIPLE CHOICE. Choose the answer which <u>best</u> answers the question or best completes the sentence.

1. A marketing hypothesis

   a) is an assumption about a specific problem or situation
   b) may prove correct or incorrect
   c) provides a basis for investigation and determination of its accuracy
   d) all of the above
   e) none of the above

2. Which of the following is <u>not</u> a source of external secondary data?

   a) state government
   b) Federal government
   c) Market Research Corporation of America
   d) record of marketing costs from the accounting department of a firm
   e) A. C. Nielson Company syndicated reports

3. M R C A

   a) stands for Market Research Corporation of America
   b) uses a panel of over 7,000 households to gather information on consumer purchases
   c) provides information that can be extremely useful in determining brand preferences and the degree of brand switching
   d) all of the above
   e) both a and b are correct

4. All of the following are types of survey methods except:

   a) telephone interviews
   b) mail interviews
   c) direct observation
   d) personal interviews
   e) focal group interviews

5. Which of the following are management complaints about marketing researchers?

   a) Research is not problem oriented.
   b) Researchers need more involvement with techniques.
   c) Research is slow, vague, and of questionable validity.
   d) Researchers tend to be inexperienced and cannot communicate in the language of management.
   e) all of the above
   f) a, c, and d only

6. An ideal marketing information system should:

   a) be a designed set of procedures and methods.

111

b) have as its purpose the generation of an orderly flow of pertinent information for use in making decisions
c) provide management with the current and future states of the market, as well as indicate market responses to company actions
d) all of the above
e) a and b only

7. Which of the following statements is not true in regard to sales forecasting?

   a) Sales forecasts are only usable in the short run.
   b) The sales forecast is an important tool for marketing control because it produces standards against which actual performance can be measured.
   c) One type of sales forecasting is the top-down method.
   d) The most typical method of sales forecasting begins with a forecast of general economic conditions.
   e) The sales forecast may be defined as the estimate of company sales for a specified future period.

8. The most common approach to sales forecasting follows these steps, in <u>order</u>:

   a) forecast national economy - develop an industry sales forecast - develop a company forecast - product forecast
   b) product forecast - industry sales forecast - forecast national economy - company forecast
   c) develop an industry sales forecast - product forecast - company forecast - forecast national economy
   d) product forecast - company forecast - industry sales forecast - forecast national economy

9. Personal interviews

   a) are typically the best means of obtaining detailed information
   b) can be conducted quickly and efficiently, and are the least expensive method of collecting survey data
   c) allow the interviewer to establish rapport with each respondent and explain confusing questions
   d) all of the above
   e) a and c only

10. The major problem of a controlled experiment is:

    a) over-control of all variables in the test situation
    b) inability to identify all variables in the test situation
    c) inability to control all the variables in a real-life situation
    d) b and c only
    e) none of the above

B. TRUE-FALSE. In the space to the left of each statement check the appropriate line to indicate whether the statement is true or false.

True False

___ ___ 1. The first important task of the market researcher is to define the problem or the opportunity precisely.

___ ___ 2. Marketing researchers often refer to internal data collection as the situation analysis and to exploratory interviews with informed persons outside the firm as the informal investigation.

___ ___ 3. The hypothesis is an assumption about a specific problem or situation that must be proven correct.

___ ___ 4. A major step in the research design is the determination of needed data to use in the testing of hypotheses.

___ ___ 5. An extremely important source of information for the marketing researcher is the use of secondary (previously published) data.

___ ___ 6. There are two types of secondary data: internal and external.

___ ___ 7. There are no advantages to using secondary data over primary data.

___ ___ 8. Observational studies are conducted by actually viewing the overt actions of the person being studied.

___ ___ 9. A simple random sample is one in which the sample is chosen in such a way so that every member has an equal chance of being selected.

___ ___ 10. Test marketing allows the marketing manager to compare actual sales with expected sales and project the figures on a nationwide basis.

This final practice test is designed to provide reinforcement of the success of your studies and the adequacy of your preparation for exams covering the material in this chapter. Like the preliminary test, the final practice test consists of 20 questions focusing on the material covered in this chapter. However, the correct answers are reprinted on the last page of the MARKETING Mastery Guide.

A.   MULTIPLE CHOICE.   Choose the answer which best answers the question or best completes the sentence.

1.   Exploratory research consists of:

   a) discussing the problem with informed sources within the firm
   b) discussing the problem with wholesalers, retailers, customers, and others outside the firm
   c) examining secondary sources of information
   d) evaluating internal company records
   e) all of the above

2.   Which of the following is not an example of internal secondary data?

   a) records of sales
   b) Census data
   c) product performance reports
   d) sales force activities
   e) marketing costs

3.   Potential limitations to the use of secondary data are:

   a) the data may be obsolete
   b) classifications of the data may not be usable in the study
   c) data must be rearranged to be usable in the study
   d) all of the above
   e) Both a and b are correct

4.   Some important advantages to the use of secondary data over primary data are:

   a) The assembly of previously collected data is almost always less expensive than the collection of primary data
   b) Less time is involved in locating secondary data.
   c) None of the above
   d) all of the above
   e) a and b only

5.   Which of the following statements is false in regard to telephone interviews?

   a) Telephone interviews account for 55-60% of all primary marketing research.

114

b) They are limited to simple, clearly worded questions.
c) Telephone inverviews have no major drawbacks in terms of responses elicited.
d) With a telephone interview, it may be extremely difficult to obtain information on respondents' personal characteristics.
e) The survey may be prejudiced by the omission of households without phones and with unlisted numbers.

6. Research is likely to be contracted to outside groups when which of the following requirements are met:

a) problem areas can be defined in terms of specific research projects
b) there is need for specialized know-how or equipment
c) intellectual detachment is necessary
d) all of the above
e) none of the above - the only consideration is cost

7. The sales forecast affects which of the following areas:

a) marketing planning
b) production scheduling
c) financial planning
d) inventory planning
e) all of the above

8. The least accurate method of forecasting general economic conditions, or GNP (Gross National Product) is:

a) trend extension
b) scatter diagram
c) least squares method
d) input-output models
e) none of the above is necessarily inaccurate; each is often used.

9. Which of the following statements is <u>not</u> true regarding mail surveys?

a) They allow the marketing researcher to conduct national studies at at reasonable cost.
b) Returned questionnaires for such studies usually average 80-90%.
c) The results of mail interviews are likely to be biased due to differences in characteristics of respondents and non-respondents.
d) Follow-up questionnaires and/or telephone interviews are used to gather additional information from non-respondents.

10. A method of obtaining a random sample, where population lists are unavailable, that utilizes blocks instead of individuals is known as:

a) taking a census
b) simple random sample
c) area sampling
d) surveying
e) none of the above

B. TRUE-FALSE. In the space to the left of each statement
check the appropriate line to indicate
whether the statement is true or false.

True False

___✓___ ___ 1. Marketing managers' main task is that of making effectieve
decisions that enable their firms to solve problems as
they arise and by anticipating and preventing future
problems.

___✓___ ___ 2. Marketing researchers deal with problem symptoms only,
such as low sales, in order to solve a problem or
enable a firm to take advantage of a potential
opportunity.

___✓___ ___ 3. Preliminary exploratory research may be undertaken in
the search for the key problem facing the decision-
maker, due to a large number of symptoms of the underlying problem.

___✓___ ___ 4. Development of the research design allows the researcher
to control each step of the research process.

___ ___✓___ 5. Three types of data are typically used in data collection:
initial, primary, and secondary data.

___✓___ ___ 6. The Federal government is the nation's most important
source of marketing data, and the most frequently used
government data are census data.

___✓___ ___ 7, Primary data is data collected for the first time during
a marketing research study.

___ ___✓___ 8. In considering the alternatives in the collection of
primary data, the controlled experiment method is the
best in most circumstances.

___✓___ ___ 9. The most widely used approach to collecting primary data
is the survey method.

___✓___ ___ 10. The controlled experiment is the least-used method of
collecting market information.

PART FOUR: PRODUCTS

Chapter 9

PRODUCT STRATEGY

Chapter Objectives

When you have finished studying this chapter you should
be able to:

Explain the broader marketing conception of the word
product.

Explain the concept of the product life cycle.

Distinguish between the adoption process and the diffusion process.

Identify the determinants of the speed of the adoption
process.

Explain the alternative methods for accelerating the
speed of adoption.

Identify the basic categories of consumer goods and
briefly describe each category.

Chapter Summary

A critical variable in the firm's marketing mix is the
products it plans to offer its market target. The best
price, most efficient distribution channel, and most effective promotional program cannot gain continuing purchases of an inferior product.

Consumers view products not only in physical terms but
more often in terms of expected want satisfaction. The
broad marketing conception of a product encompasses a
bundle of physical, service, and symbolic attributes
designed to produce this want satisfaction.

All products pass through the four stages of the product life cycle: introduction, growth, maturity, and
decline. Consumers also pass through a series of stages
in adopting new product offerings: initial product
awareness, interest, evaluation, trial purchase, and
adoption or rejection of the product.

Although first adopters of new products vary among product classes, several common characteristics have been isolated. First adopters are often younger, better educated, and more mobile, and they have higher incomes and higher social status than later adopters.

The rate of adoption for new products depends on five characteristics: (1) relative advantage--the degree of superiority of the innovation over the previous product; (2) compatibility--the degree to which the new product or idea is consistent with the value system of potential purchasers; (3) complexity of the new product; (4) divisibility--the degree to which trial purchases on a small scale are possible; and (5) communicability-- the degree to which the superiority of the innovation can be transmitted to other potential buyers.

Products are classified as either consumer goods or industrial goods. Consumer goods are used by the ultimate consumer and are not intended for resale or further use in producing other products. Industrial goods are used either directly or indirectly in producing other products. Industrial goods are used either directly or indirectly in producing other products for resale.

Differences in consumer buying habits can be used to further classify consumer goods into three categories: convenience goods, shopping goods, and speciality goods.

Once the firm's products have been classified, the marketing manager is provided with a number of insights in making decisions about distribution channels, price, and promotion--the three other variables of the marketing mix.

Directions. Match the marketing term or concept listed below with the appropriate definition chosen from the list to the right, and write the appropriate letter in the space to the left of each term or concept. The correct answers are printed upside-down at the bottom of this assignment.

_____1. ADOPTION PROCESS

_____2. COMMUNICABILITY

_____3. COMPATIBILITY

_____4. CONSUMER GOODS

_____5. CONSUMER INNOVATOR

_____6. CONVENIENCE GOODS

_____7. DIFFUSION PROCESS

_____8. DIVISIBILITY

_____9. IMPULSE GOODS

_____10. INDUSTRIAL GOODS

_____11. MAGNUSON-MOSS WARRANTY ACT (1975)

_____12. PRODUCT

_____13. PRODUCT LIFE CYCLE

_____14. RELATIVE ADVANTAGE

a. In new-product development, those individuals who purchase a new product almost as soon as it is placed on the market.

b. A bundle of physical, service, and symbolic attributes designed to produce consumer want satisfaction.

c. Degree to which a product or service innovation can be used on a limited basis.

d. A product purchased for its unique characteristics as they are perceived by the consumer. Such items are typically branded and high-priced.

e. The stages in the life of a product—introduction, growth, maturity, and decline.

f. Products destined for use by the ultimate consumer.

g. A series or stages in a consumer's relationship with a new product, beginning with awareness of the product to the ultimate decision to purchase the product regularly or to reject it.

h. Products used directly or indirectly in producing other goods for resale.

i. A guarantee to the buyer of a product that the manufacturer will replace the product or refund the purchase price if the product proves defective during a specified time period.

j. Degree to which a product or service innovation appears superior to current offerings.

119

_____15. SHOPPING GOODS

_____16. SPECIALTY GOODS

_____17. WANT SATISFACTION

_____18. WARRANTY

k. Degree to which a product or service innovation is consistent with the values and experiences of potential adopters.

l. Products that the consumer wants to purchase frequently, immediately, and with a minimum of effort.

m. Products purchased only after the consumer has made considerable comparisions between items on such bases as price, quality, style, and color.

n. Products purchased by the consumer after little or no conscious deliberation. These items are often located near the cashier in a store, to induce spur-of-the-moment purchases.

o. The degree to which the results of using a product or service innovation are observable or explainable to others.

p. A federal statute authorizing the Federal Trade Commission to develop regulations on warranty practices.

q. A state of mind achieved when a consumer's needs have been met as a result of a purchase.

r. The acceptance of new products and services by the members of a community or a social system.

The preliminary practice test is designed to help you assess your mastery of text material in this chapter. The test consists of 20 questions focusing upon materials in the chapter and is useful in indicating how well-prepared you are at this stage to take an exam covering this material. The correct answers are printed upside-down at the end of the practice test.

A. MULTIPLE CHOICE. Choose the answer which best answers the question or best completes the sentence.

1. Which of the following is true concerning the Magnunson-Moss Warranty Act?

   a) It gives regulatory power to the Securities and Exchange Commission.
   b) It regulates warranties for product costing under $15.00.
   c) It requires firms to give warranties.
   d) It assists the consumer in comparision-shopping activities.
   e) Both a and b are correct.

2. Which of the following is not a stage in the product life cycle?

   a) decline
   b) growth
   c) development
   d) maturity
   e) introduction

3. Which of the following is not characteristic of the growth stage?

   a) rapid rise in sales volume
   b) losses are common
   c) competitors are attracted
   d) mass advertising is used
   e) early customers make repeat purchases

4. Which stage of the product life cycle is characterized by sales losses and fewer competitors?

   a) maturity
   b) decline
   c) development
   d) introduction
   e) growth

5. Which of the following statements about the product life cycle are true?

   a) The length of the life cycle is roughly the same for all products.

b) Product life can never be extended.
c) Promotional emphasis must shift throughout the life cycle
d) Both b and c are correct.
e) none of the above are true

6. Which of the following steps <u>precedes</u> evaluation in the consumer adoption process?

a) awareness
b) adoption
c) trial
d) indifference
e) both a and c precede evaluation.

7. Which of the following are personal characteristics of innovators?

a) dogmatic
b) tend to be very cosmopolitan
c) tend to be older than later purchasers
d) a and b, but not c
e) all of the above

8. Which of the following is <u>not</u> true of early adoptors?

a) regarded by others as role models
b) greatest opinion leadership
c) empathic
d) tradition-oriented
e) social participation

9. Which of the following is <u>not</u> a characteristic of shopping goods?

a) staple items
b) more expensive than convenience goods
c) can be either homogeneous or heterogeneous
d) both a and c
e) none of the above

10. Extensive purchase planning time, unimportance of convenient location, and short channel length are all characteristics of:

a) convenience goods
b) specialty goods
c) impulse goods
d) industrial goods
e) shopping goods

B. TRUE-FALSE. In the space to the left of each statement check the appropriate line to indicate whether the statement is true or false.

True False

____ ____ 1. Warranty and service are considered a part of the total product.

____ ____ 2. Sales volume rises rapidly during the growth stage of the product life cycle.

____ ____ 3. The decline stage is characterized by a growing number of competitors.

____ ____ 4. Profits tend to rise for products in the decline stage.

____ ____ 5. A product life cycle may be extended by marketing managers.

____ ____ 6. Innovators tend to be highly educated and very cosmopolitan.

____ ____ 7. The late majority tend to be opinion leaders.

____ ____ 8. Convenience goods tend to be low-priced and sold by brand name.

____ ____ 9. Shopping goods can be either homogeneous or hetero-geneous.

____ ____ 10. Specialty goods can be purchased at a large number of retail outlets within the same geographic area.

ANSWERS: Multiple Choice. 1. (D); 2. (C); 3. (B); 4. (B) 5. (C); 6. (A); 7. (A); 8. (D); 9. (D); 10. (B). True-False. 1. (T); 2. (T); 3. (F); 4. (F); 5. (T); 6. (T); 7. (F); 8. (T); 9. (T); 10. (F).

FINAL PRACTICE TEST

This final practice test is designed to provide reinforce-ment of the success of your studies and the adequacy of your preparation for exams covering the material in this chapter. Like the preliminary test, the final practice test consists of 20 questions focusing on materials covered in this chapter. However, the correct answers are reprinted on the last page of the MARKETING Mastery Guide.

MULTIPLE CHOICE. Choose the answer which <u>best</u> answers the question or best completes the sentence.

1. Which of the following is the best definition of a product?

   a) an object which is purchased for a specific purpose
   b) an object or service which is manufactured in the production process
   c) a bundle of physical, service, and symbolic attributes designed to produce consumer want satisfaction
   d) both a and b are correct
   e) none of the above

2. Which of the following is <u>not</u> a component of the total product?

   a) product price
   b) warranty and service
   c) product image
   d) brand
   e) package and label

3. Which of the following tend to characterize the introductory stage of the product life cycle?

   a) stress on information about product features
   b) profits are growing
   c) an effort is made to induce middlemen to carry the product
   d) both a and b are correct
   e) both a and c are correct

4. Which stage of the product life cycle is characterized by information directed toward middlemen, extensive research and development, and lack of profits?

   a) maturity
   b) development
   c) growth
   d) decline
   e) introduction

5. Which is <u>not</u> a characteristic of the maturity stage of the product life cycle?

   a) sales reach a plateau
   b) few competitors
   c) available products exceed industry demand
   d) differences between product diminish
   e) price-cutting is common

6. Which of the following is <u>not</u> a stage in the consumer adoption process?

   a) interest
   b) indifference

c) awareness
d) trial
e) adoption

7. Which of the following is <u>not</u> one of the categories of purchasers based on relative time of adoption?

a) resisters
b) laggards
c) early majority
d) innovators
e) early adoptors

8. Which of the following is <u>not</u> true of laggards?

a) some opinion leadership
b) fear of debt
c) lowest income
d) tradition-oriented
e) little social participation

9. Convenience goods are characterized by:

a) well-known brand name
b) high price
c) frequent purchase
d) both a and b are correct
e) both a and c are correct

10. Which of the following is <u>not</u> a characteristic of speciality goods?

a) frequently branded
b) high prices
c) many retail outlets in a given geographic area
d) consumers are willing to exert much effort to get them
e) all of the above are characteristic of specialty goods

B. TRUE-FALSE. In the space to the left of each statement check the appropriate line to indicate whether the statement is true or false.

True False

____ ____   1. The Magnuson-Moss Warranty Act requires firms to give warranties.

____ ____   2. The introductory stage of the product life cycle is characterized by heavy promotion.

____ ____   3. Products begin earning big profits in the introductory stage of the life cycle.

____ ____   4. Differences among products tend to increase during the maturity stage.

True False

    ____   ____   5. The length of the life cycle is similar for all products.

    ____   ____   6. The trial stage precedes the evaluation stage in the consumer adoption process.

    ____   ____   7. Early adoptors tend to be "deliberate."

    ____   ____   8. Laggards tend to fear debt and be dogmatic.

    ____   ____   9. Shopping goods tend to be less expensive than convenience goods.

    ____   ____ 10. A specialty good tends to move through very long channels.

Chapter 10

PRODUCT MANAGEMENT DECISIONS

Chapter Objectives

When you have finished studying this chapter you should be able to:

Explain the reasons why most firms develop a line of related products rather than a single product.

Identify and explain the four organizational arrangements for new-product development.

List the stages in the product development process.

Distinguish between brands, brand names, and trademarks.

Identify the characteristics of an effective brand name.

Contrast family brands and individual brands.

Distinguish between national brands and private brands.

Differentiate generic brands and generic products.

Describe the major functions of the package.

Explain the functions of the Consumer Product Safety Commission.

Chapter Summary

Product-market strategy typically involves a line of related products. Firms usually produce several related products rather than a single product in order to achieve the objectives of growth, optimum use of company resources, and increased company importance in the market.

New-product organizational responsibility in most large firms is assigned to new-product committees, new-product departments, product managers, or venture teams. New-product ideas evolve through six stages before their market introduction: (1) idea generation, (2) screening, (3) business analysis, (4) product development, (5) test marketing, and (6) commercialization.

While new products are added to the line, old ones may
face deletion from it. The typical cause for product
eliminations are unprofitable sales and failure to fit
into the existing product line.

Product identification may take the form of brand names,
symbols, distinctive packaging, and labeling. Effective
brand names should be easy to pronounce, recognize,
and remember; they should give the right connotation
to the buyer; and they should be legally protectable.
Brand acceptance can be measured in three stages: brand
recognition, brand preference, and, finally, brand insistence. Marketing managers must decide whether to
use a single family brand for their product lines or
to use an individual brand for each product.

The package must provide protection, convenience, and
economy while achieving the company's promotional goals.
The label is also an important promotional and informational part of the package.

Product safety has become an increasingly important
component of the total product concept. This change
has occurred through voluntary attempts by product
designers to reduce hazards, through various pieces
of legislation, and through establishment of the
Consumer Product Safety Commission.

Key Terms and Concepts

Directions. Match the marketing term or concept listed below
with the appropriate definition chosen from the list to the
right, and write the appropriate letter in the space to the
left of each term or concept. The correct answers are printed
upside-down at the bottom of this assignment.

_____1.   BRAND

_____2.   BRAND INSISTENCE

_____3.   BRAND NAME

_____4.   BRAND RECOGNITION

a. A federal statute creating a regulatory agency to promote product
   safety through such means as product recalls, inspections, and consumer information, among others.

b. A brand that has been given legally
   protected status. The protection
   is granted solely to the brand's
   owner.

_____ 5. CHARTER

_____ 6. CONCEPT TESTING

_____ 7. CONSUMER PRODUCT SAFETY
          ACT (1972)

_____ 8. FAIR PACKAGING AND
          LABELING ACT (1966)

_____ 9. FAMILY BRAND

_____ 10. GENERIC NAME

_____ 11. GENERIC PRODUCT

_____ 12. INDIVIDUAL BRAND

_____ 13. LABEL

_____ 14. LANHAM ACT (1946)

_____ 15. NATIONAL BRANDS

_____ 16. PRIVATE BRANDS

_____ 17. PRODUCT LINE

_____ 18. PRODUCT MANAGER

_____ 19. TEST MARKETING

_____ 20. TRADEMARK

_____ 21. VENTURE TEAM

c. The descriptive part of a product's package, listing such items as the brand name or symbol, the name and address of the manufacturer or distributor, the ingredients, the size or quality of the product, and/or recommended uses, directions, or serving suggestions for the product.

d. A name, term, sign, symbol, design, or some combination used to identify the product of one firm and to differentiate them from competitive offerings.

e. A name used for several related products. An example is the Johnson & Johnson line of baby products.

f. In new-product development, the selection of a specific city or television coverage area considered reasonably typical of the total market and the introduction of the proposed new product in this area.

g. A consumer's awareness and familiarity with a specific brand.

h. The various related goods offered by a firm.

i. A food or household item characterized by plain labels, little or no advertising, and no brand name.

j. An organizational strategy for developing new product areas by combining the management resources of technological innovation, capital, management, and marketing expertise.

k. In new-product development, the consideration of a product idea prior to its actual development.

l. A consumer's preference for a specific brand to the point where the consumer will accept no alternatives and will search extensively for the product.

m. Products offered by a manufacturer. Also known as *manufacturers' brands*.

n. An individual in a manufacturing firm who is assigned a product or a product line, and is given complete responsibility for determining objectives and establishing marketing strategies.

o. That part of the brand consisting of words or letters that comprise a name used to identify and distinguish the firm's offerings from those of competitors.

p. A federal statute requiring that registered trademarks not contain words in general use; such *generic words* are descriptive of a particular type of product--such as "automobile" or "suntan lotion"-- and thus cannot be given trademark protection.

q. A federal statute requiring product labels to offer adequate information concerning the package contents, and a package design that facilitates value comparison among competing products.

r. The strategy of giving each item in a product line its own brand name, rather than identifying it by a single name used for all products in the line.

s. A document drawn up by a manufacturing firm specifically defining the functions, operating procedures, and other guidelines for a venture team.

t. A brand name that has become a generally descriptive term for a product (for example, nylon, zipper, and aspirin). When this happens, the original owner loses exclusive claim to the name.

u. A product that carries the name of the retailer offering it; a brand promoted by a retailer as its own. An example is the Kenmore line of appliances sold by Sears.

Preliminary Practice Test

The preliminary practice test is designed to help you assess
your mastery of text material in this chapter. The test consists of 20 questions focusing upon materials in the chapter
and is useful in indicating how well-prepared you are at this
stage to take an exam covering this material. The correct
answers are printed upside-down at the end of the practice
test.

A.   MULTIPLE CHOICE.   Choose the answer which best answers the
                       question or best completes the sentence.

1.   Which of the following alternatives is not normally used
     in locating organizational responsibility for new-product
     development, in successful medium to large-size companies?

     a) product managers
     b) new product committees
     c) engineering departments
     d) venture teams
     e) new-product departments

2.   The venture team concept is an efficient method of develo-
     ping new product ideas for the following reasons:

     a) The team is closely integrated with the organization and linked
        directly to top management.
     b) The team usually begins as a highly-structured group with defi-
        nite new-product goals.
     c) The team must meet such criteria as: return on investment,
        uniqueness of product, existence of a well-defined need, and
        patent protection.

131

d) Team members consist of top management from the major functional areas. Members meet and plan new-product strategy, but their prime job responsibilities are outside the team.
e) all of the above

3. Which of the following are potential sources for new product ideas?

   a) the markets that are served
   b) finding new uses for old products
   c) employees
   d) similar products presently on the market
   e) all of the above are possible sources

4. Geographical test markets are highly recommended in new-product development unless:

   a) management wants to maintain secrecy.
   b) the relative advantage of the new product is great.
   c) the new product could be duplicated quickly and inexpensively.
   d) all of the above
   e) none of the above

5. Which of the following functions is <u>not</u> facilitated by the use of brands?

   a) allows for repeat purchases
   b) acts as the linking factor in the consumer's mind for the image and quality of the product
   c) acts as legal protection from competitors associating similar goods to the brand
   d) allows the firm to escape some of the rigors of price competition
   e) all of the above

6. Which of the following is an argument for utilizing individual brand names?

   a) The brand name is usually related to the name of the company which is producing it.
   b) Enables promotional outlays to benefit all the products in the line
   c) products are dissimilar
   d) It facilitates the task of product introduction to the consumer and retailer.
   e) all of the above

7. Which of the following is a reason for a broad product line?

   a) increased market share
   b) optimal use of company's resources
   c) exploitation of product life cycle
   d) desire to grow
   e) all of the above

8. When responsibility of new-product development is given to one individual who has responsibility for determining objectives, the organizational arrangement is:

   a) new-product department
   b) new-product committee
   c) product manager
   d) venture team
   e) none of the above

9. Which of the following statements is correct?

   a) National brands are often referred to as private brands.
   b) National brands can be referred to as manufacturer's brands.
   c) Sears' brand such as Kenmore, is a national brand.
   d) National brands are sometimes labeled as generic products.
   e) none of the above

10. Labeling consists of which of the following characteristics?

   a) Today's packages contain labels as an integral part of marketing.
   b) Labels perform promotional functions.
   c) Labels perform informational functions.
   d) Labels should give distributor's address.
   e) all of the above

B. TRUE-FALSE. In the space to the left of each statement check the appropriate line to indicate whether the statement is true or false.

True False

____ ____ 1. A company will more readily increase its market share by offering a complimentary product line than by a single product.

____ ____ 2. The typical product manager is assigned one product or product line, and shares responsibility for determining objectives and establishing marketing strategies with the top marketing executive.

____ ____ 3. Screening is an important stage in the new product development process, since the cost to the firm will begin to accrue after this point.

____ ____ 4. Test marketing consists of offering free product samples and questioning shoppers who have evaluated competitive products.

____ ____ 5. Generic names such as Xerox, Formica, Jello, and Kodak were once brand names.

____ ____ 6. The term "battle of the brands" refers to the intense price competition resulting from the increasing market share of generic products.

_____ _____ 7. A company's first objective for its newly introduced products is to make them familiar to the consuming public.

_____ _____ 8. Brand insistence is where the consumer will accept no alternatives and will search extensively for the product.

_____ _____ 9. Procter & Gamble brand line is an example of "individual" brands.

_____ _____ 10. The Food and Drug Administration requires that nutritional contents be listed on food products.

ANSWERS: Multiple Choice. 1. (C); 2. (C); 3. (E); 4. (D); 5. (C); 6. (C); 7. (E); 8. (C); 9. (B); 10. (E).
True-False. 1. (T); 2. (F); 3. (T); 4. (F); 5. (F); 6. (F); 7. (T); 8. (T); 9. (T); 10. (T).

FINAL PRACTICE TEST

This final practice test is designed to provide reinforcement of the success of your studies and the adequacy of your preparation for exams covering the material in this chapter. Like the preliminary test, the final practice test consists of 20 questions focusing on materials covered in this chapter. However, the correct answers are reprinted on the last page of the MARKETING Mastery Guide.

A. MULTIPLE CHOICE. Choose the answer which best answers the question or best completes the sentence.

1. The development of a product line may be a result of the firm:

   a) attempting to reduce variable costs for all products
   b) seeing an opportunity to expand
   c) making certain that it does not become a victim of product obsolescence
   d) both b and c are correct
   e) all of the above

2. Which of the following job responsibilities does not pertain to the product manager?

   a) sets prices
   b) controls sales force
   c) develops advertising programs
   d) sets objectives
   e) none of the above

3. In the initial stage of screening new product ideas, which of the following factors should not be considered for elimination or continuation of the new product idea?

   a) availability of raw materials
   b) synergies of existing facilities
   c) product uniqueness
   d) return on investment
   e) compatibility of new idea with current product line

4. Which stage of the new product development process can be referred to as "concept testing"?

   a) test marketing
   b) screening
   c) product development
   d) idea generation
   e) none of the above

5. When a product has reached the late maturity and early decline stages, the firm faces these alternatives:

   a) Continue the product in order to provide a complete product line to the consumer.
   b) Discontinue the product in order to minimize losses.
   c) Continue the product and channel revenues into developing other products.
   d) Redesign the product.
   e) all of the above

6. If a company is distributing free samples or discount coupons, they are usually trying to achieve:

   a) brand insistence
   b) brand preference
   c) brand recognition
   d) none of the above
   e) all of the above

7. The packaging of a product is extremely important to its success and must accomplish which of the following objectives:

   a) convenience
   b) prevent retail pilferage
   c) be accomplished at the lowest cost possible
   d) offer physical protection
   e) all of the above

8. When a group of high-level executives are in charge of new product development, it is typically an example of:

a) new product committee
b) new product department
c) product manager
d) venture team
e) none of the above

9. The correct sequence of product development is:

a) new product ideas, screening, analysis, development, commercialization
b) idea, analysis, development, commercialization
c) idea, screening, analysis, testing, commercialization
d) idea, screening, development, testing
e) none of the above

10. Which of the following is a characteristic of generic products?

a) They are a result of inflation.
b) Little advertising is used.
c) They are usually household staples.
d) They are often distributed first in Europe.
e) all of the above

B. TRUE-FALSE.   In the space to the left of each statement check the appropriate line to indicate whether the statement is true or false.

True False

____ ____   1. By spreading the costs of company operations over a series of products, it may be possible to reduce the average costs of all products.

____ ____   2. In a new product committee, members are less concerned with reviewing and approving new product plans than with the conception and development of new product ideas.

____ ____   3. Most new product innovation comes from small organizations; venture teams enable the large firm to compete with the small firm in this area.

____ ____   4. In the business analysis stage of the new product development process, profitable product ideas are converted into a physical product.

____ ____   5. If a company feels a new product has a high probability of success, it should move directly from the product development stage to full production.

____ ____   6. National brands can be referred to as manufacturers' brands

____ ____   7. An advantage in converting to the metric system is that small firms will be better able to compete in the international market.

136

True False

____ ____ 8. Brand preference is the third stage of brand acceptance.

____ ____ 9. Heinz's product line is an example of a "family" brand.

____ ____ 10. Consumers' confusion over product sizes resulted in the passage of the Fair Packaging & Labeling Act.

Chapter 11

INDUSTRIAL PRODUCTS

Chapter Objectives

When you have finished studying this chapter you should be able to:

Describe the nature and importance of the industrial market.

Identify the major characteristics of industrial market demand.

Explain the Standard Industrial Classification system and its value to industrial marketers.

Identify and briefly explain each of the categories of industrial products.

Compare government markets to other industrial markets.

Chapter Summary

The industrial goods market consists of all entities that buy goods and service for use in producing other products for resale. The market has three distinctive characteristics: 1) geographical market concentration; 2) a relatively small number of buyers, and 3) systematic buying procedures.

The market concentration is verified by the fact that six states—California, Illinois, Michigan, New York, Ohio, and Pennsylvania - account for more than 40 percent of the value added by manufacturing in the United States. The limited number of buyers in the marketplace is illustrated by the fact that only 33 percent of all U.S. plants employ over 20 people. Industrial marketers often find the Standard Industrial Classification (SIC) codes--the categorization of all businesses into ten broadly defined industry groups--to be a useful tool in analyzing the industrial market.

The systematic nature of industrial purchasing is reflected by the use of purchasing managers who direct such efforts. Major industrial purchases may require an elaborate and lengthy decision-making process that involves many people. Purchase decisions typically depend on price, service, certainty of supply, and efficiency of item being purchased.

Industrial market demand is characterized by derived demand, joint demand, inventory adjustments, and demand variablility, all of these factors influencing the nature and extent of industrial market demand.

This chapter also presents a system for classifying industrial goods according to product use. These five categories include installations, accessory equipment, fabricated parts and materials, raw materials, and supplies. The chapter concludes with a discussion of government markets. The size, organization, market practices, and recent developments in this market are explored.

Key Terms and Concepts

Directions. Match the marketing term or concept listed below with the appropriate definition chosen from the list to the right, and write the appropriate letter in the space to the left of each term or concept. The correct answers are printed upside-down at the bottom of this assignment.

_____ 1. ACCESSORY EQUIPMENT

_____ 2. BID

_____ 3. DEMAND VARIABILITY

_____ 4. DERIVED DEMAND

_____ 5. FABRICATED PARTS AND MATERIALS

_____ 6. INDUSTRIAL GOODS MARKET

_____ 7. INSTALLATIONS

_____ 8. INVENTORY ADJUSTMENTS

a. In the industrial market, the demand for an industrial good as related to the demand for another industrial good that is necessary for the use of the first item.

b. In the industrial market, a written description of a product or a service needed by a firm. Prospective bidders use this description initially to determine whether they can manufacture the product or deliver the service, and subsequently to prepare a bid.

c. In the industrial market, the demand for an industrial product that is linked to demand for a consumer good.

d. A marketplace made up of customers who purchase goods and services for use in producing other products for resale. Examples include manufacturers, utilities, government agencies, retailers, wholesalers,

139

_____ 9. JOINT DEMAND

_____ 10. LIFE-CYCLE COSTING

_____ 11. MRO ITEMS

_____ 12. RAW MATERIALS

_____ 13. RECIPROCITY

_____ 14. SPECIFICATIONS

_____ 15. STANDARD INDUSTRIAL CLASSIFICATION (SIC)

_____ 16. SUPPLIES

_____ 17. VALUE ADDED BY MANUFACTURING

contractors, mining firms, insurance and real estate firms, and institutions, such as schools and hospitals.

e. The difference between the price charged for a manufactured good and the cost of the raw materials and other inputs.

f. In the industrial market, farm products and natural resources used in producing the final manufactured goods.

g. In the industrial market, capital assets that are less expensive and shorter-lived than installations. Examples include office machinery and hand tools.

h. In the industrial market, the finished industrial goods that actually become part of the final product.

i. In the industrial market, the highly controversial practice of extending purchasing preference to suppliers who are also customers.

j. In the industrial market, regular expense items necessary for a firm's daily operations, but not part of the final product. An example would be office stationery.

k. Changes in the amounts of raw materials or goods in process a manufacturer keeps on hand.

l. In the industrial market, the cost of using a product over its lifetime.

m. In the industrial market, the impact of derived demand on the demand for interrelated products used in producing consumer goods.

n. Supplies for an industrial firm, so called because they can be categorized as maintenance items, repair items, and operating supplies.

o. In the industrial market, such specialty goods as factories, heavy machinery, or other major capital assets.

p. In the industrial market, a written sales proposal from a vendor to a firm that wants to purchase a good or service.

q. A classification system developed by the U.S. government for use in collecting detailed information about the various industries comprising the industrial market.

Preliminary Practice Test

The preliminary practice test is designed to help you assess your mastery of text material in this chapter. The test consists of 20 questions focusing upon materials in the chapter and is useful in indicating how well-prepared you are at this stage to take an exam covering this material. The correct answers are printed upside-down at the end of the practice test.

A. MULTIPLE CHOICE. Choose the answer which best answers the question or best completes the sentence.

1. Which of the following is not a reason for the frequent use of personal selling in industrial marketing:

   a) geographical concentration
   b) wholesalers are used more frequently
   c) relatively small number of buyers
   d) unit value of product/service purchased tends to be relatively large
   e) purchases are made relatively infrequently

2. The demand for steel can be derived from the demand for automobiles. If the demand for automobiles declined, auto manufacturers may delay further purchase of steel. This is an example of which form of demand?

   a) inelastic
   b) joint demand
   c) inventory adjustments
   d) demand variability
   e) none of the above

3. Which of the following characteristics is true of accessory items?

   a) less expensive than installations
   b) longer channel of distribution
   c) less technical expertise required by seller
   d) higher importance on price in the decision process
   e) all of the above

4. The tires which come on a new Lynx are an example of what classification of industrial goods?

   a) installation
   b) accessory items
   c) fabricated parts and materials
   d) raw materials
   e) supplies.

5. Which of the following is not correct regarding the government market?

   a) less paperwork than in private industry
   b) tax exemptions
   c) timely payment for purchases
   d) enchanced opportunity for future sales to government once the first sale is made
   e) relatively stable market

6. When the demand for some industrial goods is related to the demand for other industrial goods, it is called:

   a) derived demand
   b) joint demand
   c) inventory adjustment
   d) demand variablility
   e) none of the above

7. Which of the following is not a recent development concerning government markets?

   a) increased purchase of off-the-shelf goods
   b) use of life cycle costing
   c) GSA reforms
   d) Federal Acquisition Regulation used to reduce red tape and excessive regulations
   e) all of the above

8. Geographic concentration of the industrial goods market will affect the marketing mixes of industrial marketers in the following ways:

   a) longer marketing channels to reach the 360,000 manufacturing facilities in the United States
   b) increased use of advertising
   c) increased use of personal selling
   d) relatively lower prices
   e) less research and development expenditures directed toward product innovations

9. Reciprocity is most likely to occur in the following instance:

   a) products of competing suppliers are relatively homogeneous
   b) derived demand is characteristic of the industry.
   c) prices of competing products are similar
   d) customer firms produce products needed by supplier firms
   e) a, c, and d are correct

10. MRO items are included in which of the industrial goods categories?

   a) installations
   b) supplies
   c) accessory equipment
   d) fabricated parts and materials
   e) raw materials

B. TRUE-FALSE. In the space to the left of each statement check the appropriate line to indicate whether the statement is true or false.

True False

_____ _____ 1. The majority of purchase decisions for installations are made solely by the purchasing manager.

_____ _____ 2. Reverse reciprocity is the extension of purchasing preference to suppliers who are also customers.

_____ _____ 3. When two products have a joint demand relationship, the reduction in quantity demanded for product X has a direct effect on the quantity demand of product Y.

_____ _____ 4. Accessory items are considered capital items and are depreciated over several years.

_____ _____ 5. MRO items are frequently purchased by telephone, mail, or from a local wholesaler.

_____ _____ 6. The intent of the FAR is to reduce red tape in the government market.

_____ _____ 7. Industrial goods must be products provided for direct use in consumer goods and services.

True False

_____ _____ 8. The director of purchasing at Ball State University is an industrial purchaser.

_____ _____ 9. The industrial goods classification system is based upon user buying habits.

_____ _____ 10. The purchase of installations is characterized by a longer period of negotiations than is true of accessory equipment.

FINAL PRACTICE TEST

This final practice test is designed to provide reinforcement of the success of your studies and the adequacy of your preparation for exams covering the material in this chapter. Like the preliminary test, the final practice test consists of 20 questions focusing on materials covered in this chapter. However, the correct answers are reprinted on the last page of the MARKETING Mastery Guide.

A. MULTIPLE CHOICE. Choose the answer which best answers the question or best completes the sentence.

1. Concerning the limited number of buyers and geographic concentrations of industrial markets, which of the following is not true?

   a) the Rocky Mountain and Far West Regions had the biggest increases in new plants during the 1970s
   b) the Great Lakes region with 69,558 industrial plants is still ahead of the Southern region
   c) of the 360,275 plants in the U.S., only 33 percent employ 20 or more people

144

d) none of the above are true
e) all of the above are true

2. In the case of industrial products, purchase decisions are often made on which of the following criteria?

   a) efficiency of the supplied product
   b) service
   c) certainty of supply
   d) price
   e) all of the above

3. Which of the following is not a characteristic of the installation classification of industrial goods?

   a) product life span is long, with large unit value
   b) negotiations involve a minimum number of top management, with the final decision often made by the firm's director of purchasing
   c) higher technological expertise in often supplied by the seller
   d) price plays a relatively minor role in the purchase decision
   e) most installations utilize direct channels

4. Which classification of industrial good is least likely to utilize an industrial distributor?

   a) installations
   b) accessory items
   c) parts and materials
   d) raw materials
   e) supplies

5. Which classification of industrial goods can be considered "convenience goods"?

   a) installations
   b) accessory items
   c) parts and materials
   d) raw materials
   e) supplies

6. The demand for cash registers is affected considerably by demand at the retail level. This is an example of:

   a) derived demand
   b) joint demand
   c) inventory adjustment
   d) demand elasticity
   e) none of the above

7. A raw materials supplier is bombarded with new orders, following rumors of a major price increase. This is an example of:

   a) derived demand
   b) joint demand
   c) inventory adjustment
   d) demand variability
   e) none of the above

145

8. Over 40 percent of the value added by manufacturing in the United States takes place in the following six states:

a) New York, Ohio, Michigan, Indiana, Texas, and California
b) New York, Pennsylvania, Ohio, Michigan, Illinois, and Indiana
c) New York, Pennsylvania, Ohio, Illinois, Michigan, and California
d) New York, New Jersey, Pennsylvania, Michigan, Illinois, and Florida
e) New York, New Jersey, Pennsylvania, Michigan, California, and Washington

9. The Standard Industrial Classification (SIC) codes developed by the U.S. Department of Commerce can be considered:

a) a market segmentation tool
b) the result of demand variability
c) effective in reducing reciprocity
d) made possible by the relatively small number of industrial competitors
e) in need of revision due to the recent development of new companies in DNA research, recycling, and energy which are not included in the SIC classifications.

10. Which of the following types of industrial goods are most likely to be purchased on the basis of long-term contracts?

a) installations and supplies
b) accessory equipment and raw materials
c) supplies and fabricated parts and materials
d) fabricated parts and materials and raw materials
e) accessory equipment and supplies

B. TRUE-FALSE. In the space to the left of each statement check the appropriate line to indicate whether the statement is true or false.

True False

____ ____ 1. The Mideast region with such states as New York and Pennsylvania account for the majority of the value added by manufacturing in the United States.

____ ____ 2. Inflation is greatly affected by the purchasers of industrial materials and products.

____ ____ 3. The demand for industrial goods is typically derived from demand for consumer goods.

____ ____ 4. The same classification system can be used for industrial goods that is used for consumer goods because of the interrelationship of demand.

____ ____ 5. Since fabricated parts and materials are finished products which are used in a final product flow, semi-processed products that require additional processing cannot be considered in this classification.

True False

	6.	In order for a firm to sell supplies to the government, the firm must go through the General Services Administration.
____ ____	7.	A recent trend in government purchasing is increased emphasis on special order contracts rather than relying on off-the-shelf products.
____ ____	8.	The addition of a rare stamp to a stamp collector's collection is an example of an industrial purchase.
____ ____	9.	A four-digit SIC code represents a smaller market segment than does a two-digit number.
____ ____	10.	Relatively uniform buying patterns for industrial goods results in the development of a classification system based upon product uses.

Chapter 12

SERVICES

Chapter Objectives

When you have finished studying this chapter you should
be able to:

Distinguish between goods and services.

Explain the importance of services to the economy.

Identify the key distinguishing features of services.

Relate the environmental influences to the market for
services.

Identify the similarities and differences between the
marketing mixes for services and those for tangible
products.

Chapter Summary

Almost 50 percent of all personal-consumption spending
goes for the purchase of services. This figure is expected to rise in the immediate future, according to
government forecasts. *Services* can be defined as intangible tasks that satisfy consumer and industrial user
needs when efficiently developed and distributed to
chosen market segments.

The marketing of services displays many similarities to
the marketing of goods, but there are also some significant differences. Four key features of services have
marketing implications:

1) Services are intangible.
2) Services are perishable.
3) Standardization of services is difficult.
4) Buyers are often involved in the development and distribution of services.

Important aspects of buyer behavior are also different
for services as contrasted to goods. These differences
may be grouped into three categories: attitudes, needs
and motives, and purchase behavior.

148

Although service industries have grown substantially, their development of effective marketing programs has been slow. Many service firms have not adopted the marketing concept; others, such as insurance companies, have become very efficient marketers.

Environmental factors affect service industries the same as they influence goods producers. Marketers of services must be continually aware of changes in the economic, societal, legal, and competitive environments.

An effective marketing mix is mandatory in the service industries. Service policies (service industries' versions of product planning) and pricing, distribution, and promotional strategies must all be combined into a coordinated marketing mix if the service marketer is to succeed.

Service industries will need to increase their marketing function in order to increase productivity and to attain the maximum profit from the growing demands for their varied services.

Key Terms and Concepts

Directions. Match the marketing term or concept listed below with the appropriate definition chosen from the list to the right, and write the appropriate letter in the space to the left of each term or concept. The correct answers are printed upside-down at the bottom of this assignment.

_____1.   GOODS-SERVICES
          CONTINUUM

_____2.   MARKETING MYOPIA

_____3.   PRODUCTIVITY

_____4.   SERVICES

_____5.   TERTIARY INDUSTRIES

a. The businesses that specialize in the production of services.

b. An imaginary line or spectrum, along which products are arranged in a sequence from tangible (good) to intangible (service).

c. Intangible tasks that satisfy consumer and industrial user needs when efficiently developed and distributed to chosen market segments.

d. A term coined by Theodore Levitt in his argument that executives in many industries fail to recognize the broad scope of their business. According to Levitt, future growth is endangered because these executives lack a marketing orientation.

   e. The output of a worker or a machine.

Preliminary Practice Test

The preliminary practice test is designed to help you assess your mastery of text material in this chapter. The test consists of 20 questions focusing upon materials in the chapter and is useful in indicating how well-prepared you are at this stage to take an exam covering this material. The correct answers are printed upside-down at the end of the practice test.

A. MULTIPLE CHOICE. Choose the answer which best answers the question or best completes the sentence.

1. Services such as movies, taxis, and dry cleaning can be classified as:
   a) people-based unskilled labor
   b) people-based skilled operators
   c) equipment-based unskilled operators
   d) equipment-based skilled operators
   e) none of the above

2. In contrast with goods-selection decisions, purchase behavior for the service industry is concerned with:
   a) whether to purchase the service
   b) the extent that personal service is needed, the attitude of the service source and expertise of the source
   c) proper timing of the purchase and qualifications of the source
   d) whether the service can be performed satisfactorly by the purchaser or whether the expertise, which can be purchased, is more beneficial to satisfy the need
   e) none of the above

3. Which of the following is not a reason for the sharp increase in spending for services?

a) technological advances
b) lowered productivity levels of manufacturing firms
c) shift from an agrarian economy to one based on manufacturing
d) population shifts
e) a higher standard of living for the average person

4. Which of the following societal trends are possible reasons for the rapid growth of service firms?

a) consumers' tastes shift over time
b) growing emphasis on security
c) growing concern for health
d) increase in higher education
e) all of the above

5. The advertisement utilized by a stock brokerage firm, showing a testimonial by a famous pro golfer is an example of which promotional strategy?

a) make the service more tangible by personalizing it
b) create a favorable image
c) show the tangible benefits of purchasing an intangible service
d) none of the above
e) all of the above

6. Price negotiations do not normally play an important part in which of the following?

a) foreign travel
b) medical
c) auto repair
d) insurance
e) security

7. Which service industry represents the smallest part of the total service industry?

a) medical care
b) personal business
c) recreation
d) shelter
e) travel

8. What are the key features of services?

a) intangible
b) perishable
c) not standardized
d) buyers are included with distribution
e) all of the above

9. What is a major strength service marketers have over consumer good marketers?

a) do not utilize mass merchandising
b) due to the intangible nature of the service, inventory is not a problem

151

c) can respond to market changes quicker
d) personal feeling consumers have towards servicing
e) all of the above

10. The marketing function appears to be less structured in service companies because:

a) services are less likely to have marketing departments
b) services are less likely to have an overall sales plan
c) services are less likely to develop sales training
d) less likely to spend as much on marketing when expressed as a percentage of gross sales
e) all of the above

B. TRUE-FALSE. In the space to the left of each statement check the appropriate line to indicate whether the statement is true or false.

True False

____ ____ 1. The use of sales promotion is essential to the marketing of services due to their intangible nature.

____ ____ 2. In the service firm the employee is both producer and marketer.

____ ____ 3. Due to the personal aspect of service firms, they have traditionally been more likely to utilize a customer orientation approach to their marketing than have manufacturing firms.

____ ____ 4. Nearly all service firms are subject to special forms of government regulations in addition to the usual taxes, antitrust legislation and restrictions on promotion and price discrimination.

____ ____ 5. With the increasing competition from government services, eventually most consumer services (excluding personal-care services) may be supplied through government agencies.

____ ____ 6. The decline of disco and the corresponding emergence of new wave rock shows that services have product life cycles just like goods.

____ ____ 7. Medical care will be the largest growth industry in terms of employment for the 1980s.

____ ____ 8. Hair styling is an example of a pure service.

____ ____ 9. With service retailing there is a change in the sequence of events since the sale must be made before production takes place.

____ ____ 10. It is unlikely that the characteristics of intangibility causes buyers of services to rely on subjective impressions.

FINAL PRACTICE TEST

This final practice test is designed to provide reinforcement of the success of your studies and the adequacy of your preparation for exams covering the material in this chapter. Like the preliminary test, the final practice test consists of 20 questions focusing on materials covered in this chapter. However, the correct answers are reprinted on the last page of the MARKETING Mastery Guide.

A.   MULTIPLE CHOICE.   Choose the answer which best answers the question or best completes the sentence.

1.   Services such as plumbing, appliance repair, lawn care, catering, security guards can all be classified as:

   a) people-based unskilled labor
   b) people-based skilled labor
   c) equipment-based unskilled operators
   d) equipment-based skilled operators
   e) none of the above

2.   Which of the following is not a key feature of services?

   a) generally services are perishable
   b) sellers have difficulty in developing distribution systems
   c) standarization is difficult
   d) services are intangible
   e) all of the above are features of services

3.   The marketing function appears to be less structured in service companies than in manufacturing firms and service firms:

   a) are likely to perform analysis of the various services offered
   b) are likely to utilize outside advertising agencies

c) are likely to have an overall sales plan

d) are likely to have marketing mix acticities carried out in the marketing department

e) none of the above is correct

4. Which of the following are possible reasons for the rapid growth of business services?

a) service firms often can perform a specialized function more cheaply than the purchasing company can do it itself

b) the increasing government requirements that employees of service firms be utilized

c) many companies are unable to perform certain functions themselves

d) both a and c are correct

e) all of the above

5. Which of the following is not a factor in the competitive environment of marketing services?

a) internal competition can be instrumental

b) competition from the goods manufacturers

c) price competition in unregulated services

d) many services have difficulty entering the market

e) all of the above are correct

6. Which of the following sales promotional tools is most likely to be used by a service marketer?

a) demonstrations

b) premiums

c) displays

d) sampling

e) none of the above

7. Which service industry is predicted to show the largest employment growth in the 1980s?

a) medical care

b) personal business

c) recreation

d) shelter

e) travel

8. A dinner in an exclusive restaurant is an example of which grouping on the product-service spectrum?

a) pure good

b) pure service

c) combination service-good

d) more of a pure service than pure good

e) all of the above are true

9. Differences which exist between buyers' behavior for goods and services include:

a) needs

b) motives

c) attitudes

d) purchase behavior
e) all of the above

10. Which of the following is an example of Levitt's "marketing myopia" theory?

   a) film studio head who defines the firm's activities as making movies rather than entertainment
   b) auto dealers who sells cars rather than transportation
   c) cosmetic department that sells lipstick rather than beauty
   d) the restaurant that sells steak rather than the sizzle
   e) all of the above

B. TRUE-FALSE. In the space to the left of each statement check the appropriate line to indicate whether the statement is true or false.

True False

_____ _____ 1. Although it is difficult to define services, it can generally be said that they are intangible tasks that satisfy consumer and industrial user needs.

_____ _____ 2. Standardization is much easier in the equipment-based services than in the people-based category.

_____ _____ 3. Reliance on subjective impressions as a basis for evaluating various purchase alternatives is more predominent in services than consumer goods.

_____ _____ 4. In general, manufacturing firms incur larger marketing expenditures as a percentage of gross sales than do service firms.

_____ _____ 5. Due to the personal need satisfaction that consumers desire from purchasing services, there is little direct competition between services and goods.

_____ _____ 6. Services can be classified according to their intended use, except in instances where the same service is sold to both industrial and consumer buyers.

_____ _____ 7. As a means of introducing a new service, the marketing practice of sampling is often used.

_____ _____ 8. An optometrist is an example of a pure service.

_____ _____ 9. Service marketers are typically perceived by consumers as friendlier and more cooperative than goods marketers.

_____ _____ 10. As service firms become larger they tend to lose the advantage of the consumer's personal feelings.

PART FIVE: <u>PRICE</u>

Chapter 13

PRICE DETERMINATION

Chapter Objectives

When you have finished studying this chapter you should be able to:

Describe the concept of price and its role in the economic system and in marketing strategy.

List the objectives of pricing.

Explain how prices are determined, both in economic theory and in practice.

Show how breakeven analysis, markups, mark-ons, turnover, and other criteria can be used in pricing strategy.

Contrast the decision models for pricing strategy discussed in the chapter.

Describe the role of government in pricing decisions.

Chapter Summary

Price - the exchange value of a good or service - is important because it regulates economic activity as well as determines the revenue to be received by a specific enterprise.

Pricing objectives should be the natural consequence of company and marketing goals. They can be classified under three headings:

1. Profitability objectives, including profit maximization and target return
2. Volume objectives, including sales maximization and market share
3. Objectives not related to either profitability or sales volume, including social and ethical considerations, status quo objectives, and prestige goals

Prices can be determined by theoretical or cost-oriented approaches. Economic theorists attempt to equate marginal revenue and marginal cost, while businesses tend to rely on cost-plus approaches. Both methods have practical limitations.

Breakeven analysis, the relationship between markup and turnover, and other pricing criteria are all directed toward the improvement of contemporary pricing behavior. This chapter also examines the pricing strategy decision models proposed by Oxenfeldt and Monroe, and the role of government in pricing decisions.

Directions. Match the marketing term or concept listed below with the appropriate definition chosen from the list to the right, and write the appropriate letter in the space to the left of each term or concept. The correct answers are printed upside-down at the bottom of this assignment.

_____ 1. AVERAGE COST

_____ 2. AVERAGE FIXED COST

_____ 3. BREAKEVEN ANALYSIS

_____ 4. COST-PLUS PRICING

_____ 5. CUSTOMARY PRICES

_____ 6. FULL COST PRICING

_____ 7. INCREMENTAL COST PRICING

_____ 8. MARGINAL ANALYSIS

_____ 9. MARK-ON

_____ 10. MARKUP

a. In pricing strategy, the practice of marking up a base cost figure (per unit) to cover unassigned costs and to provide a profit.

b. A market structure involving a heterogeneous product and product differentiation, allowing the marketer some degree of control over prices.

c. Total cost divided by the quantity associated with this cost.

d. A market structure characterized by homogeneous products in which there are so many buyers and sellers that none has a significant influence on price.

e. Pricing objective linked to achieving and maintaining a stated percentage of the market for a firm's product or service.

f. A pricing procedure in which only the costs directly attributable to a specific output are considered in setting a price.

g. Total fixed cost divided by the quantity associated with this cost.

_____11. MONOPOLISTIC
COMPETITION

_____12. MONOPOLY

_____13. OLIGOPOLY

_____14. PIMS STUDY

_____15. PRESTIGE GOALS

_____16. PRICE

_____17. PROFIT
MAXIMIZATION

_____18. PURE COMPETITION

_____19. SALES
MAXIMIZATION

_____20. SOCIAL AND ETHICAL
CONSIDERATIONS

_____21 STATUS-QUO OBJECTIVES

_____22. STOCK TURNOVER

_____23. TARGET RETURN
OBJECTIVE

h. In pricing strategy, the amount of markup compared against the cost of the product.

i. Major research project conducted by the Marketing Science Institute that discovered that market share and return on investment are closely linked.

j. In pricing strategy, goals based on the maintenance of stable prices.

k. A pricing objective based on setting relatively high prices so as to maintain an image of quality.

l. In pricing strategy, the traditional costs of products.

m. The exchange value of a good or service.

n. In pricing strategy, a method for comparing the profit potential of various prices.

o. A market structure involving relatively few sellers, and, because of high start-up costs, significant entry barriers to new competitors.

p. The number of times the average inventory is sold annually.

q. The practice of setting as a minimum the lowest acceptable profit level, and then seeking to enlarge sales within this framework. Under this policy, marketers believe that increased sales are more important than immediate high profits in the long run.

r. A market structure involving only one seller of a product for which no close substitutes exist.

s. A budgeting procedure, the objective of which is to allocate the same amount for an expenditure (such as promotion) that the expenditure will generate in profits.

t. In pricing strategy, the point at which the additional revenue gained by increasing the price of a product equals the increase in total cost.

u. A pricing procedure in which all costs are considered in setting a price, allowing the firm to recover all of its costs and realize a profit.

v. A pricing objective based on certain factors of society and ethics. A physician's sliding-scale fee schedule is an example.

w. In pricing strategy, the amount added to the cost of an item to determine its selling price.

ANSWERS: 1. (C); 2. (G); 3. (N); 4. (A); 5. (L); 6 (U); 7. (F); 8. (S); 9. (H); 10. (W); 11. (B); 12. (R); 13. (O); 14. (I); 15. (K); 16. (M); 17. (T); 18. (D); 19. (Q); 20. (V); 21. (J); 22. (P); 23. (E).

Preliminary Practice Test

The preliminary practice test is designed to help you assess your mastery of text material in this chapter. The test consists of 20 questions focusing upon materials in the chapter and is useful in indicating how well-prepared you are at this stage to take an exam covering this material. The correct answers are printed upside-down at the end of the practice test.

A. MULTIPLE CHOICE. Choose the answer which <u>best</u> answers the question or best completes the sentence.

1. If a firm has a marketing objective to increase market share by 10 percent, the price objective would be:

a) profitability
b) volume
c) social
d) prestige
e) none of the above

2. Target return objectives are designed to satisfy what group of people?

a) stockholders
b) general public
c) management
d) marketers
e) all of the above

3. By utilizing a market share objective in pricing strategy a firm may:

a) be subject to regulations by the government
b) realize high profits
c) realize a more competitive position in the industry
d) develop a monopoly
e) all of the above

4. Status quo pricing objectives are likely to reflect firms with which of the following?

a) maintaining a constant market share by a dominant firm
b) development of product improvements
c) competitive pricing
d) all of the above
e) none of the above

5. Which of the following is not an example of customary determination of prices?

a) reduction in the size of the Hershey candy bar, with increased price
b) division of the beer market into premium and popular prices
c) reduction in the number of first-class seats on some airlines
d) reduction in the size of soft drinks, while maintaining the same price
e) none of the above

6. Monopolistic competition is characterized by all of the following, except:

a) product differentiation
b) homogeneous product
c) control over prices

d) relatively few sellers and buyers

e) somewhat difficult to enter market

7. Monopoly is characterized by all of the following, except:

a) heterogeneous product

b) one seller

c) no close substitutes

d) considerable price control

e) all of the above are characteristic of monopolies

8. In the short run a firm will halt production in order to minimize the losses:

a) if price falls below AC

b) if price falls below AC, but remains above AVC

c) if price exceeds AVC

d) if price falls below AVC

e) none of the above

9. Which of the following is <u>not</u> true of the full cost method?

a) allocates all variable and fixed costs in setting product price

b) demand for the product is taken into account

c) method of allocation may be unrealistic

d) difficult to show cause and effect relationship between price and costs

e) all of the above

10. Which of the following is true of stock turnover?

a) avoids competitive inertia when used with flexible mark ups

b) total sales divided by beginning inventory

c) cost of goods sold divided by beginning inventory minus ending inventory.

d) is used as an important pricing tool

e) all of the above

B. TRUE-FALSE. In the space to the left of each statement check the appropriate line to indicate whether the statement is true or false.

True False

____ ____ 1. Prices are the predominant influence of a company's profit.

____ ____ 2. The only primary pricing objective is to maximize profits.

____ ____ 3. For a firm, profit is maximized at the point where marginal revenue is equal to marginal costs.

____ ____ 4. The market share price objective is the goal set for the control of a portion of the market for the firm's product.

____ ____ 5. Since World War II the major determination of price has been utilization of microeconomic theory.

161

True False

_____ _____ 6. Pure competition markets are theoretical in nature; there does not exist an industry in today's society which exhibits these characteristics.

_____ _____ 7. Variable costs include raw materials, depreciation and wages.

_____ _____ 8. The area of rational pricing behavior for the firm is the marginal cost curve above its intersection with AVC.

_____ _____ 9. Cost-plus pricing takes a base cost figure per unit and adds a markup to defined assigned costs.

_____ _____ 10. Incremental cost pricing uses those cost that can be directly assigned to output, as well as a specified method for allocating fixed costs.

FINAL PRACTICE TEST

This final practice test is designed to provide reinforcement of the success of your studies and the adequacy of your preparation for exams covering the material in this chapter. Like the preliminary test, the final practice test consists of 20 questions focusing on materials covered in this chapter. However, the correct answers are reprinted on the last page of the MARKETING Mastery Guide.

A.   MULTIPLE CHOICE.   Choose the answer which <u>best</u> answers the
                          question or best completes the sentence.

1.   The correct definition of price is:

      a) price reflects the degree of utility or want-satisfying power for
         the product
      b) price is the value of a product/service
      c) price is what the good or service can be exchanged for in the
         marketplace
      d) price is the cost of producing that good/service, plus a profit
         for the producer
      e) all of the above

2.   In today's economy many larger firms adopt a pricing
      strategy that will:

      a) maximize profits
      b) utilize the MR=MC rule
      c) result in sufficient returns on investment
      d) satisfy target return objectives
      e) yield a profit, but satisfy public pressure

3.   Which of the following statements is <u>not</u> derived from
      William Baumol's theory of pricing behavior?

      a) firms set a minimum at what they consider the lowest acceptable
         profit level
      b) firms should set price at a point where the addition to total
         revenue is just balanced by the increase in total cost
      c) maximize sales subject to a profit constraint
      d) continue to expand sales as long as total profits do not drop
         below the minimum return level
      e) all of the above

4.   Which of the following occupations would be least likely
      to utilize a social or ethical approach to pricing?

      a) optometrist
      b) physician
      c) attorney
      d) hair dresser
      e) none of the above

5.   The price strategy utilized by Clenet Coachworks is an
      example of which price objective?

      a) status-quo
      b) sales volume
      c) profitability
      d) prestige
      e) market share

6.   Pure competition is <u>not</u> characterized by which of the
      following?

a) large number of buyers and sellers
b) herterogenous products
c) no one has control over price
d) easy entry to market
e) all of the above

7. Oligopoly is not characterized by which of the following?

a) control over price
b) relatively small number of buyers and sellers
c) difficult to enter
d) common in auto industry
e) none of the above

8. The point of profit maximization is:

a) MR=MC
b) the point where MC curve intersects the AVC curve and the AC curve at the minimum points
c) the lowest point on the AFC curve
d) the lowest point on the AVC curve
e) the midpoint on the quantity axis of the curve

9. Price theory concepts are difficult to apply in practice due to:

a) difficulty in estimating demand curves
b) social pressure
c) firms do not attempt to maximize profits
d) inadequate communications
e) all of the above

10. Which of the following relationships is true at the break-even point?

a) profit is maximized
b) price is minimized
c) variable costs are covered but fixed costs are not
d) fixed costs are covered but variable costs are not
e) total variable costs and total fixed costs are covered

B. TRUE-FALSE. In the space to the left of each statement check the appropriate line to indicate whether the statement is true or false.

True False

____ ____ 1. Price serves as a means of regulating economic activity.

____ ____ 2. Price is the paramount factor in the marketing mix.

____ ____ 3. In order for the firm to maximize profits, price should be increased to the point where it causes a proportionate decrease in the number of units sold.

True False

_____ _____   4. Increased sales are more important than immediate high profits to the short-run competitive picture.

_____ _____   5. Some pricing objectives bear no relations to profitability, sales volume or social objectives.

_____ _____   6. Inflation is one of the major reasons for customary price strategies.

_____ _____   7. In the monopoly model, marginal revenue is the change in total revenue that results from selling an additional unit of output.

_____ _____   8. Marginal cost is the change in total cost that results from producing an additional unit of output.

_____ _____   9. In pure competition price is set at the AR=MR point.

_____ _____ 10. Costs do not determine prices, since the proper function of cost in pricing is to determine the profit consequences of pricing alternatives.

Chapter 14

MANAGING THE PRICING FUNCTION

Chapter Objectives

When you have finished studying this chapter you should
be able to:

Explain the organization for pricing decisions.

Describe how prices are quoted.

Identify the various pricing policy decisions that must
be made by the marketer.

Relate price to consumer perception of product quality.

Explain the relationship between price levels, advertising
expenditures, and profitability.

Contrast negotiated prices and competitive bidding.

Explain the importance of transfer pricing.

Describe pricing in the public sector.

Chapter Summary

The main elements to consider in setting a pricing strategy are the organization for pricing decisions, pricing
policies, price-quality relationships, negotiated prices,
competitive bidding, transfer pricing, and pricing in
the public sector. Methods for quoting prices depend
on factors such as cost structures, traditional practices
in a particular industry, and policies of individual
firms. Prices quoted can involve list prices, market
prices, cash discounts, trade discounts, quantity discounts, and allowances such as trade-ins, promotional
allowances, and rebates.

Shipping costs often figure heavily in the pricing of
goods. A number of alternatives exist for dealing with
these costs: FOB plant, when the price does not include
any shipping charges; freight absorption, when the buyer
can deduct transportation expenses from the bill; uniform delivered price, when the same price - including
shipping expenses - is charged to all buyers; zone
pricing, when a set price exists within each region;

and basing points, when the buyer pays a set price from a particular point, regardless of whether the goods are shipped from that point.

Pricing policies vary among firms. Among the most common are psychological pricing, unit pricing, new-product pricing, which includes skimming pricing and penetration pricing; price flexibility; relative pricing; price lining; and promotional pricing.

The relationship between price and consumer perception of quality has been the subject of much research. A well-known and accepted concept is that of price limits - limits within which the perception of product quality varies directly with price.

Sometimes, prices are negotiated through competitive bidding, a situation in which several buyers quote prices on the same service or good. At other times, prices depend on negotiated contracts, a situation in which the terms of the contract are set through talks between a particular buyer and seller.

A phenomenon of large corporations is transfer pricing, in which a company sets prices for transferring goods or services from one company profit center to another.

Pricing in the public sector has become a troublesome aspect of marketing. It involves decisions on whether the price of a public service serves as an instrument to recover costs or as a technique for accomplishing some other social or civic purpose.

Key Terms and Concepts

Directions. Match the marketing term or concept listed below with the appropriate definition chosen from the list to the right, and write the appropriate letter in the space to the left of each term or concept. The correct answers are printed upside-down at the bottom of this assignment.

167

_____ 1. BASING POINT SYSTEM

_____ 2. CASH DISCOUNT

_____ 3. COMPETITIVE BIDDING

_____ 4. EXPECTED NET PROFIT

_____ 5. FOB PLANT

_____ 6. FREIGHT ABSORPTION

_____ 7. LIST PRICE

_____ 8. LOSS LEADER

_____ 9 MARKET PRICE

_____ 10. ODD PRICING

_____ 11. PENETRATION PRICING

_____ 12. PRICE FLEXIBILITY

_____ 13. PRICING LINING

_____ 14 PROFIT CENTER

_____ 15 PROMOTIONAL ALLOWANCE

_____ 16. PROMOTIONAL PRICE

_____ 17. PSYCHOLOGICAL PRICING

a. A retail good priced at less than cost in an attempt to attract customers who will then buy other merchandise at regular prices.

b. An advertising or sales promotion grant by a manufacturer to other channel members in an attempt to integrate promotional strategy in the channel.

c. An obsolete pricing system, under which the buyer's cost included the factor price plus freight charges from a basing point nearest the buyer.

d. A price reduction granted for large volume purchases.

e. The cost of sending goods from one company profit center to another.

f. A measure of profitability equal to the rate of profit multiplied by the turnover of stock.

g. A pricing policy under which a manufacturer sets an entry price much lower than the intended long-term price, on the theory that this initial low price will help secure market acceptance.

h. A process in which potential suppliers submit price quotations to a buyer for a proposed purchase or contract.

i. A payment to a channel member or buyer for performing some marketing function normally required of the manufacturer. Also known as a *functional discount*.

j. A pricing policy based on the belief that certain prices or price ranges are more appealing than others to buyers.

k. The policy of maintaining a variable price for a product in the market.

l. A pricing system under which the market is divided into various regions and a different price is set in each region.

168

_____ 18. QUANTITY DISCOUNT

_____ 19. REBATE

_____ 20. RETURN ON INVESTMENT
(ROI)

_____ 21. SKIMMING PRICING

_____ 22. TRADE DISCOUNT

_____ 23. UNIFORM DELIVERED PRICE

_____ 24. TRADE-IN

_____ 25. TRANSFER PRICE

_____ 26. UNIT PRICING

_____ 27. ZONE PRICING

m. A pricing system under which the buyer of goods may deduct shipping expenses from the cost of the goods.

n. A price reduction made for prompt payment of a bill.

o. Any part of an organization to which revenue and controllable costs can be assigned.

p. A refund for a portion of the purchase price, usually granted by the manufacturer of a product.

q. The amount a consumer or middleman pays for a product.

r. "Free on board"; a price quotation that does not include shipping charges. The buyer is responsible for paying them.

s. A credit allowance given for an old item when a customer is purchasing a new item. An example is a used car that a customer "sells" to a car dealer in partial payment for a new car.

t. A pricing policy under which prices are stated in terms of a recognizable unit of measurement or a standard numerical count.

u. A lower-than-normal price used as an ingredient of a firm's selling strategy.

v. A pricing policy based on the theory that setting an initially high entry price will permit the manufacturer to recover its new-product costs quickly, before competition eventually drives the price down.

w. A rate normally quoted to potential buyers.

x. A formula used in competitive bidding to determine which bid shows the greatest chance of generating the most revenues.

y. The practice of marketing merchandise at a limited number of price ranges.

z. A pricing system under which all buyers are quoted the same price (including transportation expenses).

aa. A pricing policy based on the theory that a price with an uncommon last digit is more appealling than a round figure. An example would be a price of $9.99 (rather than $10.00).

ANSWERS: 1. (C); 2. (N); 3. (H); 4. (X); 5. (R); 6. (M);
7. (W); 8. (A); 9. (Õ); 10. (AA); 11. (G);
12. (K); 13. (Y); 14. (O); 15. (B); 16. (U);
17. (J); 18. (D); 19 (P); 20 (F); 21. (V);
22. (I); 23. (Z); 24. (S); 25. (E); 26. (T);
27. (L).

Preliminary Practice Test

The preliminary practice test is designed to help you assess your mastery of text material in this chapter. The test consists of 20 questions focusing upon materials in the chapter and is useful in indicating how well-prepared you are at this stage to take an exam covering this material. The correct answers are printed upside-down at the end of the practice test.

A.   MULTIPLE CHOICE.   Choose the answer which <u>best</u> answers the question or best completes the sentence.

1.   Which of the following factors does not affect price quotations?

   a) costs
   b) demand
   c) policies of individual firms
   d) practices in the industry
   e) all of the above

2.   Automobiles most frequently utilize which type of allowance?

   a) rebates
   b) promotional
   c) trade-in
   d) all of the above
   e) both b and c are correct

3.   When the seller is not responsible for any shipping charges it is referred to as:

   a) uniform delived price
   b) zone pricing
   c) FOB plant
   d) freight absorption
   e) basing points

4.   A method of handling transportation cost that is often compared to the pricing of mail service and is sometimes called "postage stamp pricing" is:

   a) uniform delivered price
   b) zone pricing
   c) FOB plant
   d) freight absorption
   e) basing points

5.   A method of handling transportation costs where the price to the customer included the price at the factory plus freight charges from a given location is:

   a) uniform delivered price
   b) zone pricing
   c) FOB plant
   d) freight absorption
   e) basing points

6.   Which of the following best describes skimming price policies?

   a) a relatively high introductory price
   b) a relatively low introductory price
   c) prices designed to drive competitors out of business

d) prices designed to capture a leading market share
e) none of the above

7. A key decision factor in utilizing penetration pricing is:

a) the size of the market share desired
b) whether the product is a consumer or industrial good
c) the amount of competition
d) the size of the product line
e) when to move the price up

8. Loss leaders are an example of what form of pricing?

a) unit pricing
b) price lining
c) promotional pricing
d) penetration pricing
e) psychological pricing

9. A firm is going to submit a bid for a job that it estimates will cost $35,000. One executive has proposed a bid of $60,000, another a bid of $50,000. There is a 40 percent chance of the buyer accepting the first bid and a 60 percent chance of accepting the second bid. From the expected net profit, which bid should they submit?

a) first bid
b) second bid
c) neither because of low profit
d) both bids generate the same expected net profit
e) problem cannot be solved without additional information

10. A functional discount can best be described as:

a) a discount based on the quantity purchased
b) a promotional discount
c) a discount given for channel service
d) a discount given for quick payment of bill
e) none of the above

B. TRUE-FALSE. In the space to the left of each statement check the appropriate line to indicate whether the statement is true or false.

True False

____ ____ 1. The market price is the amount the consumer or middle-man pays.

____ ____ 2. Payment terms such as 2/10, net 30 is an example of a cash discount.

____ ____ 3. Trade discounts tend to be based on the operating expenses of each trade category.

____ ____ 4. Trade-in allowances are synonymous with cash discounts.

True False

_____ _____   5. The basing point method of handling transportation cost no longer is used as a basis for pricing.

_____ _____   6. Skimming policies are more common in consumer markets than industrial markets.

_____ _____   7. Price level decisions are usually based on the firm's cost structure.

_____ _____   8. Studies reveal that consumers' conceptions of quality are directly related to the price of the product.

_____ _____   9. Competitive bidding strategy employs the concept of expected net profit.

_____ _____   10. Government services typically use the full cost pricing approach.

ANSWERS: Multiple Choice. 1. (E); 2. (C); 3. (C); 4. (A); 5. (E); 6. (B); 7. E 8. (C); 9. (B); 10. (C). True-False. 1. (T); 2. (T); 3. (T); 4. (F); 5. (T); 6. (F); 7. (F); 8. (T); 9. (T); 10. (F).

FINAL PRACTICE TEST

This final practice test is designed to provide reinforcement of the success of your studies and the adequacy of your preparation for exams covering the material in this chapter. Like the preliminary test, the final practice test consists of 20 questions focusing on materials covered in this chapter. However, the correct answers are reprinted on the last page of the MARKETING Mastery Guide.

A.   MULTIPLE CHOICE.   Choose the answer which best answers
                         the question or best completes the
                         sentence.

1.   According to a 1979 survey the people or groups most often
      to administer price structures are:

      a) pricing committee
      b) the president
      c) marketers
      d) Board of Directors
      c) a, b, and c are correct

2.   One firm's discount policies are as follows: an annual
      purchase of $25,000 entitles the buyer to an 8% rebate;
      purchases exceeding $50,000 bring a 15% discount.   This
      is an example of:

      a) functional discount
      b) noncumulative quantity discount
      c) cumulative quantity discount
      d) patronage discount
      e) only c and d are correct

3.   Which of the following is not a consideration when the
      marketer is dealing with shipping costs that are a
      high percentage of total costs?

      a) must determine the geographic scope the firm can serve
      b) net margins earned
      c) the ability of the firm to control or influence resale prices of
         distributors
      d) delivery terms to potential customers
      e) all of the above are considerations

4.   A method of handling transportation costs that is used
      by firms seeking to extend their market area is known
      as:

      a) uniform pricing
      b) zone pricing
      c) FOB plant
      d) freight absorption
      e) basing points

5.   A method of handling transportation costs where the
      market is divided into different regions and a price is
      set within each one is:

      a) uniform delivered price
      b) zone pricing
      c) FOB plant
      d) freight absorption
      e) basing points

6. What pricing policy is based on assumption that certain prices or price ranges are more appealing than others to buyers?

   a) psychological pricing
   b) unit pricing
   c) new-product pricing
   d) price flexibility
   e) price lining

7. What pricing policy is designed to capture a dominant market share?

   a) psychological pricing
   b) unit pricing
   c) penetration pricing
   d) skimming pricing
   e) none of the above

8. Which pricing policy depends on the market segments being clearly identified?

   a) unit pricing
   b) pricing lining
   c) psychological pricing
   d) penetration pricing
   e) none of the above

9. Which of the following is <u>not</u> a consideration when using promotional pricing?

   a) may result in consumers' misconceptions
   b) loss of profits could result from prolonged use
   c) some consumers are not influenced by price appeals
   d) may violate unfair trade laws
   e) all of the above are considerations

10. Which of the following is not a consideration in the pricing of the public sector?

    a) should use the full cost approach
    b) taxes act as an indirect price
    c) utilize an ability-to-pay base
    d) Should the price function as an instrument to recover costs?
    e) none of the above

B. TRUE-FALSE. In the space to the left of each statement check the appropriate line to indicate whether the statement is true or false.

True False

_____ _____   1. The list price is the rate normally quoted to potential buyers and is always determined by cost-plus procedures.

____ ____ 2. Cash discounts are reductions from the list price which constitute the variation from the market price.

____ ____ 3. Quantity discounts are frequently referred to as functional discounts.

____ ____ 4. Large purchases reduce selling expenses and may shift part of the storing, transporting and financing functions to the buyer.

____ ____ 5. The seller has several alternatives in handling transportation cost including FOB, freight absorption, and zone pricing.

____ ____ 6. A skimming price policy attempts to maximize profits received from a new product before competition enters the market.

____ ____ 7. Price flexibility is frequently utilized when mass selling is employed.

____ ____ 8. Pricing strategies are usually decided on by considering the product's relationship with the firm's other products in the product line.

____ ____ 9. The average return on investment is greater for firms with high-price-advertising consistency.

____ ____ 10. Transfer price problems referred to shipping cost from seller to buyer.

PART SIX: <u>DISTRIBUTION</u>

Chapter 15

CHANNEL STRATEGY

Chapter Objectives

When you have finished studying this chapter you should be able to:

Identify the types of utility created by marketing channels.

Describe the major marketing channels for consumer and industrial goods.

Explain the factors that determine the optimum marketing channel for a product or service.

Explain the concept of reverse channels and the problems in their development.

Identify the three degrees of intensity of marketing coverage.

Explain the sources of vertical and horizontal channel conflict.

Explain the three major types of vertical marketing systems.

Chapter Summary

Marketing channels bridge the gap between producer and consumer. By making products available when the consumer wants to buy and at a convenient location and by arranging for transfer of title to the goods, marketing channels create time, place, and ownership utility.

The marketing manager faces a host of alternative channels for the firm's products - from contacting the consumer directly through catalog sales or the use of salespersons to using a variety of independent wholesaling middlemen and retailers. In fact, manufacturers of similar products often utilize multiple channels. The choice of optimum channels is based on careful analysis of the firm's market target, characteristics of the manufacturer, product characteristics, and a number of environmental factors.

The degree of intensity of market coverage for products may vary from a single dealer in a given territory (exclusive distribution) to the use of a few dealers (selective distribution) to a total saturation of the market using every dealer who will agree to handle the product (intensive distribution). Exclusive distribution policies may present legal problems, since the concept of limiting the number of dealers who can handle a firm's output carries with it overtones of restraint of trade.

Cooperation among channel members is essential for efficient distribution. The channel captain, the dominant member of the channel, typically assumes responsibility for obtaining cooperation from channel members. Although channel captains have traditionally been manufacturers or wholesalers, large retailers are increasingly assuming this role in the marketing channel.

The need for channel cooperation has resulted in the development of vertical marketing systems (VMS). Whether formed through single ownership of each stage in the marketing channel, through contractual relationships among channel members, or through voluntary cooperation, these systems have proven effective and efficient in managing the operations of the marketing channel.

Key Terms and Concepts

Directions. Match the marketing term or concept listed below with the appropriate definition chosen from the list to the right, and write the appropriate letter in the space to the left of each term or concept. The correct answers are printed upside-down at the bottom of this assignment.

____ 1. CHANNEL CAPTAIN

____ 2. CLOSED SALES TERRITORIES

a. An understanding between a dealer and a manufacturer that requires the dealer to carry the manufacturer's full product line in exchange for an exclusive dealership.

178

a	3.	EXCLUSIVE DEALING AGREEMENT	b. Institutions, such as insurance companies, banks, and transportation companies, which provide specialized assistance to channel members in moving the product from producer to consumer.
o	4.	EXCLUSIVE DISTRIBUTION	
b	5.	FACILITATING AGENCIES	c. An individual who aids wholesalers and retailers by providing information about a firm's products, and generally acts as a management consultant for members of the channel.
h	6.	FRANCHISE	
f	7.	INDUSTRIAL DISTRIBUTORS	
N	8.	INTENSIVE DISTRIBUTION	d. The paths goods follow from consumer to manufacturer, in an effort to recycle used products.
g	9	JOB-ORDER PRODUCTION	e. The dominant and controlling member of a marketing channel.
f	10.	MARKETING CHANNELS	f. The activities of those who sell to retailers, other wholesalers, and industrial users, but not in significant amounts to ultimate consumers.
i	11.	MIDDLEMAN	
c	12.	MISSIONARY SALESPERSON	g. A production system in which products are manufactured to fill customer orders.
g	13.	OWNERSHIP UTILITY	
k	14.	PLACE UTILITY	h. A contractual arrangement in which a dealer agrees to meet the operating requirements of a manufacturer.
s	15.	RETAILER	
d	16.	REVERSE CHANNELS	i. A business firm, either wholesale or retail, that operates between the producer of goods and the consumer or industrial user.
f	17.	SELECTIVE DISTRIBUTION	
j	18.	SPECULATIVE PRODUCTION	j. Production based on the firm's estimate of the demand for its product.
m	19.	TIME UTILITY	

k. A want-satisfying power created by marketers who have products available where consumers want to buy them.

l. An understanding betwen a manufacturer and a middleman that prohibits the middleman from handling the product lines of the manufacturer's competitors.

_____ 20. TYING AGREEMENT

_____ 21. VERTICAL MARKETING
SYSTEM (VMS)

_____ 22. WHOLESALING

m. A want-satisfying power created by marketers having products available when consumers want to buy them.

n. A policy under which a manufacturer of a convenience good attempts to saturate the market with the product.

o. A policy under which a firm grants exclusive rights to a wholesaler or retailer to sell in a particular geographic area.

p. A policy under which a firm chooses only a limited number of retailers to handle the product line.

q. A want-satisfying power created by marketers when title to a product is transferred to the customer at the time of purchase.

r. Restricted geographic selling regions ordered by a manufacturer for its distributors.

s. One who sells products or services to the ultimate consumer and not for resale.

t. The steps a good or service follows from producer to final consumer.

u. A professionally managed and centrally programmed network structured to achieve operating economy and maximum impact.

v. In the industrial market, wholesalers who represent a manufacturer of accessory equipment in the sale and distribution of the manufacturer's product.

ANSWERS: 1. (E); 2. (R); 3. (L); 4. (O); 5. (B); 6. (H); 7. (V); 8. (N); 9. (G); 10. (T); 11. (I); 12. (C); 13. (Q); 14. (K); 15. (S); 16. (D); 17. (P); 18. (J); 19. (M); 20. (A); 21. (U); 22. (F).

The preliminary practice test is designed to help you assess your mastery of text material in this chapter. The test consists of 20 questions focusing upon materials in the chapter and is useful in indicating how well-prepared you are at this stage to take an exam covering this material. The correct answers are printed upside-down at the end of the practice test.

A. MULTIPLE CHOICE. Choose the answer which <u>best</u> answers the question or best completes the sentence.

1. One reason for Japan's relatively inefficient distribution system includes:

   a) size of the country
   b) rugged terrain
   c) emphasis on production
   d) inefficient production processes
   e) all of the above

2. Which of the following illustrates creation of <u>place</u> utility?

   a) mail order catalogues
   b) vending machines
   c) retail stores
   d) all of the above
   e) a and b, but not c

3. The reason that industrial product channels tend to be shorter than consumer goods channels is:

   a) retailers are only found in consumer goods channels
   b) industrial buyers are concentrated
   c) there are a limited number of purchasers
   d) all of the above
   e) none of the above; consumer goods channels tend to be shorter than channels for industrial products

4. Which of the following is least likely to affect channel choice?

   a) whether product is intended for the consumer or industrial market
   b) geographical location
   c) needs of the firm's potential market
   d) size of the product
   e) shifts in consumer buying patterns

5. Channels tend to be shorter when:

   a) the products are perishable
   b) the products are highly technical

c) the products have a low unit value
d) both a and b
e) both a and c

6. The following are all examples of intensive distribution except:

   a) television viewer's sets
   b) TV Guide
   c) soft drinks
   d) chewing gum
   e) cigarettes

7. The following regulations all deal with competition violations except:

   a) The Clayton Act
   b) The Sherman Act
   c) The Norris-Baker Act
   d) The Federal Trade Commission Act

8. The following is true about vertical channel conflict except:

   a) it occurs between channel members at the same level
   b) it occurs frequently
   c) it occurs between channel members at different levels
   d) it is often the most severe form of conflict in the channel
   e) none of the above; all the statements are true

9. Retailers, as channel captains, are likely to be:

   a) more often in the nineteenth century than today
   b) in channels where they purchase most of their goods from large merchant wholesalers
   c) in industries where manufacturers are strong and provide considerable service and continuing new-product innovations
   d) in channels where by-passing the wholesaler is common
   e) none of the above

10. Which of the following is not a type of contractual system?

    a) Wholesaler - sponsored voluntary chain
    b) Wholesaler cooperative
    c) Retailer Cooperative
    d) Franchise
    e) none of the above

B. TRUE-FALSE. In the space to the left of each statement check the appropriate line to indicate whether the statement is true or false.

True False

____ ____   1. Speculative production is rarely used in modern manufacturing.

True	False		
✓		2.	Marketing channels are the paths that goods and title to them follow from producer to consumer.
	✓	3.	Wholesalers sell a large portion of their stock to ultimate consumers.
	✓	4.	The simplest, most direct channel is always the best choice.
	✓	5.	Retailers are important members of industrial product channels.
✓		6.	A major determinant of channel structure is whether the product is intended for consumer or industrial markets.
	✓	7.	Perishable products are required to pass through the longest channels.
✓		8.	The lower the unit value of the product, the longer the channel.
	✓	9.	The more selective the distribution, the more likely price cutting becomes.
	✓	10.	The Disclosure Requirements and Prohibitions Concerning Franchising and Business Opportunities ruling of 1979 prohibits franchisers from owning franchised operations opened after January 1, 1981.

ANSWERS: Multiple Choice. 1. (B); 2. (D); 3. (D); 4. (D); 5. (D); 6. (A); 7. (A); 8. (C); 9. (D); 10. (B). True-False. 1. (F); 2. (T); 3. (F); 4. (F); 5. (F); 6. (T); 7. (F); 8. (T); 9. (F); 10. (F).

FINAL PRACTICE TEST

This final practice test is designed to provide reinforcement of the success of your studies and the adequacy of your preparation for exams covering the material in this chapter. Like the preliminary test, the final practice test consists of 20 questions focusing on materials covered in this chapter. However, the correct answers are reprinted on the last page of the MARKETING Mastery Guide.

A.   MULTIPLE CHOICE.   Choose the answer which <u>best</u> answers the
                           question or best completes the sentence.

1.   Which of the following does <u>not</u> characterize a job-order
      production system?

      a) order is placed and customer receives products from inventory
      b) few marketing risks
      b) many products are purchased this way
      c) both a and b
      e) both a and c

2.   Which of the following types of utility are <u>not</u> created
      by marketing channels?

      a) place utility
      b) ownership utility
      c) service utility
      d) time utility
      e) both a and b

3.   The traditional marketing channel for consumer goods is:

      a) from manufacturer to wholesaler to retailer to consumer
      b) from manufacturer to retailer to wholesaler to consumer
      c) from manufacturer to jobber to wholesaler to industrial user
      d) from wholesaler to broker to retailer to consumer
      e) none of the above; there is no "traditional" channel

4.   Firms with broad product lines are usually able to mar-
      ket their products directly to retailers or industrial
      users because:

      a) the sales force can offer a variety of products
      b) selling costs can be spread over the variety of products
      c) large firms have the financial resources to shorten the
         channel length
      d) both a and c
      e) both a and b

5.   Which of the following factors is <u>not</u> in the text as
      affecting choice of marketing channels:

      a) consumer characteristics
      b) economic factors
      c) product characteristics
      d) manufacturer characteristics
      e) environmental factors

6.   All of the following characterize exclusive distribution
      except:

      a) some loss of market coverage
      b) image of quality and prestige for products
      c) reduced marketing costs

d) little contact between manufacturer and retailer
e) small number of accounts

7. Horizontal channel conflict occurs:

   a) between channel members on different levels
   b) between large retailers and large wholesalers
   c) between retail giants such as Sears and larger limited-line stores handling the same lines of products
   d) a and b
   e) b and c

8. Which of the following are not types of vertical marketing systems?

   a) industrial system
   b) corporate system
   c) contractual system
   d) administered system
   e) both a and d

9. Which of the following is <u>not</u> a function of missionary salesperson?

   a) order taking
   b) providing information about the firm's products
   c) assisting in developing firm's most effective promotion strategy
   d) creating store layout designs
   e) acting as management consultants

10. The best marketing channel available is through a:

    a) wholesaler - retailer - consumer combination
    b) retailer - consumer combination
    c) there is no one best marketing channel
    d) rack jobber - supermarket - consumer combination
    e) distributor - industrial user combination

B. TRUE-FALSE. In the space to the left of each statement check the appropriate line to indicate whether the statement is true or false.

True False

____ ____ 1. Job-order production tends to result in large inventories of finished products.

____ ____ 2. Japan has one of the most efficient distribution systems in the world.

____ ____ 3. Channels create three types of utility: Time, Place and Ownership.

____ ____ 4. Once a channel has been selected for a product, it should not be changed.

185

___ ___ 5. In general, industrial product channels tend to be shorter than consumer channels.

___ ___ 6. Facilitating agencies help direct the flow of goods and services through the channel.

___ ___ 7. Reverse channels will become more important as raw materials become more expensive.

___ ___ 8. In general, the more standardized the product, the longer the channel.

___ ___ 9. Shopping goods are characterized by intensive distribution.

___ ___ 10. Horizontal conflict occurs between channel members at the same level.

Chapter 16

WHOLESALING

Chapter Objectives

Chapter Objectives

When you have finished studying this chapter you should
be able to:

Identify the functions performed by wholesaling middlemen.

Explain the channel options available to a manufacturer
who desires to bypass independent wholesaling middlemen.

Identify the conditions under which a manufacturer is
likely to assume wholesaling functions rather than use
independents.

Distinguish between merchant wholesalers and agents and
brokers.

Identify the major types of merchant wholesalers and
instances where each type might be used.

Describe the major types of agents and brokers.

Summarize the changes in the relative shares of total
wholesale trade between merchant wholesalers, agents
and brokers, and manufacturer-owned wholesale facilities since 1929.

Chapter Summary

Wholesalers are one of the two major institutions that
make up a firm's marketing channel. They are persons
or firms who sell to retailers and other wholesalers
or to industrial users but who do not sell in significant amounts to ultimte consumers. The three types
of wholesaling middlemen are manufactured-owned facilities, merchant wholesalers, and agents and brokers.
Merchant wholesalers take title to the goods they handle.
Agents and brokers may take possession of the goods,
but do not take title. Merchant wholesalers include
full function wholesalers, rack jobbers, cash-and-carry
wholesalers, truck wholesalers, and drop shippers.

187

Commission merchants, auction houses, brokers, selling agents, and manufacturers' agents are classified as agent wholesaling middlemen because they do not take title to goods.

The operating expenses of wholesaling middlemen vary considerably, depending on the number of services provided and the costs involved. The services include storage facilities in conveniently located warehouses, market coverage by a sales force, financing for retailers and manufacturers, market information for retailers and manufacturers, transportation, and, specifically for retailers, management services, retail sales training, and merchandising assistance and advice.

While the percentage of wholesale trade by manufacturer-owned facilities has increased since 1929, independent wholesaling middlemen continue to account for 87 percent of all wholesale establishments and nearly two-thirds of total wholesale trade. They accomplish this by continuing to provide desired services to manufacturers and retailers.

Key Terms and Concepts

Directions. Match the marketing term or concept listed below with the appropriate definition chosen from the list to the right, and write the appropriate letter in the space to the left of each term or concept. The correct answers are printed upside-down at the bottom of this assignment.

_e_ 1. AUCTION HOUSE

_l_ 2. BROKER

_h_ 3. CASH-AND-CARRY WHOLESALER

_c_ 4. COMMISSION MERCHANT

_a_ 5. MANUFACTURERS' AGENT

a. A merchant wholesaler whose services to retailers include supplying a display case, pricing the merchandise, stocking the case, and returning regularly to replenish the case.

b. Merchant wholesaler who operates in the marketing of perishable food items and tobacco products.

c. One who takes possession of goods when they are shipped to a central market for sale, acts as the producer's agent, and collects an agreed-upon fee at the time of sale.

_j_ 6. MERCHANDISE MART

_f_ 7. MERCHANT WHOLESALERS

_n_ 8. PUBLIC WAREHOUSE

_a_ 9. RACK JOBBER

_k_ 10. SALES BRANCH

_p_ 11. SALES OFFICE

_d_ 12. SELLING AGENT

_i_ 13. TRADE FAIR

_b_ 14. TRUCK WHOLESALER

_m_ 15. WHOLESALER

_g_ 16. WHOLESALING
        MIDDLEMAN

d. Agent wholesaling middleman who is responsible for the total marketing program of a firm's product line.

e. An establishment that brings buyers and sellers together in one location for the purpose of permitting buyers to examine merchandise before purchasing it.

f. An independent wholesaling middleman who takes title to the goods handled.

g. Channel members who take title to the goods they handle; also, agents and brokers who perform important wholesaling activities without taking title to the goods.

h. One who performs most wholesaling functions except financing and delivery.

i. A regularly scheduled show, at which manufacturers of a particular industry display their wares for visitng wholesale and retail buyers.

j. A facility in which manufacturers rent space for relatively permanent exhibits of their product offerings.

k. An installation of a firm that carries inventory and processes customer orders from available stock.

l. An independent wholesaling middleman who does not take title or possession to goods, and whose primary function is bringing buyers and sellers together.

m. A middleman who takes title to the goods he or she handles.

o. An independent salesperson who works for a number of manufacturers of related but non-competiting products; the salesperson receives a commission based on a specified percentage of sales.

n ? where ol ol .

189

p. A regional installation for a
firm's sales personnel.

Preliminary Practice Test

The preliminary practice test is designed to help you assess
your mastery of text material in this chapter. The test consists of 20 questions focusing upon materials in the chapter
and is useful in indicating how well-prepared you are at this
stage to take an exam covering this material. The correct
answers are printed upside-down at the end of the practice test.

A.   MULTIPLE CHOICE. Choose the answer which best answers the
                      question or best completes the sentence.

1.   All of the following are services provided by middlemen
      except:

      a) selecting
      b) storing
      c) financing
      d) transporting
      e) selling

2.   Which of the following is not one of the three basic
      types of ownership by wholesaling middlemen?

      a) retailer-owned cooperatives
      b) independent cooperatives
      c) manufacturer-owned sales offices
      d) independent wholesaling middleman

e) none of the above

3. Which of the following services is <u>not</u> normally performed by full-function merchant wholesalers?

   a) storing merchandise in convenient locations
   b) maintain sales forces to call regularly on retailers
   c) make deliveries
   d) extend credit to qualified buyers
   e) all of the above are commonly done by full-function merchant wholesalers

4. The "TOPS" ordering system described in the chapter performs all the following functions except:

   a) immediate visual data on item availability
   b) enters orders
   c) initiates sales
   d) maintains accurate computer purchasing records
   e) furnishes a quarterly item transaction report.

5. Which of the following is <u>not</u> one of the categories of agent wholesaling middlemen?

   a) commission merchants
   b) auction houses
   c) brokers
   d) rack jobbers
   e) selling agents

6. Manufacturers'agents are used to develop marketing channels for several reasons. Which of the following is <u>not</u> one of the reasons given in the text?

   a) They reduce selling costs by spreading the cost over several different products.
   b) They take possession of the products and provide storage.
   c) Agents are paid on a commission basis and often cost less than sales force.
   d) Firms with unrelated lines typically need more than one channel.
   e) They provide access to the market for small firms with no sales force.

7. None of the following take title to the goods they handle except:

   a) rack jobbers
   b) merchant wholesalers
   c) agents
   d) brokers
   e) auction houses

8. Which of the following is <u>not</u> included in the service category of <u>providing market information</u>?

   a) regular contacts with retail and industrial buyers
   b) provides information about new products
   c) reports on competitor activities

d) reports on industry trends
e) all of the above are included in the service of providing market information

9. Wholesaling middlemen can be bypassed if the manufacturers are willing to:

a) lose sales,
b) limit their product lines
c) lower prices
d) assume the functions they perform
e) all of the above

10. Electronics Corporation of America is a small firm with limited financial resources and virtually no marketing capability. Its sole product is a low-pricedtelephone answering/recording device. Which of the following wholesalers appears most appropriate?

a) auction company
b) sales agent
c) merchant wholesaler
d) broker
e. Commission merchant

B. TRUE-FALSE. In the space to the left of each statement check the appropriate line to indicate whether the statement is true or false.

True False

_____ _✓_ 1. There is little risk-taking ivolved in the job of the wholesaling middlemen.

_____ _✓_ 2. Wholesaling middleman cannot be bypassed by the manu-facturers without reducing overall sales.

_____ _✓_ 3. Manufacturers seldom market their products directly.

_✓_ _____ 4. Agents and brokers do not take title to goods.

_____ _✓_ 5. Brokers take title to the goods they handle, but not possession.

_____ _✓_ 6. Cash-and-carry wholesalers perform financing and delivery functions.

_____ _✓_ 7. Drop shippers always maintain an inventory and, as such, incur added costs.

_✓_ _____ 8. Selling agents can be responsible for the total mar-keting program of a firm's product line.

_____ _✓_ 9. Rack-jobbers are not considered merchant wholesalers.

_____ _✓_ 10. Commission merchants always take title to the agri-cultural products they sell.

192

FINAL PRACTICE TEST

This final practice test is designed to provide reinforcement of the success of your studies and the adequacy of your
preparation for exams covering the material in this chapter.
Like the preliminary test, the final practice test consists
of 20 questions focusing on materials covered in this chapter.
However, the correct answers are reprinted on the last page
of the MARKETING Mastery Guide.

A.   MULTIPLE CHOICE.   Choose the answer which best answers the
                         question or best completes the sentence.

1.   Wholesalers are individuals or firms who sell to everyone
      except:

      a) other wholesalers
      b) ultimate consumers
      c) retailers
      d) industrial users
      e) middlemen

2.   Which of the following is not a reason for products being
      marketed directly by manufacturers?

      a) some products are perishable
      b) some require complex installation
      c) some need aggressive promotion
      d) some are low unit value goods
      e) all of the above are reasons for direct marketing

3.   Sales branches and offices are prevalent in the market-
      ing of all of the following except:

      a) petroleum products
      b) commercial machinery
      c) food products

d) chemicals
e) motor vehicles

4. Rack jobbers perform all the following functions except:

a) extend credit to retailers
b) supplies the racks
c) stocks the merchandise
d) prices the goods
e) refills the shelves on regular visits

5. The following statements about drop shippers are all true except:

a) they take title to the goods
b) they store the goods
c) they receive orders from customers
d) they operate in fields where products are bulky
e) they do not maintain an inventory

6. The following statements about commission merchants are all true except:

a) they have little latitude in their decisions
b) they predominate in agricultural products marketing
c) they take possession of the goods
d) they act as the producer's agent
e) they receive an agreed-upon fee

7. All of the following take title to the goods they handle except:

a) manufacturers' agents
b) auction houses
c) drop shippers
d) truck wholesalers
e) both a and b

8. Which of the following is not included in the wholesaling service category of buying?

a) providing a sales force
b) anticipating customer demands
c) knowledge of alternative sources of supply
d) acts as purchasing agent to the customer
e) all of the above are included in the buying service category

9. Which of the following is not included in the risk-taking service category?

a) evaluating credit risks of customers
b) extension of credit to customers
c) anticipation of customer demands
d) transportation of goods
e) inventory risks

10. Which of the following are reasons for products being
     marketed directly by manufacturers?

     a) some products are perishable
     b) some need agressive promotion
     c) some require complex installation
     d) some products are high-unit value goods
     e) all of the above

B.   TRUE-FALSE.   In the space to the left of each statement
                   check the appropriate line to indicate
                   whether the statement is true or false.

True False

__✓__ _____   1. The term wholesaler is applied only to wholesaling
                   middlemen who take title to the product they handle.

__✓__ _____   2. Wholesalers serve as important information links for <u>both</u>
                   manufacturers and their customers.

_____ __✓__   3. Some marketing functions can be eliminated when the eco-
                   nomy is in a downturn.

__✓__ _____   4. Merchant wholesalers take title to goods.

_____ __✓__   5. Sales branches carry inventory but do not process orders.

__✓__ _____   6. Full function merchant wholesalers prevail in industries
                   where retailers are small and carry relatively in-
                   expensive items.

__✓__ _____   7. Drop shippers operate in fields where products are bulky.

__✓__ _____   8. The task of a broker is to bring buyers and sellers
                   together.

_____ __✓__   9. Since 1929, agents and brokers have become increasingly
                   important to manufacturers.

_____ __✓__ 10. Operating expenses of middlemen tend to be relatively
                   constant in every industry.

Chapter 17
RETAILING

Chapter Objectives

When you have finished studying this chapter you should be able to:

Distinguish between limited line stores and general merchandise retailers.

Explain and illustrate the methods of classifying retailers.

Identify the major types of mass mechandisers.

Explain the types of nonstore retailing.

Distinguish between chain and independent retailers and identify those industries dominated by chains.

Contrast the three types of planned shopping centers.

Explain the wheel-of-retailing theory and give examples of its application.

Chapter Summary

The two million retail establishments in the United States are vital members of the marketing channels for consumer products. They play a major role in the creation of time, place, and possession utility. Retailers can be categorized on five bases: (1) shopping effort expended by customers; (2) services provided to customers; (3) product lines; (4) location of retail transactions; and (5) form of ownership.

Retailers - like consumer goods - may be divided into convenience, shopping, and specialty categories based upon the efforts shoppers are willing to expend in purchasing products. A second method of classification categorizes retailers on a spectrum ranging from self-service to full-service. The third method divides retailers into three categories: *limited-line stores,* which compete by carrying a large assortment of one or two lines of products; *specialty stores,* which carry a very large assortment of only part of a single line

of products; and *general merchandise retailers*, such
as department stores, variety stores, and such mass
merchandisers as discount houses, hypermarkets, and
catalog retailers - all handling a wide variety or
products.

A fourth classification method distinguishes between
retail stores and non-store retailing. While more than
97 percent of total retail sales in the United States
takes place in retail stores, such nonstore retailing
as house-to-house retailing, mail-order establishments,
automatic merchandising machines are important in marketing many types of products and services.

The fifth method of classification categorizes retailers
by form of ownership. The major types include corporate
chain stores, independent retailers, and independents
who have banded together to form retail cooperatives
or to join wholesaler-sponsored voluntary chains or
franchises.

Chains are groups of retail stores that are centrally
owned and managed, and that handle the same lines of
products. Chain stores dominate retailing in four
fields: department stores, variety stores, food stores,
and shoe stores. They account for approximately one-
third of all retail sales.

A pronounced shift in retailing away from the down-
town business districts and toward planned suburban
shopping centers has taken place. These shopping centers account for almost 40 percent of all retail sales.

The changes in retailing practices and the development
of new retailing forms reflect retailers' attempt to
keep up with changing consumer demands. Retailers are
a vital institution in the firm's marketing channel.

Key Terms and Concepts

Directions. Match the marketing term or concept listed
below with the appropriate definition chosen from the
list to the right, and write the appropriate letter
in the space to the left of each term or concept. The
correct answers are printed upside-down at the bottom
of this assignment.

197

_____ 1. CATALOG RETAILER

_____ 2. CHAIN STORE

_____ 3. COMMUNITY SHOPPING CENTER

_____ 4. CONVENIENCE RETAILER

_____ 5. DEPARTMENT STORE

_____ 6. DISCOUNT HOUSE

_____ 7. GENERAL MERCHANDISE RETAILER

_____ 8. HOUSE-TO-HOUSE RETAILING

_____ 9. HYPERMARKET

_____ 10. LIMITED-LINE STORE

_____ 11. MASS MERCHANDISER

_____ 12. NEIGHBORHOOD SHOPPING CENTER

a. A retailer who sells to the ultimate consumer and focuses chiefly on a central location, long store hours, rapid checkout, and adequate parking facilities.

b. A giant mass merchandiser who operates on a low-price, self-service basis and carries lines of soft goods and groceries.

c. An establishment that typically handles only part of a single line of products.

d. A group of retail stores planned, coordinated, and marketed as a unit to shoppers in a geographic trade area.

e. All of the activities involved in the sale of products and services to the ultimate consumer.

f. A merchant who operates from a showroom displaying samples of the product line. Customers order from the store's catalog and orders are filled from a warehouse, usually on the premises.

g. A store that charges lower-than-normal prices but does not offer many typical retail services, such as credit, sales assistance by clerks, and home delivery.

h. A merchant who stocks a wider line of goods than that offered by a department store, but usually does not offer the same depth of assortment.

i. A hypothesis by M.P. McNair stating that new types of retailers gain a competitive foothold by offering lower prices through reduction or elimination of services. Once they are established, however, they add more services and their prices gradually rise. They then are vulnerable to the emergence of a new low-price retailer with minimum services.

_____ 13. PARTY-PLAN SELLING

_____ 14. PLANNED SHOPPING CENTER

_____ 15. REGIONAL SHOPPING CENTER

_____ 16. RETAIL LIFE CYCLE

_____ 17. RETAILING

_____ 18. SCRAMBLED MERCHANDISING

_____ 19. SHOPPING STORE

_____ 20. SPECIALTY RETAILER

_____ 21. SPECIALTY STORE

_____ 22. SUPERMARKET

_____ 23. TELESHOPPING

_____ 24. WHEEL OF RETAILING

j. A distribution strategy under which a company's representative makes a presentation of the product(s) in a party setting. Orders are taken and the host or hostess receives a commission or gift based on the amount of sales.

k. A group of retail stores that are centrally owned and managed and that handle essentially the same product lines.

l. An innovative method of shopping by which consumers order merchandise that is displayed on their television set.

m. The concept that retail institutions pass through a series of stages in their existence - introduction, growth, maturity, and decline.

n. An establishment carrying a wide variety of product lines, all of which are stocked in some depth.

o. An establishment at which customers typically compare prices, assortments, and quality levels with those of competing outlets before making a purchase decision.

p. A large-scale departmentalized retail store offering a variety of food products and various nonfood items. It typically operates on a self-service basis and emphasizes low prices and adequate parking facilities.

q. A distribution strategy under which the transaction occurs between the seller and the consumer in the consumer's home.

r. A group of 15 to 50 retail stores, often including a branch of a department store as the primary tenant. This type of center typically serves 20,000 to 100,000 persons within a radius of a few miles.

s. The practice of carrying dissimilar product lines in an attempt to generate added sales volume.

t. An establishment that offers a large assortment of one product line, or a few related product lines.

u. A large retail firm handling a variety of merchandise, including clothing, household goods, appliances, and furniture.

v. A geographical cluster of stores, usually consisting of a supermarket and about 5 to 15 smaller stores. The center provides convenient shopping for 5,000 to 15,000 shoppers in its vicinity.

w. One who provides a combination of product lines, service, and/or reputation in an attempt to attract customer preference.

x. The largest type of planned cluster of retail stores, usually involving one or more major department stores and as many as 200 other stores. A center of this size typically is located in an area with at least 250,000 people within 30 minutes driving time of the center.

ANSWERS: 1. (F); 2. (K); 3. (R); 4. (A); 5. (U); 6. (G); 7. (N); 8. (O); 9. (B); 10. (T); 11. (H); 12. (V); 13. (J); 14. (D); 15. (X); 16. (M); 17. (E); 18. (S); 19 (O); 20. (W); 21. (C); 22. (P); 23. (L); 24. (I).

The preliminary practice test is designed to help you assess your mastery of text material in this chapter. The test consists of 20 questions focusing upon materials in the chapter and is useful in indicating how well-prepared you are at this stage to take an exam covering this material. The correct answers are printed upside-down at the end of the practice test.

A. MULTIPLE CHOICE: Choose the answer which <u>best</u> answers the question or best completes the sentence.

1.   The following are all "limited-line" stores except:

a) Sears
b) Radio Shack
c) Toys-R-Us
d) Lerner's Shops
e) Handy Man

2.   Convenience retailers focus upon all of the following except:

a) elegant decor
b) convenient location
c) adequate parking
d) long store hours
e) rapid checkout service

3.   When the customer purchases the most readily available brand of the product at the nearest store, this describes:

a) a convenience store - specialty good
b) a convenience store - convenience good
c) a specialty store - convenience good
d) a specialty store - shopping good
e) none of the above

4.   Such characteristics as restricted services, price appeal, staple goods, and convenience goods describe:

a) self-selection
b) full-service
c) self-service
d) limited-service
e) none of the above

5.   Which of the following does <u>not</u> characterize a Supermarket?

a) large profit margin
b) departmentalized
c) adequate parking facilities

d) low prices
e) self-service

6. Which of the following is <u>not</u> characteristic of house-to-house retailing?

   a) direct contact between seller and customer
   b) a low-cost method of distribution
   c) maximum consumer convenience
   d) manufacturer controls the marketing channels
   e) used by firms emphasizing product demonstrations

7. Which of the following is <u>not</u> characteristic of scrambled merchandising?

   a) satisfies consumer demands for one-stop shopping
   b) complicates channel decisions for manufacturers
   c) generates added sales volume
   d) lowers retailers' costs
   e) all of the above

8. Which of the following areas is <u>not</u> dominated by chain stores according to the text?

   a) department stores
   b) variety stores
   c) jewelry stores
   d) food stores
   e) shoe stores

9. An example of a "limited line" retailer would be:

   a) furniture store
   b) hardware store
   c) sporting goods store
   d) appliance store
   e) all of the above

10. The life cycle concept:

   a) can be applied to retailers as well as people and products
   b) describes the emergence, growth, and eventual decline of the general store
   c) categorizes hypermarkets as in the early growth stage
   d) indicates that retail life cycles can be extended in a similar manner as in the case of products
   e) all of the above are correct

ANSWERS: Multiple Choice. 1. (A); 2. (A); 3. (B); 4. (A); 5. (A); 6. (B); 7. (D); 8. (C); 9. (E); 10. (E).
True-False. 1. (T); 2. (F); 3. (F); 4. (T); 5. (F); 6. (T); 7. (T); 8. (T); 9. (F); 10. (T).

This final practice test is designed to provide reinforcement of the success of your studies and the adequacy of your preparation for exams covering the material in this chapter. Like the preliminary test, the final practice test consists of 20 questions focusing on materials covered in this chapter. However, the correct answers are reprinted on the last page of the MARKETING Mastery Guide.

A. MULTIPLE CHOICE. Choose the answer which best answers the question or best completes the sentence.

1. The reason for the general store's virtual extinction can be traced to:

    a) high prices resulting from inefficient order quantities
    b) poor service
    c) inability to compete with specialized stores
    d) all of the above
    e) none of the above

2. Which of the following is not a base upon which retailers may be classified?

    a) shopping effort expended by customer
    b) product lines
    c) form of ownership
    d) all of the above are used in classifying retail stores
    e) none of the above are used to classify retailers

3. Shopping stores include all of the following except:

    a) Levitz Furniture
    b) General Electric appliance store
    c) clothing outlet
    d) sporting goods store
    e) 7-Eleven food store

4. When the customer is indifferent to the brand purchased and shopping is done at competing stores to obtain the best price, this describes:

    a) shopping store - shopping good
    b) shopping store - convenience good
    c) specialty store - specialty good
    d) convenience store - convenience good
    e) convenience store - specialty good

5. Which of the following characteristics does not describe a limited service retailer classification?

    a) staple goods

b) convenience goods
c) shopping goods
d) both a and b
e) none of the above

6. Which of the following characteristics best describes department stores?

   a) buyers often run their departments almost as independent businesses
   b) willingness to adapt to changing consumer desires
   c) limited number of services
   d) both a and b
   e) both b and c

7. The main advantage possessed by chain operations over independent retailers is:

   a) convenience of location
   b) economies of scale
   c) personalized service
   d) both a and b
   e) all of the above

8. Which of the following is <u>not</u> classified as a general merchandise retailer?

   a) department stores
   b) discount houses
   c) hypermarkets
   d) catalog retailers
   e) all of the above are general merchandise retailers

9. When the consumer has a strong preference for both a particular store and a particular brand, this describes:

   a) convenience store - convenience good
   b) convenience store - specialty good
   c) shopping store - shopping good
   d) shopping store - specialty good
   e) none of the above

10. All of the following are examples of retail transactions except:

    a) purchase of fresh vegetables at a roadside stand
    b) purchase of this book at the college bookstore
    c) preparation of personal income tax report by a local accounting firm
    d) purchase of paint by a contractor
    e) all of the above are retail transactions

B.   TRUE-FALSE.   In the space to the left of each statement check the appropriate line to indicate whether the statement is true or false.

True False

____ ____ 1. The first important retail institution in the United States was the department store.

____ ____ 2. Convenience retailers tend to focus on low prices.

____ ____ 3. Lord & Taylor is used in the text as an example of a specialty retailer.

____ ____ 4. Self-service stores tend to carry fashion merchandise.

____ ____ 5. Mail order retailing is an example of full service.

____ ____ 6. Retail location and price are unimportant to self-service retailers.

____ ____ 7. Decisions in a department store tend to be made by one central figure.

____ ____ 8. A hypermarket is a giant mass merchandising operation which operates on a low-price, low-service basis.

____ ____ 9. Mail order selling is a recent development in retailing.

____ ____ 10. Scrambled merchandising is defined as the practice of carrying dissimilar lines in an attempt to generate added sales volume.

Chapter 18

MANAGEMENT OF PHYSICAL DISTRIBUTION

Chapter Objectives

When you have finished studying this chapter you should be able to:

Explain the role of physical distribution in an effective marketing strategy.

Describe the objective of physical distribution.

List the three concepts that make up the physical distribution concept.

Explain what is meant by customer service standards and how they affect physical distribution decisions.

Identify and compare the major elements of a physical distribution system.

Relate the major transportation alternatives to such factors as speed, dependability, and cost.

Chapter Summary

Physical distribution, as a system, consists of six elements: (1) customer service, (2) transportation, (3) inventory control, (4) materials handling, (5) order processing and (6) warehousing. These elements are interrelated and must be balanced for a smoothly functioning distribution system. The physical distribution department is one of the classic examples of the systems approach to business problems. Three basic concepts of the systems approach - the total cost approach, the avoidance of suboptimization, and cost trade-offs - combine to form the physical distribution concept.

The goal of a physical distribution department can be stated as follows: to produce a specified level of customer service while minimizing the costs involved in physically moving and storing the product from its production point to the point where it is ultimately purchased.

The physical distribution manager has available five transportation alternatives: railroads, motor carriers, water carriers, pipelines, and air freight. Inter-modal transport systems are also available and are increasingly being used. Other elements of the physical distribution department include customer service, inventory control, materials handling, protective packaging, order processing, transportation, warehouse site selection, and warehousing. Efficient international physical distribution allows U. S. firms to compete effectively in foreign markets.

Physical distribution, by its very nature, involves keeping track of thousands of details, such as transport rates, inventory locations, and customer locations. Computerization is an invaluable aid for the logistics manager.

Key Terms and Concepts

Directions. Match the marketing term or concept listed below with the appropriate definition chosen from the list to the right, and write the appropriate letter in the space to the left of each term or concept. The correct answers are printed upside-down at the bottom of this assignment.

_____1. BREAK-BULK CENTER

_____2. CLASS RATE

_____3. COMMODITY RATE

_____4. COMMON CARRIERS

_____5. CONTAINERIZATION

_____6. CONTRACT CARRIERS

_____7. COST TRADE-OFF

a. warehouse used to assemble and redistribute products.

b. transportation middlemen who consolidate shipments in order to reduce shipping costs for their customers.

c. an addition to a predetermined optimal inventory level of a particular product in order to compensate for demand fluctuations.

d. the quality of service that the organization's customers will receive.

e. warehouses used to store products for moderate to long periods of time in an attempt to balance supply and demand for producers and purchasers.

_____8. CUSTOMER SERVICE STANDARDS

_____9. DISTRIBUTION WAREHOUSES

_____10. ECONOMIC ORDER QUANTITY

_____11. FOREIGN FREIGHT FORWARDERS

_____12. FREIGHT FORWARDERS

_____13. MAKE-BULK CENTER

_____14. MATERIALS HANDLING

_____15. PHYSICAL DISTRIBUTION

_____16. PHYSICAL DISTRIBUTION CONCEPT

_____17. PRIVATE CARRIERS

_____18. SAFETY STOCK

_____19. STORAGE WAREHOUSES

f. integration of the three basic concepts of efficient movement of finished goods to consumers: the total cost approach, avoidance of suboptimizaion, and cost trade-offs.

g. a condition in which the attempt to minimize costs in a single department results in increased overall costs for the organization as a result of the interrelationships among the various departments.

h. transportation middlemen who specialize in physical distribution outside the United States.

i. organized group of parts or components linked together according to a plan to achieve specific objectives.

j. for-hire carriers who serve the general public.

k. a time-and money-saving service provided by railroads to large-volume customers, in which a train is loaded with the shipments of only one company and transports solely for that customer.

l. attempt to minimize materials handling costs through the combination of several unitized loads.

m. broad range of activities concerned with efficient movement of finished products from the end of the production line to the customer.

n. central distribution center in which consolidated shipments are made to be broken down into smaller shipments for individual customers.

o. the rate, sometimes called a special rate, that is given to carriers by shippers as a reward for either regular use or large quantity shipments.

20. SUBOPTIMIZATION

21. SYSTEM

22. TOTAL COST APPROACH

23. UNIT TRAINS

p. distribution center in which smaller shipments are assembled and then consolidated into one shipment.

q. for-hire carriers who do not serve the general public, but instead establish specific contracts with certain customers and operate exclusively for a particular industry.

r. the standard rate applied to every commodity moving between any two destinations.

s. component of the total cost approach in physical distribution in which some functional areas may experience less than minimal costs in order to achieve minimal overall costs.

t. all the activities associated in moving products within the manufacturer's plants, warehouses, and transportation company terminals.

u. not-for-hire carriers who transport products only for a particular firm and who cannot solicit other transportation business.

v. optimal inventory order size determined by balancing inventory holding costs and order costs.

w. the premise that all relevant factors in physically moving and storing products should be considered as a whole and not individually.

The preliminary practice test is designed to help you assess your mastery of text material in this chapter. The test consists of 20 questions focusing upon materials in the chapter and is useful in indicating how well-prepared you are at this stage to take an exam covering this material. The correct answers are printed upside-down at the end of the practice test.

A. MULTIPLE CHOICE. Choose the answer which best answers the question or best completes the sentence.

1. Which of the following concepts are not vital to effective physical distribution?

    a) sub-optimization
    b) cost tradeoff
    c) total cost approach
    d) avoidance of sub-optimization
    e) all of the above are essential in effective management

2. According to the text, a unified physical distribution department is initially:

    a) staff-oriented
    b) line-oriented
    c) market-oriented
    d) cost-oriented
    e) none of the above

3. The physical distribution system should be designed to minimize total costs of all of the following except:

    a) market research
    b) inventory control
    c) materials handling
    d) order processing
    e) warehouses and their location

4. Which of the following are not classes of carriers?

    a) contract carriers
    b) regulated carriers
    c) private carriers
    d) common carriers
    e) both a and b

5. Which of the following carriers have experienced significant decreases in use since 1940?

    a) pipelines
    b) railroads

c) water carriers
d) motor carriers
e) air carriers

6. Which of the following carriers have experienced substantial increases over the years?

a) pipelines
b) motor carriers
c) water carriers
d) railroads
e) both a and b

7. Which of the following statements concerning pipelines is true?

a) It is second only to railroads in the number of ton-miles transported.
b) There is a slow rate of growth in the use of "slurry" pipelines.
c) Pipelines are relatively inexpensive.
d) Pipelines are very efficient.
e) all of the above are true statements.

8. Which of the following is **not** a form of intermodal coordination?

a) piggyback
b) railback
c) birdy back
d) fishy back
e) all of the above are forms of intermodal coordination

9. All of the following are mentioned in the text as factors to be considered in deciding the location of warehouses except:

a) local climate
b) local taxes
c) police and fire protection
d) attitude of the community toward the warehouse
e) availability of a trained labor force

10. All of the following are advantages of automated warehouses except:

a) reduced labor costs
b) reduced breakage
c) reduced costs for low volume distributors
d) assistance in inventory control
e) reduced worker injuries

B. TRUE-FALSE. In the space to the left of each statement check the appropriate line to indicate whether the statement is true or false.

True False

____ ✓   1. Physical distribution functions account for less than 25 percent of all marketing costs.

____ ✓   2. Cost trade-offs require a sacrifice of the established level of customer satisfaction to reduce costs.

✓ ____   3. The chief role of the physical distribution department in determining customer service levels is to point out costs involved in proposed standards.

____ ✓   4. The commodity freight rate is the "standard rate."

✓ ____   5. Common carriers are regulated and they serve the general public.

____ ✓   6. Private carriers are subject to the same regulations which apply to common carriers.

____ ✓   7. Water carriers tend to be very slow and expensive.

✓ ____   8. Air carriers are considered fast but expensive.

✓ ____   9. Automated warehouses can provide major savings to high volume distributors.

✓ ____   10. Containerization refers to a combination of several unitized loads.

ANSWERS: Multiple Choice. 1. (A); 2. (A); 3. (A); 4. (B); 5. (B); 6. (E); 7. (E); 8. (B); 9. (A); 10. (C). True-False. 1. (F); 2. (F); 3. (T); 4. (F); 5. (T); 6. (F); 7. (F); 8. (T); 9. (T); 10. (T).

FINAL PRACTICE TEST

This final practice test is designed to provide reinforcement of the success of your studies and the adequacy of your preparation for exams covering the material in this chapter. Like the preliminary test, the final practice test consists of 20 questions focusing on materials covered in this chapter. However, the correct answers are reprinted on the last page of the MARKETING Mastery Guide.

A.   MULTIPLE CHOICE.   Choose the answer which <u>best</u> answers the question or best completes the sentence.

1.   Physical distribution activities include all of the following except:

a) warehousing
b) credit approval
c) materials handling
d) order processing
e) customer service

2.   The physical distribution concept is based upon the following systems concepts:

a) total cost approach
b) avoidance of sub-optimization
c) cost trade-offs
d) none of the above
e) all of the above

3.   The chief role of the physical distribution department in determining customer service standards is to:

a) minimize costs
b) find out what the customers require
c) determine the maximum level of service possible
d) determine costs involved in providing proposed standards
e) none of the above

4.   Which of the following is <u>not</u> regulated by the Interstate Commerce Commission?

a) railroads
b) trans-Atlantic freighters
c) pipelines
d) motor carriers
e) inland water carriers

5.   Which of the following is <u>not</u> a major transportation alternative?

a) courier service
b) railroads
c) water carriers
d) pipelines
e) air carriers

6.   Which of the following carriers' rate of use has remained generally stable over the years?

a) pipelines
b) railroads
c) water carriers
d) motor carriers
e) air carriers

7. The trucking industry's primary appeal as a carrier is:

   a) superior service
   b) lower cost
   c) lack of regulation
   d) all of the above
   e) both b and c.

8. Which of the following statements about air carriers is not true?

   a) air freight use has been growing
   b) fast delivery service is possible
   c) significantly lower costs on large shipments is an advantage
   d) both a and b
   e) both a and c

9. Which of the following characteristics of pipelines limit their use?

   a) pipelines are dependable
   b) they are fast
   c) they are inexpensive
   d) a relatively small number of products can be transported through them
   e) they require little maintenance

10. Which of the following are advantages of freight forwarders?

    a) lower costs on small shipments
    b) fast delivery service
    c) lower costs on large shipments
    d) a and b, but not c
    e) a and c, but not b

B. TRUE-FALSE. In the space to the left of each statement check the appropriate line to indicate whether the statement is true or false.

True False

___✓___ _____ 1. Physical distribution activities include decision areas such as warehousing, transportation and order processing.

_____ ___✓___ 2. Physical distribution has little impact on customer service.

___✓___ _____ 3. There is a current trend toward centralized physical distribution management.

214

True False

____ ____✓ 4. Transportation in the United States is a minimally regulated industry.

____ ____✓ 5. The class rate is referred to as the "special rate."

____✓ ____ 6. Contract carriers do not offer service to the general public.

____✓ ____ 7. The trucking industry has shown dramatic growth over past decades because of fast consistent service.

____✓ ____ 8. Freight forwarders consolidate shipments to get lower rates for their customers.

____ ____✓ 9. Pipelines tend to be relatively inefficient carriers.

____ ____✓ 10. The EOQ model emphasizes cost trade-offs between holding costs and order costs.

PART SEVEN: <u>PROMOTION</u>

Chapter 19

PROMOTION: A CONCEPTUAL FOUNDATION

Chapter Objectives

When you have finished studying this chapter you should
be able to:

Relate the communications process to promotional strategy.

Explain the concept and components of the promotional mix.

List the objectives of promotion.

Describe how a firm should budget for promotional expenditures.

Explain how to effectively integrate a promotional plan.

Defend promotion against the public criticisms that are
sometimes raised.

Chapter Summary

This chapter provides an introduction to promotion, fourth
variable in the marketing mix (product, pricing, distribution, and promotional strategies). Promotional strategy is closely related to the marketing communications
system, which includes the elements of sender, message,
encoding, transfer mechanism, decoding, receiver, feedback, and noise. Its major components are personal
selling and nonpersonal selling (advertising, sales
promotion, and public relations). These elements are
discussed in the two chapters that follow.

Developing an effective promotional stragegy is a complex matter. The elements of promotion are related to
the type and value of the product being promoted as
well as to the timing of the promotional effort. Personal
selling is used primarily for industrial goods, higher
value items, and during the transactional phase. Advertising, by contrast, is used primarily for consumer
goods, lower value items, and during the pretransactional and posttransactional phases.

216

A pulling strategy concentrates on stimulating user demands primarily through advertising and sales promtion.
A pushing strategy, which relies on personal selling,
attempts to promote the product to the members of the
marketing channel rather than to the ultimate user.

The five basic objectives of promotion are to (1) provide
information, (2) stimulate demand, (3) differentiate
the product, (4) accentuate its value, and (5) stabilize
sales. There are several problems involved in promotional budgeting and in measuring the effectiveness
of promotional expenditures. The coordination of the
entire promotional effort can be accomplished by the
eight-stage adaptive planning and control sequence.

Although it has become the target of much criticism,
promotion plays an important role in the business, economic, and social spheres of influence.

Key Terms and Concepts

Directions. Match the marketing term or concept listed below
with the appropriate definition chosen from the list to the
right, and write the appropriate letter in the space to the
left of each term or concept. The correct answers are printed
upside-down at the bottom of this assignment.

_____1. ADAPTIVE PLANNING AND
         CONTROL SEQUENCE (APACS)

_____2. ADVERTISING

_____3. DECODING

_____4. DIRECT-SALES RESULTS
         TEST

_____5. ENCODING

_____6. FEEDBACK

a. A budget allocation method, under
   which a predetermined promotional
   amount is allocated, either on a
   historical or forecasted basis.

b. A firm's communications and relationships with its various publics.

c A budget allocation method, under
   which a firm defines its goals and
   then determines the amount needed
   to accomplish them.

d. A promotional effort by the seller
   of a product to members of the
   marketing channel to stimulate
   personal selling of a product.

e. A budget allocation method under
   which a fixed percentage of funds,
   based on past or forecasted sales
   volumes, is allocated for promotion.

_____7. FIXED SUM PER UNIT

_____8. MARKETING COMMUNICATIONS

_____9. NOISE

_____10. PERCENTAGE OF SALES

_____11. PERSONAL SELLING

_____12. PROMOTION

_____13. PUBLIC RELATIONS

_____14. PUBLICITY

_____15. PULLING STRATEGY

_____16. PUSHING STRATEGY

_____17. SALES PROMOTION

_____18. TASK OBJECTIVE METHOD

_____19. TRANSFER MECHANISM

f. An eight-step process developed by Marketing Science Institute for promotional decision making, from defining the problem and setting objectives, to getting feedback and adapting the program as needed.

g. In marketing communications, the means of delivering a message.

h. The function of informing, persuading, and influencing the consumer's purchase decision.

i. A nonpersonal sales presentation, usually directed at a large number of potential customers.

j. In marketing communications, the translation of a message into understandable terms and its transmittal through a communications medium.

k. All marketiing activities (other than personal selling, advertising, and publicity) that stimulate consumer purchasing and dealer effectiveness. Examples are displays, shows and expositions, demonstrations, and various nonrecurrent selling efforts.

l. That part of a company's public relations function that is most directly related to promoting the firm's products or services.

m. The messages that deal with buyer-seller relationships.

n. A promotional effort by the seller to stimulate final user demand, exerting pressure on the distribution channel.

o. In marketing communications, the receiver's response to a message.

p. In marketing communications, the receiver's interpretation of a message.

q. In marketing communications, interference in a transmitted message.

r. A seller's promotional presentation conducted on a person-to-person basis with the buyer.

s. A tool for measuring the effectiveness of promotional expenditures,
by ascertaining the increase in
revenue per dollar spent.

Preliminary Practice Test

The preliminary practice test is designed to help you assess
your mastery of text material in this chapter. The test consists of 20 questions focusing upon materials in the chapter
and is useful in indicating how well-prepared you are at this
stage to take an exam covering this material. The correct
answers are printed upside-down at the end of the practice test.

A. MULTIPLE CHOICE. Choose the answer which <u>best</u> answers the
question or best completes the sentence.

1. A message must accomplish which of the following tasks to
be effective?

a) gain the attention of the receiver
b) be understood by the receiver
c) be understood by the sender
d) all of the above
e) both a and b are correct

2. Which of the following types of non-personal selling is
considered the most important form?

a) advertising

219

b) sales promotion
c) publicity
d) public relations
e) all are considered equally important

3. A "pushing" strategy relies upon:

a) personal selling
b) trade discounts
c) consumer advertising
d) a and b
e) a and c, but not b

4. Which of the following is <u>not</u> a method of allocating a promotional budget?

a) total costs
b) percentage of sales
c) fixed sums per unit
d) meeting the competition
e) task objective

5. The fixed sum per unit approach differs from percentage of sales in only one respect:

a) it assumes that the productivity of each dollar is measureable
b) it assumes that some of the promotional dollar will be wasted
c) it applies a predetermined dollar amount to each sales or product unit
d) it requires use of a computer
e) it assumes that each sales unit contributes the same amount

6. Probably the most effective way to measure the effectiveness of promotion is through:

a) marginal analysis
b) polling
c) direct-sales results test
d) task-objective method
e) readership research studies

7. Which of the following is a reason for economic importance of promotion?

a) it is responsible for the employment of millions of people
b) it increases units sold, thereby assisting in reducing production costs and prices
c) advertising subsidizes the informational content of newspapers
d) all of the above
e) both a and c are correct

8. The five basic objectives of promotion include all of the following except:

a) to stabilize demand
b) to stabilize sales
c) to provide information

d) to accentuate the value of the product
e) to differentiate the product

9. Which of the following tasks must be accomplished if a promotional message is to be considered effective?

a) it must gain the attention of the receiver
b) it must stimulate the needs of the receiver
c) it must be understood by both the receiver and the sender
d) it must suggest an appropriate method of satisfying the needs that have been stimulated in the receiver
e) all of the above

10. A "pulling" strategy is best illustrated by:

a) offering middlemen bonuses for above-average sales
b) heavy advertising aimed at consumers
c) cooperative advertising
d) sales training programs for retail sales personnel
e) discounts for additional shelf space and sizable retail orders

B. TRUE-FALSE. In the space to the left of each statement check the appropriate line to indicate whether the statement is true or false.

True False

____ ____ 1. Promotion accounts for the largest part of a firm's marketing budget.

____ ____ 2. Public relations is classified as nonpersonal selling.

____ ____ 3. Encoding is the receiver's interpretation of the message.

____ ____ 4. Sales promotion is one of the two major elements of the promotional mix.

____ ____ 5. Advertising is defined as a non-personal sales presentation, usually directed to a large number of potential customers.

____ ____ 6. The "public" in public relations refers primarily to customers.

____ ____ 7. The decision to emphasize personal selling or advertising depends primarily on the size of the overall promotional budget.

____ ____ 8. It is more difficult to promote lower-value goods through advertising.

____ ____ 9. During the pretransactional period, personal selling is usually more important than advertising.

____ ____ 10. A pushing strategy is the promotion of the product to the members of the channel.

FINAL PRACTICE TEST

This final practice test is designed to provide reinforcement of the success of your studies and the adequacy of your preparation for exams covering the material in this chapter. Like the preliminary test, the final practice test consists of 20 questions focusing on materials covered in this chapter. However, the correct answers are reprinted on the last page of the MARKETING Mastery Guide.

A.   MULTIPLE CHOICE.   Choose the answer which best answers the question or best completes the sentence.

1.   Promotion includes all of the following except:

   a) informing the consumer
   b) defining more precisely the organization's market target
   c) persuading the consumer
   d) influencing the consumer's purchase decision
   e) all of the above

2.   The following terms are all parts of the communications process except:

   a) feedback
   b) coding
   c) encoding
   d) decoding
   e) noise

3.   Which of the following items are most amenable to personal selling?

   a) chewing gum
   b) food products
   c) clothing
   d) industrial goods
   e) television sets

4. Which of the following is <u>not</u> considered an objective of promotion?

   a) to provide information
   b) to increase demand
   c) to stabilize sales
   d) to differentiate the product
   e) all of the above are objectives

5. The crucial assumption underlying the task objective approach is:

   a) that the firm can afford to spend as much as its competition
   b) that the productivity of each promotional dollar is measureable
   c) that the emphasis will always fall upon advertising
   d) that a computer is available for the task
   e) all of the above

6. The most common way of allocating promotion budgets is:

   a) marginal analysis
   b) percentage of sales
   c) fixed sum per unit
   d) task objective method
   e) there is no one most common way of allocating promotion budgets

7. Which of the following is <u>not</u> an element of the APACS:

   a) define the problem and set objectives
   b) appraise the overall situation
   c) estimate expected results
   d) review decisions by management
   e) all of the above are elements of APACS.

8. Advertising is used primarily in:

   a) marketing lower value items
   b) marketing industrial goods
   c) the pretransactional stages of the sales process
   d) a and c, but not b
   e) all of the above

9. Which of the following is <u>not</u> among the five objectives of promotion?

   a) to provide information
   b) to stabilize sales
   c) to stabilize demand
   d) product differentiation
   e) all are possible promotional objectives

10. Encoding is best characterized by:

    a) a potential buyer views an advertisement for Firestone tires and decides to purchase a set
    b) a $10 million advertising campaign Pearl Beer's <u>J.R. Ewing's Private Stock</u> results in a 5 percent market share for the brand

223

c) Ford Motor Company relies heavily on television advertising to promote the fuel economy of its Escort "world car"

d) Hershey Chocolate Co. decides to advertise after "holding out" for more than 50 years

e) total advertising expenditures of $500,000 results in the election of a U.S. Senator from the Democratic Party as a result of his acquiring 25 percent of the votes of registered Republicans

B. TRUE-FALSE. In the space to the left of each statement check the appropriate line to indicate whether the statement is true or false.

True False

____ ____ 1. Promotion is the function of informing, persuading and influencing the consumer's purchase decision.

____ ____ 2. Encoding is the process of interpreting incoming messages.

____ ____ 3. Noise is a valuable part of the marketing communication process.

____ ____ 4. The components of the marketing mix are personal and non-personal selling.

____ ____ 5. Public relations accounts for most of a firm's promotional expenditure.

____ ____ 6. Publicity is a significant part of effective public relations.

____ ____ 7. The most critical promotional problem facing the marketing manager is finding the proper promotional mix.

____ ____ 8. Personal selling is typically more effective than advertising.

____ ____ 9. A pulling strategy is a promotional effort by the seller to stimulate final user demand.

____ ____ 10. In the post-transactional stage, advertising is the primary promotional effort.

Chapter 20

PROMOTIONAL STRATEGY: ADVERTISING, SALES PROMOTION, PUBLIC RELATIONS, AND PUBLICITY

Chapter Objectives

When you have finished studying this chapter you should be able to:

Explain the current status and historical development of advertising in the United States.

Identify the major types of advertising.

List and discuss the various advertising media.

Explain how advertising effectiveness is determined.

Outline the organization of the advertising function.

Describe the process of creating an advertisement.

Identify the methods of sales promotion.

Explain the role of public relations and publicity.

Chapter Summary

Advertising, sales promotion, public relations, and publicity - the nonpersonal selling elements of promotion - are not twentieth century phenomena. Advertising, for instance, can trace its origin to very early times. Today, these elements of promotion have gained professional status and serve as vital aspects of most organizations - both profit and nonprofit.

Advertising, a nonpersonal sales presentation usually directed to a large number of potential customers, seeks to achieve communications goals rather than direct sales objectives. It strives to inform, persuade, and remind potential consumers of the product or service being promoted.

Advertising planning starts with effective research, which permits the development of a strategy. Tactical decisions about copy and scheduling are then made. Finally, advertisements are evaluated, and appropriate feedback is provided to management. There are six basic types of advertising: (1) informative product advertising, (2) persuasive product advertising, (3) reminder-oriented product advertising. (4) informative institutional advertising, (5) persuasive institutional advertising, and (6) reminder-oriented institutional advertising. One of the most vital decisions in developing an advertising strategy is the selection of the media to be employed.

The major tasks of advertising departments are advertising research, art, copywriting, media analysis, and sales promotion. Many advertisers use independent advertising agencies to provide them with the creativity and objectivity missing in their own organizations and to reduce the cost of advertising. The final step in the advertising process is developing and preparing the advertisement.

The principal methods of sales promotion are point-of-purchase advertising; specialty advertising; trade shows; samples, coupons, and premiums; contests; and trading stamps. Public relations and publicity also play major roles in developing promotional strategies.

Key Terms and Concepts

Directions. Match the marketing term or concept listed below with the appropriate definition chosen from the list to the right, and write the appropriate letter in the space to the left of each term or concept. The correct answers are printed upside-down at the bottom of this assignment.

_____	1.	ADVERTISING
_____	2.	COMPARATIVE ADVERTISING
_____	3.	COOPERATIVE ADVERTISING
_____	4.	COUPONS

a. that part of public relations that is most directly related to promoting a company's products or services.

b. assessing an advertisement's effectiveness after it has been used.

c. the nonpersonal selling of a particular good or service.

d. the nonpersonal selling of a concept, an idea, a philosophy, or the good will of an industry, company, or organization.

_____ 5. DEMOGRAPHICS

_____ 6. INSTITUTIONAL ADVERTISING

_____ 7. PREMIUMS

_____ 8. PRODUCT ADVERTISING

_____ 9. POSITIONING

_____ 10. POSTTESTING

_____ 11. PRETESTING

_____ 12. PUBLIC RELATIONS

_____ 13. PUBLICITY

_____ 14. RETAIL ADVERTISING

_____ 15. SALES PROMOTION

_____ 16. SAMPLING

_____ 17. SPECIALTY ADVERTISING

_____ 18. TRADING STAMPS

e. in promotion, the free distribution of a product in an attempt to obtain future sales for it.

f. a category of nonpersonal selling efforts designed to supplement and extend the other aspects of promotional strategy.

g. all nonpersonal sales presentations by stores that sell goods or services directly to the consuming public.

h. a sales promotion technique involving redeemable stamps which are given as a purchase premium in some retail establishments.

i. a sales promotional medium that utilizes useful articles carrying the advertiser's name, address, and advertising message to reach the target consumers.

j. a nonpersonal sales presentation usually directed to a large number of potential customers.

k. characteristics such as age, sex, and income levels that may be utilized to segment consumer markets.

l. the sharing of advertising costs between the retailer and the manufacturer or vendor.

m. the practice of making direct promotional comparisons with leading competitive brands.

n. specialty advertising tool offering a discount on the purchase of a product when redeemed at retail outlets.

o. development of a marketing strategy aimed at a particular segment of the market and designed to achieve a desired position in the mind of the prospective buyer.

p. assessing an advertisement's effectiveness before it is actually used.

227

q. the organization's communications and relationships with its various publics, including customers, suppliers, stockholders, employees, the government, and the society in which it operates.

r. gift items given free with the purchase of another product and utilized in attempting to motivate consumers to try new products or brands.

ANSWERS: 1. (J); 2. (M); 3. (L); 4. (N); 5. (K); 6. (D); 7. (R); 8. (C); 9. (O); 10. (B); 11. (P); 12. (Q); 13. (A); 14. (G); 15. (F); 16. (E); 17. (I); 18. (H).

Preliminary Practice Test

The preliminary practice test is designed to help you assess your mastery of text materials in this chapter. The test consists of 20 questions focusing upon materials in the chapter and is useful in indicating how well-prepared you are at this stage to take an exam covering this material. The correct answers are printed upside-down at the end of the practice test.

A.   MULTIPLE CHOICE.   Choose the answer which best answers the question or best completes the sentence.

1.   Originally advertising agencies sold:

   a) copywriting
   b) research
   c) space
   d) magazines and newspapers in addition to advertising
   e) all of the above

2. Early advertising research dealt primarily with:

   a) demographics
   b) psychographics
   c) media selection
   d) motivation research
   e) advertising effectiveness

3. The starting place for advertising planning is:

   a) scheduling
   b) research
   c) copywriting
   d) budgeting
   e) positioning

4. Comparative advertising is usually used by:

   a) firms leading the market
   b) products which stress low-cost
   c) consumer products
   d) firms not leading the market
   e) none of the above

5. Institutional advertising deals with:

   a) non-personal selling of a good
   b) personal selling of a service
   c) promoting a philosophy
   d) promoting good will
   e) both c and d

6. Informative advertising is usually used in which stage of the product life cycle?

   a) maturity
   b) introductory
   c) decline
   d) growth
   e) all stages

7. Reminder-oriented advertising is used in which stages of the product life cycle?

   a) introduction
   b) maturity
   c) decline
   d) growth
   e) both b and c

8. Which of the following is not an advantage of magazine advertising?

   a) quality reproduction
   b) flexibility
   c) long life
   d) selectivity of market target
   e) extra services.

9. Which of the following are disadvantages of television advertising?

   a) high cost
   b) public distrust
   c) high mortality rates
   d) lack of selectivity
   e) all of the above

10. Which of the following is <u>not</u> an advantage of direct mail?

   a) high cost per contact
   b) speed
   c) intensive coverage
   d) selectivity
   e) flexibility of format

B. TRUE-FALSE. In the space to the left of each statement check the appropriate line to indicate whether the statement is true or false.

True False

____ ____ 1. Post-testing is a more desirable method of testing advertising effectiveness than pretesting.

____ ____ 2. Inquiry tests are a popular method of post-testing.

____ ____ 3. Establishing a relationship with a company's other products is always helpful in advertising a new product.

____ ____ 4. Retail advertising typically makes effective use of newspapers since sales and new product are "newsworthy" and attention-getting.

____ ____ 5. Specialty advertising includes items such as life-size displays of a celebrity from a TV ad in a store.

____ ____ 6. Premiums need not be related to the purchased item.

____ ____ 7. Public relations is an important component of personal selling.

____ ____ 8. The earliest advertisements were carried in newspapers.

____ ____ 9. Psychographics have been of limited use in advertising.

____ ____ 10. Comparative advertising is most often used by firms whose products do not lead their markets.

FINAL PRACTICE TEST

This final practice test is designed to provide reinforcement of the success of your studies and the adequacy of your preparation for exams covering the material in this chapter. Like the preliminary test, the final practice test consists of 20 questions focusing on materials covered in this chapter. However, the correct answers are reprinted on the last page of the MARKETING Mastery Guide.

A.   MULTIPLE CHOICE.   Choose the answer which best answers the question or best completes the sentence.

1.   Which of the following were the earliest common elements of advertising?

   a) magazine and newspaper ads
   b) signs
   c) criers and hawkers
   d) both b and c
   e) all of the above

2.   The reformist movement in advertising began:

   a) in the early 1900s
   b) after the depression
   c) in the 1960s
   d) during the industrial revolution
   e) after World War II

3.   All of the following are communications objectives of advertising except:

   a) informing
   b) persuading

c) critiquing
d) reminding
e) all of the above are objectives

4. Positioning is especially important in advertising:

a) products which are not leaders in their field
b) products which are leaders in their field
c) consumer products
d) industrial products
e) low-cost products

5. Which of the following is not one of the two types of advertising?

a) service
b) product
c) institutional
d) communicative
e) both a and d

6. Informative product advertising seeks to:

a) create good will
b) promote a philosophy
c) develop initial demand
d) remind former customers of a previously-sampled product
e) reinforce previous buying behavior

7. Persuasive product advertising is typically used in which stage of the product life cycle?

a) growth
b) introductory
c) decline
d) development
e) all stages

8. The largest share of total advertising revenues is spent on:

a) television
b) newspapers
c) radio
d) magazines
e) none of the above

9. Which of the following is not an advantage of television advertising?

a) impact
b) mass coverage
c) prestige
d) high cost
e) repetition

10. Which of the following are disadvantages of radio?

    a) high cost
    b) fragmentation
    c) flexibility
    d) public distrust
    e) all of the above

B. TRUE-FALSE.   In the space to the left of each statement
                  check the appropriate line to indicate
                  whether the statement is true or false.

True False

____ ____ 1. Determination of advertising effectiveness includes pre-
              testing and post-testing.

____ ____ 2. Unaided recall tests are a method of pretesting.

____ ____ 3. An advantage of an independent advertising agency is a
              great degree of objectivity.

____ ____ 4. Retail advertising consists of all advertising by stores
              that sell goods and services directly to the consuming
              public.

____ ____ 5. Cooperative advertising resulted from offering lower rates
              to national advertisers.

____ ____ 6. Trade shows are rarely used for consumer products.

____ ____ 7. The part of public relations that is most directly re-
              lated to promoting a company's product is publicity.

____ ____ 8. Advertising is typically directed at small numbers of
              potential customers.

____ ____ 9. The reformist movement in advertising developed during
              the early 1900s.

____ ____ 10. Advertising planning begins with the budget.

Chapter 21

PROMOTIONAL STRATEGY: PERSONAL SELLING AND SALES MANAGEMENT

Chapter Objectives

When you have finished studying this chapter you should be able to:

Explain the role of personal selling in the organization's marketing mix.

Identify the three basic sales tasks.

Explain why some salespeople fail.

Outline the steps in the sales process.

Describe the major problems faced by sales management.

List the functions of sales management.

Chapter Summary

Personal selling is the seller's promotional presentation conducted on a person-to-person basis with the buyer. It is inherent in all business enterprises. The earliest sellers were known as peddlers, and some of the negative stereotyping associated with them remains today.

Three basic selling tasks exist: order processing, creative selling, and missionary selling. The successful salesperson is self-motivated and prepared to meet the demands of the competitive marketplace.

The basic steps involved in selling are (1) prospecting and qualifying, (2) approach, (3) presentation, (4) demonstration, (5) handling of objections, (6) closing, and (7) follow-up.

Retail selling is different from other kinds of selling, primarily in that the customer comes to the salesperson. Also, salespeople in stores are concerned with responsibilities other than selling. Two selling techniques particularly applicable to retailing are selling up and suggestion selling.

Sales management involves six basic functions: (1) recruitment and selection, (2) training, (3) organization, (4) supervision, (5) compensation, and (6) evaluation and control. Poor utilization of time and planned sales effort ranks as the leading problem faced by sales management today.

Key Terms and Concepts

Directions. Match the marketing term or concept listed below with the appropriate definition chosen from the list to the right, and write the appropriate letter in the space to the left of each term or concept. The correct answers are printed upside-down at the bottom of this assignment.

_____ 1.	APPROACH
_____ 2.	CANNED APPROACH
_____ 3.	CLOSING
_____ 4.	COMBINATION PLAN
_____ 5.	COMMISSION
_____ 6.	DETAILER
_____ 7.	FOLLOW-UP
_____ 8.	HANDLING OBJECTIONS
_____ 9.	MISSIONARY SALES
_____ 10.	ORDER PROCESSING

a. the third step in the sales process, during which the initial contact between the salesperson and the prospective customer occurs.

b. the second step in the sales process during which the salesperson determines whether a prospect is a potential customer.

c. persons selling at the wholesale or retail level in which the majority of the selling function involves processing of orders for customers.

d. a memorized sales presentation used to ensure uniform coverage of the points deemed important by management.

e. a method of compensating sales personnel by using a base salary along with a commission incentive.

f. a missionary salesperson in the health care industry who provides product information to physicians, hospitals, and retail durggists.

g. the management activities of securing, maintaining, motivating, supervising, evaluating, and controlling an effective sales force.

_____11. PERSONAL SELLING

_____12. PRESENTATION

_____13. PROSPECTING:

_____14. QUALIFYING

_____15. QUOTA

_____16. SALARY

_____17. SALES MANAGEMENT

_____18. SELLING-UP

_____19. SUGGESTION SELLING

h. the fifth step in the sales process, during which the salesperson
answers questions and attempts to
overcome objections of the potential
customers.

i. fixed payment made on a periodic
basis to employees, including some
sales personnel.

j. retailing sales technique designed
to convince the customer to purchase a higher-priced item than that
under current consideration.

k. post-sales activities designed to
remedy problems involved with the
purchase and to ensure customer
satisfaction.

l. form of compensation that is directly related to the sales or profits achieved by a salesperson.

m. the fourth step in the sales process, during which the salesperson
gives the sales message to the
prospective customer.

n. the sixth step in the sales process, during which the salesperson
asks the prospective customer to
conclude the purchase.

o. a seller's promotional presentation
conducted on a person-to-person
basis with a potential buyer.

p. an indirect type of selling in
which sales personnel are responsible for the creation and maintenance of good will of the selling firm by providing the customer with specialized assistance
and advice.

q. the first step in the sales process in which potential customers
are identified.

r. a specified sales or profit target that a salesperson is expected
to achieve.

s. retailing sales technique designed to broaden the customer's original purchase with related items, special promotions, or seasonal merchandise.

ANSWERS: 1. (A); 2. (D); 3. (N); 4. (E); 5. (L); 6. (F); 7. (K); 8. (H); 9. (P); 10. (C); 11. (O); 12. (M); 13. (Q); 14. (B); 15. (R); 16. (I); 17. (G); 18. (J); 19. (S).

Preliminary Practice Test

The preliminary practice test is designed to help you assess your mastery of text material in this chapter. The test consists of 20 questions focusing upon materials in the chapter and is useful in indicating how well-prepared you are at this stage to take an exam covering this material. The correct answers are printed upside-down at the end of the practice test.

1. Which of the following is <u>not</u> one of the basic sales tasks?

    a) sales promotion
    b) missionary selling
    c) order processing
    d) creative selling
    e) all of the above are basic sales tasks.

2. Which of the following is <u>not</u> a task of order processing sales people?

   a) identify customer needs
   b) seek out new customers
   c) point out the need to the customer
   d) complete the order
   e) all of the above are order processing tasks

3. All sales personnel perform the following function(s):

   a) providing sales intelligence to the marketing organization
   b) order taking
   c) creating good will
   d) creative selling
   e) all of the above

4. Which of the following is <u>not</u> one of the steps in the sales process?

   a) demonstration
   b) presentation
   c) initiation
   d) follow-up
   e) closing

5. Which of the following is <u>not</u> a basic technique for closing a sale?

   a) the SRO technique
   b) the AIO technique
   c) silence
   d) alternative-decision technique
   e) emotional close

6. Sales management activities discussed in the text include all of the following except:

   a) securing the sales force
   b) motivating the sales force
   c) evaluating the sales force
   d) budgeting the sales force
   e) supervising the sales force

7. Methods used in training a sales force include:

   a) role-playing
   b) on-the-job training
   c) lectures
   d) training films
   e) all of the above

8. According to the text, the key to good supervision is:

   a) authority
   b) experience
   c) communication

d) clearly-defined authority-responsibility relationship
e) well-trained subordinates

9. Which of the following are disadvantages of the commission system?

a) little company loyalty is generated
b) service aspect of selling may be slighted
c) excessive turnover of personnel when business declines
d) both a and b
e) all of the above

10. Which of the following are disadvantages of straight salary compensation?

a) little financial incentive
b) salary compression may occur
c) little company loyalty is generated
d) tend to increase direct selling costs
e) all of the above are disadvantages

B. TRUE-FALSE. In the space to the left of each statement check the appropriate line to indicate whether the statement is true or false.

True False

____ ____ 1. Combination compensation compensates sales personnel for all activities.

____ ____ 2. Combination plans are inexpensive to administer.

____ ____ 3. Personal selling is inherent in all business enterprises.

____ ____ 4. Selling has always been a function separate from ownership interests.

____ ____ 5. Completing the order is not a function of order processing.

____ ____ 6. Missionary sales are an indirect type of selling.

____ ____ 7. The "canned approach" of sales presentation is the most widely used technique.

____ ____ 8. The public is more aware of retail selling than any other kind.

____ ____ 9. Selling up seeks to broaden the customer's original purchase with related items.

____ ____ 10. An industrial marketer's promotional mix is more likely to emphasize personal selling than would the mix of a customer goods marketer.

FINAL PRACTICE TEST

This final practice test is designed to provide reinforcement of the success of your studies and the adequacy of your
preparation for exams covering the material in this chapter.
Like the preliminary test, the final practice test consists
of 20 questions focusing on materials covered in this chapter.
However, the correct answers are reprinted on the last page
of the MARKETING Mastery Guide.

A.   MULTIPLE CHOICE.   Choose the answer which best answers the
                        question or best completes the sentence.

1.   Which of the following statements are true about selling?

      a) early sellers sometimes used questionable sales practices
      b) the sales task has evolved into a professional occupation
      c) the negative sales stereotype has largely vanished
      d) all of the above are true
      e) both a and b

2.   Salespeople engaged in order-processing must:

      a) identify customer needs
      b) create customer wants
      c) point out the need to the customer
      d) all of the above
      e) both a and c

3.   Order processing becomes the primary task when:

      a) customers must be persuaded on their need
      b) needs can be readily identified by the salesperson
      c) purchases require extensive review by customer
      d) the sales person seeks to create good will
      e) order processing is never the primary task of salespeople

4. Which of the following is <u>not</u> part of the marketing intelligence provided by field sales personnel?

a) current assesments of competitive efforts
b) report on new product launches
c) assess customer reactions
d) both a and c
e) all of the above are considered part of the salesperson's marketing intelligence responsibility

5. The "canned approach" is:

a) a memorized sales talk used to ensure uniform coverage of important points
b) no longer used by salespeople
c) more effective in industrial selling
d) illegal in some states
e) none of the above

6. Which of the following is <u>not</u> a distinctive feature of retail selling?

a) the customer comes to the salesperson
b) retail salespeople have major nonselling responsibilities
c) creativity is more important in retail selling than in other sales fields
d) selling-up is frequently employed in retail selling
e) suggestion selling is frequently employed in retail selling

7. A successful career in sales offers all the following opportunities except:

a) security
b) high earnings
c) independence
d) a definite hierarchy of advancement
e) variety

8. Which of the following is <u>not</u> mentioned in the text as a basis for a territory allocation decision?

a) seniority of sales personnel
b) company objectives
c) personnel qualifications
d) equality of workloads
e) all of the above are mentioned

9. Which of the following are <u>not</u> advantages of straight commission plans?

a) pay relates directly to performance
b) regular income is assured
c) salespeople have the greatest possible incentive
d) company selling investment is reduced
e) system is readily understood

10. Which of the following are advantages of straight salary
compensation?

   a) regular income is assured
   b) provides great incentive
   c) easy administration
   d) both a and c
   e) all of the above are advantages

B   TRUE-FALSE. In the space to the left of each statement
check the appropriate line to indicate
whether the statement is true or false.

True False

____ ____ 1. Combination compensation plans offer a greater range of
earnings possibilities than straight salary.

____ ____ 2. Combination plans are easily understood.

____ ____ 3. Combination plans offer the advantages of both salary
and commission.

____ ____ 4. Retail selling is very similar to other kinds of
selling.

____ ____ 5. The negative stereotype of sales has vanished.

____ ____ 6. Creative selling is often required for new products.

____ ____ 7. All sales personnel provide sales intelligence to the
marketing organization.

____ ____ 8. The key to a good demonstration is confidence.

____ ____ 9. Suggestion selling uses the technique of convincing
the customer to buy a higher-rpiced item than he or
she originally intended.

____ ____ 10. A career in sales provides independence and variety but
no security.

PART EIGHT: EMERGING DIMENSIONS IN MARKETING

Chapter 22

INTERNATIONAL MARKETING

Chapter Objectives

When you have finished studying this chapter you should
be able to:

Explain the role that exporting, importing, balance of
trade, balance of payments, exchange rate adjustments,
and bartering play in international marketing.

Contrast the concepts of absolute advantage and comparative advantage.

Describe how marketing strategy differs in the international marketplace.

Identify the levels of involvement in international
marketing.

Outline the environment for international marketing.

List the various formats for multinational economic
integration.

Explain why the United States is an attractive market
for the marketers of other nations.

Chapter Summary

International marketing has become increasingly important
to the United States. Many U.S. firms depend on their
ability to market their goods abroad, while others depend on buying raw materials from other countries.

International marketing is often considered in terms
of a nation's balance of trade (the relationship between exports and imports) and balance of payments
(flow of money into or out of the country). Countries
must sometimes adjust their exchange rates (the rates
at which their currency can be exchanged for others
or for gold). Bartering, or the swapping of goods, is
now playing an increased role in international marketing, particularly in East-West trade.

243

Two of the basic concepts in international marketing
are absolute advantage and comparative advantage. An
absolute advantage exists if a nation is the sole producer of an item or can produce it for less than any
other nation. A comparative advantage exists if a
country can produce an item more efficiently than it
can produce alternate ones.

Competing in overseas markets is often considerably
different from competing at home. Market size, buying
behavior, and marketing practices may all differ. International marketers must make significant adaptations
in their product, pricing, distribution, and promotional
strategies to fit different markets abroad.

Several levels of involvement in international marketing
can be identified: casual or accidental exporting, active exporting, foreign licensing, overseas marketing,
and foreign production and marketing.

The world's largest firms are usually multinational
in their orientation. Such companies operate in several
countries and view the world as their market.

Various environmental factors can influence international
marketing strategy. Cultural, economic, and societal
factors can hinder international marketing. So can
assorted trade restrictions and some political and legal
factors.

Since the end of World War II, there has been a notice-
able trend toward multinational economic integration.
Three basic formats for integration are free trade a-
reas, customs unions, and common markets.

The United States is now viewed as an attractive market target for marketers from abroad. Thus U.S. firms
can expect to face stiff foreign competition in their
own domestic market.

Key Terms and Concepts

Directions. Match the marketing term or concept listed below
with the appropriate definition chosen from the list to the
right, and write the appropriate letter in the space to the
left of each term or concept. The correct answers are printed
upside-down at the bottom of this assignment.

_____ 1. ABSOLUTE ADVANTAGE

_____ 2. ACTIVE EXPORTING

_____ 3. BALANCE OF PAYMENTS

_____ 4. BALANCE OF TRADE

_____ 5. BARTERING

_____ 6. CARTELS

_____ 7. CASUAL EXPORTING

_____ 8. COMMON MARKET

_____ 9. COMPARATIVE ADVANTAGE

_____ 10. CUSTOMS UNION

_____ 11. DEVALUATION

_____ 12. DUMPING

_____ 13. EMBARGO

_____ 14. EXCHANGE CONTROL

_____ 15. EXCHANGE RATE

_____ 16. EXPORTING

_____ 17. FLOATING EXCHANGE RATE

_____ 18. FOREIGN CORRUPT
          PRACTICE ACT

a   prohibits bribery of foreign offici-
    als in order to obtain new or re-
    peat sales abroad and requires suf-
    ficient accounting controls to
    monitor internal compliance.

b. the flow of money into or out of a
    country as a result of exports,
    imports, tourism, military ex-
    penditures abroad, investment a-
    broad, and foreign aid.

c. a tax levied against imported pro-
    ducts to generate funds for the
    government and/or to protect mar-
    kets for domestic producers.

d. in international marketing, a for-
    mat for multinational economic
    integration that sets up a free
    trade area for member nations and
    a uniform tariff for nonmember
    nations.

e. the rate at which a nation's cur-
    rency can be exchanged for other
    currencies or gold.

f. the activities of a firm that
    takes a passive level of invol-
    vement in international market-
    ing.

g. international trade concept in
    which a nation is the sole pro-
    ducer of a product or can produce
    the product for less than any
    other nation.

h. limitation on the amount of pro-
    ducts in certain categories that
    can be imported.

i. exempts from antitrust laws vari-
    ous combinations of U.S. firms
    who act together outside the
    United States to match the econo-
    mic powers of cartels.

j. selling goods abroad.

k. the exchange of goods for goods,
    in contrast with the traditional
    exchange of currency for goods.

l. an increase in the value of a
    nation's currency in relation to
    gold or some other currency.

_____ 19. FOREIGN LICENSING

_____ 20. FRIENDSHIP, COMMERCE, AND NAVIGATION (FCN) TREATIES

_____ 21. GENERAL AGREEMENT ON TARIFFS AND TRADE (GATT)

_____ 22. IMPORTING

_____ 23. IMPORT QUOTA

_____ 24. JOINT VENTURE

_____ 25. MULTINATIONAL CORPORATION

_____ 26. REVALUATION

_____ 27. TARIFF

_____ 28. TOKYO ROUND

_____ 29. WEBB-POMERENE EXPORT TRADE ACT of 1918

m. an international trade accord designed to reduce the overall level of tariffs throughout the world.

n. selling a product at a lower price in a foreign market that it sells for in the producer's domestic market.

o. in international marketing, a format for multinational economic integration involving a customs union and continuing efforts to standardize trade regulations of all governments.

p. the latest series of negotiations attempting to bring about tariff reductions among nations.

q. the complete ban on importing certain products.

r. in international marketing, the activities of a firm that has made a commitment to seek export business.

s. agreements among nations that deal with various aspects of their commercial relations.

t. international trade concept in which a nation chooses to produce those products that can be produced more efficiently than alternative products.

u. a firm that operates in several countries and literally views the world as its market.

v. the relationship between a nation's imports and exports.

w. attempt to regulate international trade by requiring exporting firms receiving foreign exchange to sell this exchange to the nation's central bank or agency, and importers requiring foreign exchange to purchase it from the same agency.

x. the reduction of the value of a nation's currency in relation to gold or some other currency.

y. method of international marketing
in which a domestic firm enters
into an agreement with a partner
who is usually a national of
the host nation and who shares
the risks, costs, and management
of the foreign operation.

z. monopolistic organizations of
foreign firms.

aa. buying foreign goods and raw
materials.

bb. those exchange rates that are
allowed to adjust to market
conditions.

cc. in international marketing, an
agreement between a firm and a
foreign company, whereby the
foreign company produces and dis-
tributes the firm's goods in the
foreign country.

ANSWERS: 1. (G); 2. (R); 3. (B); 4. (V); 5. (K); 6. (Z);
7. (F); 8. (O); 9. (T); 10. (D); 11. (X);
12. (N); 13. (O); 14. (W); 15. (E); 16. (J);
17. (BB); 18. (A); 19. (CC); 20. (S); 21. (M);
22. (AA); 23. (H); 24. (Y); 25. (U); 26. (L);
27. (C); 28. (P); 29. (I).

Preliminary Practice Test

The preliminary practice test is designed to help you assess
your mastery of text material in this chapter. The test consists of 20 questions focusing upon materials in the chapter
and is useful in indicating how well-prepared you are at this
stage to take an exam covering this material. The correct
answers are printed upside-down at the end of the practice test.

A.   MULTIPLE CHOICE.   Choose the answer which <u>best</u> answers the question or best completes the sentence.

1. Which of the following is <u>not</u> true concerning the United States's foreign trade activities?

    a) foreign trade is more critical in terms of percent of GNP to the U.S. than to West Germany
    b) the U.S. is the world's largest importer
    c) the U.S. is the world's largest exporter
    d) the leading import of the U.S. is petroleum
    e) the U.S.'s leading export items are motor vehicles.

2. Which of the following are mentioned in the text as having an impact on a nation's balance of payments?

    a) tourism
    b) military expenditures abroad
    c) investments abroad
    d) all of the above
    e) none of the above

3. The growing popularity of bartering can be explained by:

    a) marketers' attempts to expand sales
    b) attempts to reduce balance of payments problems
    c) attempts to increase sales of lower quality products
    d) attempts to increase sales of higher quality products
    e) a, b, and c are correct

4. Which of the following conditions are experienced by marketers who venture abroad?

    a) different market sizes
    b) similar buyer behavior
    c) different marketing practices
    d) foreign marketing is very similar to domestic marketing
    e) both a and c are correct

5. Which of the following types of adaptations in product strategy for international markets are mentioned by the text?

    a) modification of the product itself
    b) packaging modification
    c) product identification
    d) all of the above
    e) both a and b

6. Which of the following is <u>not</u> true concerning foreign promotional strategy?

    a) many firms have taken a firm stand against illicit business practices
    b) overseas marketing practices by U.S. firms are not evaluated in terms of U.S. standards

248

c) effective personal selling is still vital
d) advertising has gained in importance
e) all of the above are true

7. Which of the following is an advantage concerning foreign licensing?

a) availability of local marketing information
b) availability of local marketing channels
c) lack of conflict between parties involved
d) protection from various legal barriers
e) a, b, and d are correct

8. Which of the following is <u>not</u> mentioned by the text as an environmental influence in international marketing?

a) cultural bias
b) economic bias
c) societal bias
d) trade restrictions
e) all of the above are mentioned by the text

9. What is the purpose of a protective tariff?

a) to impose political sanctions
b) to raise funds for the government
c) to reduce trade activity
d) to raise the price of imported products
e) none of the above

10. Which of the following is/are <u>not</u> among the three dimensions of the legal environment for firms practicing abroad?

a) Sherman Act
b) U.S. law
c) international law
d) laws of the host nation
e) none of the above

B. TRUE-FALSE. In the space to the left of each statement check the appropriate line to indicate whether the statement is true or false.

True False

_____ _____ 1. The Webb-Pomerene Export Trade Act of 1918 applied anti-trust laws to combinations of U.S. firms developing foreign markets.

_____ _____ 2. FCN treaties have been considered illegal in the U.S. for many years.

249

True False

____ ____ 3. The U.S. is an unattractive target for foreign marketers due to a number of anti-dumping laws passed during the 1970s.

____ ____ 4. Foreign trade consists of importing and exporting.

____ ____ 5. The U.S.'s leading export is petroleum.

____ ____ 6. An unfavorable balance of trade exists when exports exceed imports.

____ ____ 7. Floating exchange rates are allowed to adjust to market conditions.

____ ____ 8. Japan is very rich in raw materials.

____ ____ 9. Only about 8 percent of U.S. manufacturing firms export their products.

____ ____ 10. Buyer behavior often differs significantly from one country to another.

ANSWERS   Multiple Choice. 1. (A); 2. (D); 3. (E); 4. (D); 5. (D); 6. (D); 7. (E); 8. (E); 9. (D); 10. (A). True-False. 1. (F); 2. (F); 3. (F); 4. (T); 5. (F); 6. (F); 7. (T); 8. (F); 9. (T); 10. (T).

FINAL PRACTICE TEST

This final practice test is designed to provide reinforcement of the success of your studies and the adequacy of your preparation for exams covering the material in this chapter. Like the preliminary test, the final practice test consists of 20 questions focusing on materials covered in this chapter. However, the correct answers are reprinted on the last page of the MARKETING Mastery Guide.

A.   MULTIPLE CHOICE: Choose the answer which <u>best</u> answers the
                        question or best completes the sentence.

1.   Which of the following is true concerning the United
     States's foreign trade activities?

     a) the leading export items are motor vehicles and parts
     b) the U.S. is the world's largest importer
     c) the U.S. is the world's largest exporter
     d) the leading import of the U.S. is petroleum
     e) all of the above

2.   A favorable balance of trade results:

     a) when imports exceed exports
     b) when exports exceed imports
     c) when tariffs are high
     d) when tariffs are low
     e) when money flows are outward, all other things being equal

3.   What do the examples of Japan and Nauru suggest with
     regard to marketing activities?

     a) on the whole, small nations are superior marketers
     b) international marketing is heavily dependent upon a nation's
        raw materials
     c) nations benefit if they specialize in certain markets
     d) nations benefit from diversification
     e) the physical size of the Pacific Ocean force island nations
        to engage in international trade

4.   A nation has an absolute advantage when it:

     a) produces highly specialized products
     b) it is the sole producer of the product
     c) it can produce a prodduct cheaper than anyone else
     d) all of the above
     e) both b and c are correct

5.   Which of the following facts concerning world market
     statistics is <u>not</u> true?

     a) death rates are rising in many nations
     b) birth rates are dropping in many nations
     c) international markets are increasingly urbanized
     d) international markets are still gorwing in size
     e) the U.S. is no longer the world's wealthiest industrialized
        nation

6.   Which of the following is <u>not</u> true about pricing strate-
     gies in foreign markets?

     a) export pricing is the least affected of the marketing
        mix variables
     b) price strategies are affected by varying economic conditions
        in different nations

251

c) pricing strategies are subject to competitive constraints
d) pricing strategies are subject to political constraints
e) pricing strategies are subject to legal constraints

7. Which of the following is <u>not</u> one of the levels of involvement mentioned by the text?

a) casual exporting
b) active exporting
c) domestic licensing
d) accidental exporting
e) overseas marketing

8. Which of the following are ways of achieving the ultimate degree of company involvement in the international marketing arena?

a) a firm can set up its own production/marketing operation in the foreign country
b) acquisition of an existing firm in the country
c) formation of a joint venture with a partner who is a national in the host nation
d) none of the above
e) all of the above

9. What is the purpose of a revenue tariff?

a) to impose political sanctions
b) to raise funds for the government of the importing nation
c) to reduce trade activity
d) to raise the price of imported products
e) all of the above

10. Which of the following statements is true about protective tariffs?

a) they raise the price of imported products
b) they are usually higher than revenue tariffs
c) they are usually lower than revenue tariffs
d) both a and c are correct
e) both a and b are correct

B.   TRUE-FALSE.   In the space to the left of each statement check the appropriate line to indicate whether the statement is true or false.

True False

____ ____ 1. The Foreign Corrupt Practices Act states it is legal to bribe a foreign official only if it is legal in the host nation.

252

True False

True	False		
✓	____	2.	Today Webb-Pomerene associations account for less than 2 percent of United States exports.
✓	____	3.	The simplest approach to multinational economic intergration is a free trade area.
____	✓	4.	Foreign competition in the United States is expected to decline in the future.
✓	____	5.	The United States is the largest importer and exporter in the world.
____	✓	6.	A nation's balance of trade is determined by imports only.
____	✓	7.	Balance of trade does not affect balance of payments.
____	✓	8.	Revaluation occurs when a country adjusts the value of its currency upward only.
____	✓	9.	The concept of comparative advantage is a less practical approach to international trade specialization than absolute advantage.
✓	____	10.	The international market place is expected to continue to grow in size during the 1980s.

Chapter 23

MARKETING IN NONPROFIT SETTINGS

Chapter Objectives

When you have finished studying this chapter you should be able to:

Outline the primary characteristics of nonprofit organizations.

Describe the evolution of the broadening concept.

Identify the steps involved in introducing marketing to a nonprofit institution.

Explain how a marketing mix might be developed in a nonprofit setting.

Suggest some variables that may be used in the evaluation and control of a nonprofit marketing program.

Chapter Summary

Nonprofit organizations are those enterprises whose primary objective is something other than returning a profit to its owners. Nonprofit organizations are often characterized by the intangible nature of many of their services; minimal control by customers; professional rather than organizational orientation of their employees; involvement of resources contributors; lack of an overall bottom line; and the lack of a clear organizational structure.

The introduction of marketing into nonprofit settings has been associated with the broadening concept, which extends the marketing concept to nontraditional exchange processes. The broadening concept was introduced by Philip Kotler and Sidney J. Levy in 1969.

Marketing is now viewed as integral to many nonprofit settings, although it is too often defined largely in terms of promotional strategy. There are six steps involved in the introduction of marketing to a nonprofit institution: (1) appoint a marketing committee; (2) set up task forces; (3) contract marketing specialist firms; (4) hire a marketing consultant; (5)

employ a marketing director, and (6) hire a marketing vice president.

Nonprofit agencies require a comprehensive marketing mix strategy based on accurate marketing research. An effective evaluation and control system must be set up to monitor the marketing strategy. This system might be based on one or more of the following variables: total market response; market share; cost per dollar of market response; efficiency measures; and market attitudes.

Key Terms and Concepts

Directions. Match the marketing term or concept listed below with the appropriate definition chosen from the list to the right, and write the appropriate letter in the space to the left of each term or concept. The correct answers are printed upside-down at the bottom of this assignment.

_____1. BOTTOM LINE

_____2. BROADENING CONCEPT

_____3. MARKET DEINCENTIVIZATION

_____4. MARKET INCENTIVIZATION

_____5. NONPROFIT ORGANIZATION

a. pricing strategy for nonprofit organization designed to discourage consumption.

b. pricing strategy for nonprofit organization designed to encourage increased usage of the product or service.

c. the extension of the marketing concept to nontraditional exchange processes based upon the theoretical justification that marketing is a generic activity for all organizations.

d. organizations whose primary objectives do not inlcude returning a profit to their owners.

e. business jargon referring to the overall profitability measure of performance.

ANSWERS: 1. (E); 2. (C); 3. (A); 4. (B); 5. (D).

The preliminary practice test is designed to help you assess
your mastery of text material in this chapter. The test consists of 20 questions focusing upon materials in the chapter
and is useful in indicating how well-prepared you are at this
stage to take an exam covering this material. The correct
answers are printed upside-down at the end of the practice test.

A.   MULTIPLE CHOICE.   Choose the answer which <u>best</u> answers the
                       question or best completes the sentence.

1.   Which of the following is <u>not</u> an example of a private
     sector, nonprofit organization?

     a) University of Florida football team
     b) art institutes
     c) labor unions
     d) hospitals
     e) the United Fund

2.   The most commonly noted feature of nonprofit organiza-
     tions cited by the text is:

     a) lack of organizational structure
     b) lack of control over resources
     c) lack of "bottom line"
     d) lack of power
     e) lack of tangibility

3.   The comprehensive marketing approach in the nonprofit
     sector should include:

     a) market analysis
     b) analysis of resources
     c) analysis of mission
     d) all of the above
     e) both a and b

4.   Which of the following alternatives were/was <u>not</u> sug-
     gested by Kotler for introducing marketing to a non-
     profit organization?

     a) set up a task force
     b) hire an account specialist
     c) hire a consultant
     d) hire a marketing director
     e) all of the above were suggested by Kotler

5.   The ultimate step in integrating marketing activities
     into a nonprofit institution, according to Kotler, is:

     a) appoint a marketing committee

b) hire a marketing consultant
c) hire a marketing director
d) hire a marketing vice president
e) contract a marketing specialist firm

6. Pricing strategy can be used to accomplish all of the following goals in a nonprofit organization except:

   a) cost recovery
   b) profit maximization
   c) market polarization
   d) market incentivization
   e) market deincentivization

7. Which of the following variables can be used to measure the effectiveness of nonprofit marketing efforts?

   a) total market response
   b) market share
   c) cost per dollar of market response
   d) both a and c
   e) all of the above

8. Marketing in nonprofit organizations:

   a) lacks sophistication
   b) often is seen as a "quick fix" solution
   c) is still viewed with suspicion by many of the people involved
   d) has not been accepted to any degree in the nonprofit sector
   e) all of the above apply

9. Which of the following statements about nonprofit organizations are not true?

   a) the primary objective is something other than profit
   b) they can be found in the public and private sector
   c) they are diverse
   d) both b and c are false
   e) all of the above are true

10. The comprehensive marketing approach in the nonprofit sector typically does not include:

    a) image analysis
    b) market analysis
    c) resource analysis
    d) mission analysis
    e) all of the above should be included

B. TRUE-FALSE. In the space to the left of each statement check the appropriate line to indicate whether the statement is true or false.

True False

_____ _____ 1. Nonprofit organizations are found only in the public sector.

_____ _____ 2. The Lions Club is an example of a private sector non-profit organization.

_____ _____ 3. Products offered by nonprofit organizatins tend to be intangible.

_____ _____ 4. The most commonly noted feature of the nonprofit sector is its lack of a "bottom line."

_____ _____ 5. The broadening concept was an extension of the marketing concept to non-traditional exchange processes.

_____ _____ 6. Most nonprofit organizations take a comprehensive market-ing approach.

_____ _____ 7. Marketing has not yet been accepted as part of the operational environment of successful nonprofit organi-zations.

_____ _____ 8. Decisions in nonprofit settings tend to be based upon extensive research.

_____ _____ 9. A common failure among nonprofit organizations is the assumption that heavy promotional efforts can overcome a poor marketing mix.

_____ _____ 10. Nonprofit organizations are often incautious in planning their disttribution strategy.

FINAL PRACTICE TEST

This final practice test is designed to provide reinforce-ment of the success of your studies and the adequacy of your preparation for exams covering the material in this chapter. Like the preliminary test, the final practice test consists of 20 questions focusing on materials covered in this chapter. However, the correct answers are reprinted on the last page of the MARKETING Mastery Guide.

A.   MULTIPLE CHOICE.   Choose the answer which best answers the question or best completes the sentence.

1.   Which of the following statements about nonprofit organizations are true?

   a) they represent a substantial portion of the U.S. economy
   b) their primary objective is something other than returning a profit
   c) not all of the marketing mix variables are present
   d) all of the above are true
   e) both a and b are true

2.   Which of the following is not a characteristic of nonprofit organizations?

   a) products offered are often intangible
   b) service users exercise control over the organization's destiny
   c) customers have little control over the organization's destiny
   d) they often posess a degree of monopoly power in a given area
   e) resource contributors often can interfere with the marketing program

3.   The current status of nonprofit marketing is the result of:

   a) new federal regulations
   b) an evolutionary process
   c) resistance from the profit sector
   d) all of the above
   e) none of the above

4.   Which of the following practices were implemented before marketing in nonprofit organizations?

   a) strategic planning
   b) personnel selection
   c) accounting
   d) both a and b
   e) all of the above

5.   According to the text, Kotler believes that the marketing director should report to:

   a) the vice president of planning
   b) the vice president of marketing
   c) the sales manager
   d) the company president
   e) none of the above

6.   Which of the following elements is not an element of the marketing mix in the nonprofit sector?

   a) promotional strategy
   b) product strategy
   c) pricing strategy
   d) distribution strategy
   e) all of the above are elements of the marketing mix

7. All of the following are examples of cost recovery
    venture except:

    a) mass transit
    b) public supported colleges
    c) churches
    d) bridges
    e) all of the above are examples

8. Which of the following is not one of the variables listed
    in the text to measure effectiveness of nonprofit
    marketing efforts?

    a) market attitudes
    b) rate of return
    c) market share
    d) total market response
    e) efficiency measure

9. The broadening concept:

    a) restricts marketing to the profit sector
    b) extends the marketing concept to other countries
    c) extends the marketing concept to non-traditional exchange
       processes
    d) both b and c are correct
    e) does none of the above

10. Which of the following are examples of private sector,
    nonprofit organizations?

    a) University of Texas football team
    b) art institute
    c) labor unions
    d) both b and c are examples
    e) all of the above are examples

B. TRUE-FALSE. In the space to the left of each statement
                 check the appropriate line to indicate
                 whether the statement is true or false.

True False

____ ____   1. Nonprofit organizations are found only in the private
               sector.

____ ____   2. Nonprofit organizations are found in both the public and
               private sectors.

____ ____   3. The public sector offers a greater diversity of non-
               profit settings than the private sector.

____ ____   4. Resource contributors often interfere with the marketing
               program in the nonprofit sector.

True False

_____ _____   5. Nonprofit organizations tend to have clear-cut organizational structures.

_____ _____   6. The broadening concept was an extension of the marketing concept to other countries.

_____ _____   7. Nonprofit organizations typically implemented accounting practices before marketing.

_____ _____   8. Kotler believes that the marketing director should report to the vice president of planning.

_____ _____   9. Marketing research is less important in nonprofit organizations.

_____ _____ 10. Pricing is a less important element in the marketing mix for nonprofit organizations.

Chapter 24

MARKETING AND SOCIETY

Chapter Objectives

When you have finished studying this chapter you should
be able to:

Describe marketing's contemporary environment.

Outline the need for measuring social performance.

Identify the major societalissues in marketing.

Explain how the contemporary societal issues in marketing might be resolved.

Chapter Summary

There are many important issues in contemporary marketing's societal environment. Marketing's environmental relationships have expanded in scope and importance. In fact, some companies have even set up
public responsibility committees at the board level
to deal with some of these issues.

The current issues in marketing can be categorized as
consumerism, marketing ethics, and social responsibility. Consumerism is a protest against abuse and mal-
practice in the marketing system as well as a plea
for greater attention to consumer wants and desires.
Marketing ethics is a complex subject since it can be
considered from the viewpoints of individual, organizational, or professional ethics. Ethical problems
exist in marketing research, product management, pricing, distribution strategy, and promotion. Another
issue is the relationship between social responsibility
in marketing and the profit motive and the process for
making socially responsible marketing decisions in the
organization.

Increased regulation, better public information, and
a more responsible marketing philosophy are possible
alternatives for resolving these issues. All are expected to play a greater role in the years ahead.

Directions. Match the marketing term or concept listed below with the appropriate definition chosen from the list to the right, and write the appropriate letter in the space to the left of each term or concept. The correct answers are printed upside-down at the bottom of this assignment.

_i_ 1. CLASS ACTION SUIT

_D_ 2. CONSUMER RIGHTS

_h_ 3. CONSUMERISM

_a_ 4. ECOLOGY

_f_ 5. GREEN RIVER ORDINANCES

_g_ 6. OPEN DATING

_k_ 7. PLANNED OBSOLESCENCE

_B_ 8. POLLUTION

_e_ 9. PUBLIC RESPONSIBILITY COMMITTEE

_J_ 10. RECYCLING

_C_ 11. RESOURCE CONSERVATION RECOVERY ACT

a. the relationship between people and their environment.

b. a broad term that is usually defined as "making unclean" and can be categorized as either environmental or cultural.

c. Federal legislation requiring all refuse dumps to be closed by 1983, in an attempt to reclaim natural resources.

d. list of rights delieneated by President John F. Kennedy in 1962, including the rights to safety, to be informed, to choose, and to be heard.

e. permanent committee made up of the boards of directors of a number of the major corporations in the United States which considers matters of corporate social responsibility.

f. municipal ordinances designed to place limitations on door-to-door sales solicitations.

g. the listing of the last possible date that an item can be sold on the package or label of perishable foods.

h. a demand that marketers give greater attention to consumer wants and desires in making their decisions.

i. a legal suit brought by private citizens on behalf of any group of consumers for damages caused by unfair business practices.

j. reuse of such items as packaging materials to provide a new source of raw materials while simultaneously alleviating a major factor in environmental pollution.

k. a policy of producing products with only a limited life span. This can occur where the producers uses materials of lower cost with no compensating benefits to the consumer, such as lower prices or improved performance characteristics.

ANSWERS: 1. (I); 2. (D); 3. (H); 4. (A); 5. (F); 6. (G); 7. (K); 8. (B); 9. (E); 10. (J); 11. (C).

Preliminary Practice Test

The preliminary practice test is designed to help you assess your mastery of text material in this chapter. The tests consists of 20 questions focusing upon materials in the chapter and is useful in indicating how well-prepared you are at this stage to take an exam covering this material. The correct answers are printed upside-down at the end of the practice test.

A. MULTIPLE CHOICE. Choose the answer which <u>best</u> answers the question or best completes the sentence.

1. The Green River ordinances were enacted to:

   a) prevent payoffs to suppliers
   b) limit door-to-door selling
   c) limit telephone selling
   d) eliminate questionable advertising practices
   e) promote efficient marketing in non-urban areas

2. Many arguments of marketing critics are based upon the theme that:

   a) materialsim ignores the quality of life
   b) competition destroys the marketplace
   c) marketing is too powerful in today's organizations
   d) marketing dictates rather than costs determine product price
   e) all of the above

3. Which of the following are included in the major issues in marketing?

   a) consumerism
   b) conservatism
   c) marketing ethics
   d) all of the above
   e) both a and c

4. The argument that the rise in consumerism is proof that the marketing concept has failed is based upon:

   a) the fact that not enough firms have adopted the marketing concept
   b) the concept itself has not made firms more responsive
   c) the concept places undue emphasis on profit
   d) all of the above
   e) both a and b

5. Which of the following is/are included in consumerism's indictment of marketing?

   a) not enough is spent on marketing expenditures designed to measure consumer needs
   b) service suffers because of emphasis on product quality
   c) the system has produced health and safety hazards
   d) both a and b
   e) all of the above

6. John F. Kennedy's rights of the consumer included all the following except:

   a) the right to return faulty products
   b) the right to be informed on product choice matters
   c) the right to choose
   d) the right to be heard
   e) the right to safety

7. The most promising long-term solution to consumer problems is expected to result from:

   a) consumer legislation
   b) consumer education
   c) class action suits
   d) new legal actions at the local levels
   e) consumer agencies

8. The most regulated aspect of a firm's marketing strategy is:

   a) pricing
   b) promotion
   c) advertising
   d) packaging
   e) distribution

9. The "kid-vid" Rule of 1978 proposed that:

   a) advertising be prohibited during times when children of certain ages made up a specified proportion of the viewers
   b) advertising of heavily sugared products be prohibited
   c) advertisers be required to underwrite health announcements
   d) all of the above
   e) both a and b

10. All of the following are ecological problems for marketers, except:

    a) planned obsolecence
    b) pollution
    c) recycling
    d) preservation of resources
    e) all of the above are ecological problems for marketers

B. TRUE-FALSE. In the space to the left of each statement check the appropriate line to indicate whether the statement is true or false.

True False

___ ___ 1. Open dating sets the last date a perishable food can be sold.

___ ___ 2. The Green River ordinances limit door-to-door selling.

___ ___ 3. Consumerism has charged marketing with being inefficient.

___ ___ 4. Marketers admit that product quality is poor.

___ ___ 5. Consumer protection agencies exist primarily at the federal level of government.

___ ___ 6. The best long-term solution to consumer problems is consumer education.

___ ___ 7. Professional ethics are based on a concept which transcends organizational and individual ethics.

___ ___ 8. Marketing research has occasionally been castigated as an invasion of personal privacy.

True False

_____ ___✓___ 9. Pricing is the least regulated aspect of the marketing mix.

_____ ___✓___ 10. Promotion is the component of the marketing mix where most ethical questions arise.

FINAL PRACTICE TEST

This final practice test is designed to provide reinforcement of the success of your studies and the adequacy of your preparation for exams covering the material in this chapter. Like the preliminary test, the final practice test consists of 20 questions focusing on materials covered in this chapter. However, the correct answers are reprinted on the last page of the MARKETING Mastery Guide.

A. MULTIPLE CHOICE. Choose the answer which best answers the question or best completes the sentence.

1. Environmental relationships in marketing include:

    a) customers
    b) employees
    c) government
    d) vendors
    e) all of the above

2. Adam Smith saw _____ as the watchdog that kept the economy on the correct course.

    a) competition
    b) public opinion

267

c) democracy
d) regulations
e) materialism

3. Which of the following is <u>not</u> a traditional measure of social contributions of the firm?

a) employment
b) environment
c) wages
d) profits
e) bank deposits

4. Which of the following are <u>not</u> included in the major issues in marketing?

a) marketing ethics
b) consumerism
c) social responsibility
d) all of the above are included
e) both a and b

5. Which of the following is/are <u>not</u> included in consumerism's indictment of marketing?

a) marketing costs are too high
b) not enough is spent on marketing expenditures designed to measure consumer needs
c) the system is inefficient
d) marketers are guilty of collusion and price fixing
e) product quality is poor

6. Marketing "pleads guilty" to all the following charges except:

a) the system is sometimes inefficient
b) marketing costs are frequently too high
c) product quality is poor
d) service is often poor
e) consumers do not receive complete information

7. Which of the following are termed "consumer weapons?"

a) consumer legislation
b) class action suits
c) consumer protection agencies
d) all of the above
e) both a and b

8. The types of ethic mentioned in the text include all the following except:

a) individual ethic
b) organizational ethic
c) religious ethic
d) professional ethic
e) all of the above are mentioned

9. The component of the marketing mix where the majority of ethical questions arise is:

    a) pricing
    b) distribution
    c) advertising
    d) product design
    e) promotion

10. The concept of business responsibility has traditionally concerned the relationship with all of the following except:

    a) managers and customers
    b) managers and society
    c) managers and employees
    d) managers and stockholders
    e) managers and subordinates

B. TRUE-FALSE. In the space to the left of each statement check the appropriate line to indicate whether the statement is true or false.

True False

_____ _____   1. Marketers feel that regulations in the area of pricing will decrease in the future.

_____ _____   2. Internal relationships form the basis of the social issues in marketing.

_____ _____   3. Consumerism has charged that marketing costs are too high.

_____ _____   4. Marketers have successfully refuted consumerism's charges.

_____ _____   5. All consumer demands are being met by consumer-oriented firms.

_____ _____   6. Class action suits have proven largely ineffective as consumer weapons.

_____ _____   7. Individual ethics seldom differ with organizational ethics.

_____ _____   8. Professional ethics are based on a combination of organizational and individual ethics.

_____ _____   9. Promotion is the most regulated aspect of the marketing mix.

_____ _____ 10. Pricing is the component of the marketing mix where most ethical questions arise.

Chapter 25

EVALUATION AND CONTROL

Chapter Objectives

When you have finished studying this chapter you should be able to:

Explain the marketing control process.

Outline the conclusions reached in the PIMS study and the contributions of the Boston Consulting Group.

Describe the use of sales analysis and marketing cost analysis.

Explain how ROI and ratio analysis are used in evaluating marketing performance.

Identify and discuss the various aspects of conducting a marketing audit.

Chapter Summary

The control process is an important part of marketing. *Evaluation and control* refers to all the various assessments that marketers employ to determine if the marketing opportunity analysis, the objectives and the standards set during the marketing planning phase, and/or the implementation of the marketing program itself has been effective. Evaluation and control permits marketers to determine whether corrective actions are needed. Control charts are sometimes used to set both upper and lower control limits for such assessments.

Chapter 25 examines the question of how marketing performance should be measured. The PIMS study said that market share and ROI data were closely linked. The Boston Consulting Group (BCG) decided that higher market shares led to lower production cost, giving high market share firms a distinct advantage over competitors. Still other have disagreed with both PIMS and BCG premises.

Several techniques or procedures are useful in marketing evaluation and control. Sales analysis is an in-depth evaluation of a firm's sales designed to obtain meaningful information from existing data. Marketing cost analysis is the evaluation of such items as selling costs, billing, warehousing, advertising, and delivery expenses in order to determine the profitability of particular customers, territories, or product lines. ROI is a quantitative tool that seeks to relate the activity or project's profitability to its required investment. Also, the calculation of various ratios helps in analyzing specific aspects of marketing performance. The marketing audit, which entails a thorough study of a firm's marketing program, is extremely useful in improving overall effectiveness.

Key Terms and Concepts

Directions. Match the marketing term or concept listed below with the appropriate definition chosen from the list to the right, and write the appropriate letter in the space to the left of each term or concept. The correct answers are printed upside-down at the bottom of this assignment.

_____ 1.   CONTROL CHARTS

_____ 2.   EVALUATION AND CONTROL

_____ 3.   EXPERIENCE CURVE

_____ 4.   FUNCTIONAL ACCOUNTS

_____ 5.   ICEBERG PRINCIPLE

_____ 6.   INVENTORY TURNOVER

_____ 7.   MARKET SHARE

a. the possibility of obscuring important evaluative information through the process of aggregating data.

b. financial ratio designed to show the percentage of each dollar of sales that remains after all costs and taxes; calculated by dividing net profit after taxes by sales.

c. a thorough, objective evaluation of an organization's marketing philosophy, goals, policies, tactics, practices, and results.

d. reclassification of traditional accounting data to reflect the purpose for which expenditures were made for use in marketing cost analysis.

_____8.   MARKETING AUDIT

_____9.   MARKETING COST
          ANALYSIS

_____10. NATURAL ACCOUNTS

_____11. PROFIT CENTER

_____12. PROFIT IMPACT OF
          MARKET STRATEGIES
          (PIMS)

_____13. PROFIT MARGIN ON
          SALES

_____14. RATE OF RETURN ON
          COMMON EQUITY

_____15. RATE OF RETURN ON
          TOTAL ASSETS

_____16. RETURN ON
          INVESTMENT (ROI)

_____17. SALES ANALYSIS

_____18. SALES QUOTA

e. research studies revealing the close, positive relationship between the percentage of a market controlled by a firm and its return on investment.

f. evaluation of such items as selling costs, billing, warehousing, advertising, and delivery expenses in order to determine the profitability of particular customers, territories, or product lines.

g. the various assessments utilized by the marketer to determine whether the marketing opportunity analysis, the objectives and standards set during the marketing planning phase, and/or the implementation of the marketing program itself has been effective.

h. financial ratio designed to measure the rate of return of the firm's total investment; calculated by dividing net profit after taxes by total assets.

i. performance objective for a particular salesperson, product, or territory.

j. the percentage of a market controlled by a firm.

k. an administrative unit whose contribution to corporate earnings can be measured.

l. traditional accounting classifications such as salary expenses or supplies expenses.

m. diagrams that plot actual performance against established control limits.

n. financial ratio designed to show how many times each year the average investment in inventory turns over; calculated by dividing sales by inventory.

272

o. a quantitative tool designed to relate the activity or project's profitability to its investment.

p. reduction in costs as a result of learning, increased specialization, higher investment, and economies of scale.

q. financial ratio designed to show the success of management in earning returns on stockholders' investment; calculated by dividing net income available to common stock by common equity.

r. in-depth evaluation of a firm's sales by dividing overall sales into such breakdowns as geographical, product, type of sale, or type of customer.

ANSWERS: 1. (M); 2. (G); 3. (P); 4. (D); 5. (A); 6. (N); 7. (J); 8. (C); 9. (F); 10. (L); 11. (K); 12. (E); 13. (B); 14. (Q); 15. (H); 16. (O); 17. (R); 18. (I).

Preliminary Practice Test

The preliminary practice test is designed to help you assess your mastery of text material in this chapter. The test consists of 20 questions focusing upon materials in the chapter and is useful in indicating how well-prepared you are at this stage to take an exam covering this material. The correct answers are printed upside-down at the end of the practice test.

A.   MULTIPLE CHOICE.   Choose the answer which <u>best</u> answers the question or best completes the sentence.

1.   Which of the following are evaluative methods used for measuring marketing performance?

   a) financial ratios
   b) extensive field tests
   c) questions about organizational achievements
   d) both b and c
   e) all of the above

2.   The experience curve:

   a) does not affect costs
   b) will result in increased costs
   c) states that higher market shares reduce costs
   d) both a and b
   e) none of the above

3.   The iceberg principle:

   a) cautions marketers against putting too much blind faith in research
   b) suggests that important data are often hidden by aggregate data
   c) shows the relationship between ROI and market share
   d) is a cost-cutting method
   e) is none of the above

4.   Marketing cost analysis evaluates all the following items except:

   a) selling costs
   b) supplier costs
   c) warehousing
   d) advertising
   e) billing

5.   Which of the following factors does not affect ROI calculations?

   a) book value of assets
   b) industry concentration
   c) market value of assets
   d) transfer pricing
   e) time periods

6.   Which of the following ratios are profitability-oriented?

   a) inventory turnover
   b) rate of return on common equity
   c) rate of return on total assets
   d) all of the above
   e) both b and c

7. All of the following are profitability-oriented ratios except:

a) rate of return on total assets
b) rate of return on common equity
c) inventory turnover
d) profit margin on sales
e) none of the above are profitability-oriented

8. Which of the following is <u>not</u> one of the elements on which the ratios' significance depends?

a) company's past performance
b) sales forecasts
c) industry averages
d) alternatives available
e) none of the above are significant for the ratios

9. Which of the following are elements evaluated in the marketing audit?

a) marketing practices
b) marketing goals
c) markeing tactics
d) both a and c
e) all of the above

10. Which of the following are potential sources of auditors?

a) special marketing audit staffs
b) outside marketing consultants
c) federal regulatory agencies
d) both a and b
e) all of the above

B. TRUE-FALSE. In the space to the left of each statement check the appropriate line to indicate whether the statement is true or false.

True False

____ ____ 1. The PIMS study showed that market share and ROI results are positively linked.

____ ____ 2. BCG consultants suggest that profitability is a better measure of performance than market share.

____ ____ 3. The purpose of sales analysis is to obtain meaningful information from existing data.

____ ____ 4. Sales analysis is one of the most expensive sources of marketing information.

True False

_____ _✓_ 5. Profit margin on sales is a volume-oriented assessment.

_____ _✓_ 6. Marketing audits apply only to profit-oriented organizations.

_____ _✓_ 7. Marketing audits always follow a precise procedure.

_____ _✓_ 8. The control process is a relatively minor part of marketing.

_____ _✓_ 9. A limited number of evaluative methods exist for measuring marketing performance.

_____ _✓_ 10. Most organizations select one best evaluative method to use in assessing marketing performance.

ANSWERS: Multiple Choice. 1. (E); 2. (C); 3. (B); 4. (B); 5. (C); 6. (E); 7. (C); 8. (B); 9. (E); 10. (D). True-False. 1. (T); 2. (F); 3. (T); 4. (F); 5. (F); 6. (F); 7. (F); 8. (F); 9. (F); 10. (F).

FINAL PRACTICE TEST

This final practice test is designed to provide reinforcement of the success of your studies and the adequacy of your preparation for exams covering the material in this chapter. Like the preliminary test, the final practice test consists of 20 questions focusing on materials covered in this chapter. However, the correct answers are reprinted on the last page of the MARKETING Mastery Guide.

A. MULTIPLE CHOICE. Choose the answer which best answers the question or best completes the sentence.

1. The marketing control model described in the text asks all of the following questions except:

   a) is performance satisfactory?
   b) is the implementation at fault?
   c) are the standards at fault?
   d) is the plan itself at fault?
   e) are the customer's actions at fault?

2. The PIMS study concluded that:

   a) market share and ROI are linked
   b) market share and ROI are negatively correlated
   c) market share and total sales are linked
   d) market share and total sales are negatively correlated
   e) none of the above

3. Basic financial statements:

   a) are very useful in marketing evaluation
   b) are not very useful in marketing evaluation, but very useful in control
   c) are very useful in both control and marketing evaluation
   d) are not very useful in either market evaluation or control
   e) none of the above

4. Possible breakdowns for sales analysis include:

   a) customer type
   b) product
   c) method of sale
   d) geographic area
   e) all of the above

5. All of the following factors can affect ROI calculations except:

   a) book value of assets
   b) market value of assets
   c) industry pricing structures
   d) industry concentration
   e) transfer pricing

6. A profit center is:

   a) any administrative unit whose contribution to corporate earnings can be measured
   b) is a company which earns a profit
   c) an area of the company which earns a profit
   d) both a and c
   e) all of the above

7. Which of the following ratios is volume-oriented?

   a) profit margin on sales
   b) inventory turnover
   c) rate of return on common equity
   d) rate of return on total assets
   e) all of the above

8. The significance of these ratios depends upon:

   a) industry averages
   b) company's past performance
   c) alternatives available
   d) all of the above
   e) none of the above

9. Which of the following is <u>not</u> one of the elements evaluated in the marketing audit?

   a) marketing goals
   b) marketing tactics
   c) marketing practices
   d) marketing history
   e) marketing policies

10. The following are all potential sources of auditors except:

   a) special marketing audit staffs
   b) regular corporate executives
   c) federal regulatory agencies
   d) outside marketing consultants
   e) all of the above are potential sources

B. TRUE-FALSE. In the space to the left of each statement check the appropriate line to indicate whether the statement is true or false.

True False

____ ____ 1. The key to effective control is keeping the variations within the control limits.

____ ____ 2. The experience curve indicates that higher market shares increase costs.

____ ____ 3. Financial statements are often too broad to be useful in marketing evaluation and control.

____ ____ 4. The Iceberg Principle suggests that important evaluative information is often hidden by aggregate data.

____ ____ 5. Inventory turnover is a profitablility-oriented ratio.

____ ____ 6. The marketing audit goes beyond the normal control system.

____ ____ 7. The number of firms using marketing audits is expected to grow.

____ ____ 8. The real value of the marketing audit is revealed when the final report is presented.

True False

    ____   ____   9. The PIMS and BCG premises have been accepted by virtually all major U.S. firms.

    ____   ____ 10. Most marketing objectives and performance standards can be categorized as either volume-oriented or profitability-oriented.

PART III.

MARKETING Assignments

This Part of the MARKETING Mastery Guide is designed to provide experiences in applying the marketing concepts discussed in class and in the text. The ability to apply learned concepts is the ultimate test of learning.

At least two assignments are included for each chapter. Some assignments represent short cases which you are asked to solve by utilizing marketing knowledge from the text. In other instances, the assignment involves local applications of marketing concepts from the college or university or the local community. Still other assignments will require the use of library materials for their completion.

These assignments are typically utilized by the instructor as homework designed to ensure that the students have understood the materials covered in class and in the text and that they are able to apply fundamental marketing concepts. To facilitate their use as assignments, each exercise contains space for recording the name of the student and the course, section, and professor.

Name *Susee Stone*   Course & Section *Sect. 7*

Instructor *Benno*   Time *8:30 MWF*

Chapter 1. THE MARKETING PROCESS

Assignment 1

Olde Frothingslosh

Pittsburgh Brewing was able to take a disc jockey's skit and convert it into a major marketing success. Back in the 1950s, a Pittsburgh disc jockey would use part of his show to satirize local personalities and happenings. One morning he created a British gentleman name Sir Reginald Frothingslosh who had been asked to develop "a new old ale, a pale, stale ale." The mythical brew was "Olde Frothingslosh," so light that "it floated on top of the foam. With the foam on the bottom, there were no more messy mustaches."

Pittsburgh Brewing, makers of Iron City beer, bought the disc jockey's rights in the pretend beverage and in 1957 began producing the Olde Frothingslosh label as a Christmas business gift. The idea caught on, and the firm began to market some of its Iron City beer under the Olde Frothingslosh label every Christmas. By 1959, sales had reached eighty thousand cases.

Originally, the disc jockey appeared on the label as Sir Reginald. Later ve sions included a medieval dame and gentleman spoofing a British ale and two unsteady British lions having a beer while hanging over a coat of arms. Then, in 1965, Pittsburgh Brewing found a three hundred pound go-go dancer known as "The Blonde Bomber." Renamed "Miss Olde Frothlingslosh," she began to make promotional visits to Pittsburgh taverns, where she would autograph the Olde Frothlingslosh calendar and photographs that the firm used as promotional items.

Today, beer can collecting is a popular hobby, and Olde Frothlingslosh is a must in any collection. In fact, Pittsburgh Brewing now produces it year round. The company also sells the popular promotional calendars it once gave away, and it has made available a bountiful supply of empty Olde Frothlingslosh cans--at one dollar each. The three hundred pound Miss Olde Frothlingslosh is still a major part of the brewery's promotional efforts.

Pittsburgh Brewing's marketing manager, Dan McCann, has explained the firm's marketing strategy this way: "It was a unique thing for us to do, and it gives us a chance to have people sample our regular product." McCann also has noted that the popularity of Olde Frothlingslosh helps keep Pittsburghers from switching to a national brand and that it was a major asset in introducing the company's new light beer, Sierra.*

Directions. In the space below explain how Pittsburgh Brewing creates each type of utility with its products.

Time- *Christmas time gift giving*

Place- *Novelty store + later more stores*

Ownership- *available*

*Adapted from "Pittsburgh Brewing Co.'s Olde Frothingslosh May Have the Foam at the Bottom, But Its Profits Are in the Top: A Heady Story," Sales & Marketing Management, April 3, 1978, pp. 49ff. Reprinted by permission from Sales & Marketing Management magazine. Copyright 1978.

Describe the likely market target for Olde Frothingslosh.

_The Business world for gag gifts—
mustache wearers, beer drinkers._

Relate the elements of the marketing mix to the Olde Frothlingslosh example.

a. _Pricing_
_Pricing worked - people were probably
willing to pay a bit more for a gag gift._

b. _Product_
_Beer — there own - brought others
awareness to them. The product
was very unique._

c. _Promotion_
_Something besides beer to laugh at
ex. fat lady, collector's bottles,
business world as gifts_

d. _Distribution_
_By having to go somewhere special
to get it, made it more valuable._

284

Name _____   Course & Section _____

Instructor _____   Time _____

Assignment 2

AT&T Discovers Marketing

Many consumers do not realize that their monthly telephone bill accounts for less than half of the Bell System's business. AT&T's revenues are in excess of $36 billion, but only 43 percent comes from residential rates. Businesses account for 50 percent, directory advertising for 4 percent, and coin phones for 3 percent. For many years, AT&T was in the position of a regulated monopoly. But today the firm finds itself in a highly competitive communications market, particularly for its business customers. This situation is vastly different from when the company prided itself on good service but was never threatened by competition.

Competition took a $700 million chunk of the telephone market from AT&T in 1977 alone. The PBX (switchboard) market has witnessed some sizable defections to foreign competitors. And even AT&T's private line customers have been buying specialized equipment provided by other firms. AT&T has good reason to fear firms like IBM, whose satellite business systems could skip the Bell network entirely in solving business communications problems.

Now AT&T is fighting back. The firm that long ignored marketing because it was protected by its monopolistic position has become an aggressive marketer. Six years ago, board chairman John De Butts announced that his goal was to "develop a marketing capability to match our technological capability."

The communications giant has since brought in marketing personnel from outside AT&T ranks and has set up a comprehensive sales program called the Bell Marketing System (BMS). Bell's 8,500 account executives (sales personnel) now specialize in the particular industries of their customers. They are backed by a substantial corps of technical support personnel, and they are evaluated on the basis of revenue performance.

As expected, many Bell employees still prefer to do things as they did in the monopolistic past. Perhaps AT&T's chief marketer, executive vice-president Kenneth J. Whelan, put it best: "It took us over 100 years before we discovered we could sell telephones in a color other than black." But times are changing at AT&T as Ma Bell enters the marketing era.*

After reading Chapter 1, how would you state the moral of this story?

Companys have to change in reaction
to their environment - here, to competition
It's a current changeover from production
to consumer oriented operations

*Information from Thayer C. Taylor, "Can Ma Bell End Its Marketing Hangup?" Sales & Marketing Management, May 1978, pp. 49-52, 54, 56.

Describe the market target for AT&T.

They are targeting at large corporations
to figure out ___ phone systems
within. They want to get more
of their business back & become
more specialized

Marketing decisions--including those made by AT&T--take place in a dynamic
environment involving variables over which the marketing executive has little
control. In the space below, list each environmental variable and include
an example relevant to AT&T.

a. ___Legal -___

b. ___Economic -___
AT&T was loosing money to ⊖ competitors
& therefore, business

c. ___Societal-___
It wasn't residents who were the main
customers anymore - It was business

d. ___Competetive -___
The whole reason for "marketing emphasis"
for the first time. AT&T was losing its
monopoly & had to urn over theirscustomers.

Name _____   Course & Section _____

Instructor _____   Time _____

Chapter 2. THE ENVIRONMENT FOR MARKETING DECISIONS

Assignment 1

Write a brief statement on how inflation has impacted your personal
consumption patterns.

_____   _____

_____   _____

_____   _____

_____   _____

_____   _____

_____   _____

Assignment 2

Contrast the impact of inflation on yourself with the likely impact on
individuals in the following categories:

a. young married couples with no children

b. young married couples with two children under ten

c. fixed income households

Assignment 3

a. Give two examples of industries that are severely handicapped by recent
    inflation rates.

_____   _____

_____   _____

_____   _____

_____   _____

b. Give two examples of industries or product categories that have bene-
    fitted from recent rates of inflation.

_____

_____

Assignment 4

Identify the consumer protection agencies that are currently operating in
your community or state. In the space below, list each agency and include
a brief description of their activities.

_____
_____
_____
_____
_____
_____
_____
_____
_____
_____
_____
_____
_____
_____
_____
_____
_____
_____
_____
_____
_____
_____
_____
_____
_____

Chapter 3. CONSUMER BEHAVIOR: BASIC CONCEPTS

Assignment 1

In the space below, list each stage in Maslow's needs hierarchy. Then list an example of a current advertising campaign in which that specific need is utilized.

a. _____

    Example:

b. _____

    Example:

c. _____

    Example:

d. _____

    Example:

e. _____

    Example:

Assignment 2

Market growth for any organization typically requires attitude change. In the space below, list the components of an attitude and indicate how each component might be utilized in producing attitude change.

a. _____

b. _____

c. _____

Assignment 3

Identify and give an example of each component in the learning process.

a. _____

   Example:

b. _____

   Example:

c. _____

   Example:

d. _____

   Example:

Name _____   Course & Section _____

Instructor _____   Time _____

Chapter 4.   CONSUMER BEHAVIOR: ENVIRONMENTAL INFLUENCES AND THE
CONSUMER DECISION PROCESS

Assignment 1

Choosing a College for Jeff Nixon

Jeff Nixon, a senior at Memorial High School, faces the dilemma of choosing a college. He is a good student and has made all-state (second team) as a defensive end. His father is a graduate of a well-known western university and would like to see Jeff go there. Two schools in his state (including one in his home town) have offered him football scholarships. One has a great football tradition, which includes one of the nation's longest winning streaks. Jeff's best girl friend has decided to live at home and go to the local university, while his best friend on the team has decided to sign with an Atlantic Coast Conference university several hundred miles away. Jeff applied to all of these schools and has been accepted. He needs financial aid and plans to become an engineer.

Jeff accepts the football tender at the school in his state which had such a fine reputation during the 1960s. In addition, the university has a strong engineering curriculum. The problem, though, is that he has no friends there and has no real desire to join one of the social groups, the apparent key to popularity.

Directions. Using the model of the consumer decision process in Figure 4.5, relate what must have happened during and after this decision. Make any assumptions that are necessary.

Assignment 2

What impact is each of the following factors likely to have on the relative influence of the wife in household decision making? Defend your answer.

a. employment status of wife

b. rural vs. urban location

c. social class

d. number of years married

Assignment 3

Explain the concept of cognitive dissonance as it might apply in a retail setting.

Under what conditions is cognitive dissonance most likely to occur?

Make several specific recommendations for reducing dissonance.

Name _____   Course & Section _____

Instructor _____   Time _____

Chapter 5. MARKETING PLANNING AND FORECASTING

Assignment 1

The Boston Consulting Group has made a number of important contributions to
marketing planning. The BCG matrix contains a number of quadrants for various
products in a firm's "portfolio." In the space below, identify each of these
quadrants, provide an example of a product that appears to be in this
quadrant, and advice the company concerning the product.

Quadrant 1. _____

_____

_____

_____

_____

_____

Quadrant 2. _____

_____

_____

_____

_____

_____

Quadrant 3. _____

_____

_____

_____

_____

_____

Quadrant 4. _____

_____

_____

_____

_____

_____

_____

Assignment 2

Total sales for the organization during the past five years are shown below.

Year	Sales
Last Year	$ 28,500,000
Two Years Ago	23,500,000
Three Years Ago	21,500,000
Four Years Ago	18,500,000
Five Years Ago	15,500,000

Growth in total industry sales are expected to remain constant for the coming year. In the space below, utilize the above data to forecast company sales for the coming year. Indicate the assumptions you have made in developing your forecast.

Name _____   Course & Section _____ _____ ___

Instructor _____   Time _____

Chapter 6. MARKET SEGMENTATION

Assignment 1

a. Briefly explain the bases for the superiority of family life cycle
    analysis over traditional demographic variables as a predictor variable
    in market segmentation.

    _____

    _____

    _____

    _____

b. Identify each stage of the family life cycle and give an example of a
    product or firm for which each stage represents an important market
    segment.

    _____

    _____

    _____

    _____

    _____

    _____

    _____

    _____

    _____

    _____

    _____

    _____

    _____

    _____

    _____

    _____

    _____

    _____

Assignment 2

In the space below, list the generalizations referred to as *Engel's Laws*.

_____
_____
_____
_____
_____
_____

Which of the above laws are <u>not</u> supported by statistical evidence?

_____
_____
_____
_____
_____
_____

Assignment 3

What impact would you expect the expected growth in the two age groups to have on the current geographic population shifts?

_____
_____
_____
_____
_____
_____
_____
_____
_____
_____

Chapter 7. MARKET SEGMENTATION STRATEGY

Assignment 1

Capri Carpets

Capri Carpets, a 22-year-old firm located in eastern Wisconsin, has been managed since its inception by its founder, Harold Wakestein. Wakestein had announced at the last stockholders' meeting his plans to assume the position of chairman of the eight-member board of directors and to promote Gary Kintner as Capri's second president. Kintner, 32, has been employed with Capri for the past eight years since his graduation from the School of Business Administration at the University of Wisconsin.

Until now, Capri has marketed its entire output of carpet as an industrial product to the building industry for use in new-home construction and in commercial buildings. Kintner's first major decision as company president was to ask his marketing staff to evaluate the possibility of entering the consumer goods market.

Directions. In the space below, show how market target decision analysis can assist Capri Carpets in analyzing the consumer market for carpet.

Assignment 2

Suggest a market segmentation base for each of the following products. Defend your suggestions.

a. Irish Spring soap.   Base: _____

_____

_____

_____

_____

b. Toro Snowblower.   Base: _____

_____

_____

_____

_____

c. Interval Ownership in a Condominium
    in Snowmass, Colorado   Base: _____

_____

_____

_____

_____

d. J.R. Ewing's Private Stock (new
    brand of beer by Pearl Brewing Co.)   Base: _____

_____

_____

_____

_____

e. Space Invaders video game   Base: _____

_____

_____

_____

_____

Chapter 8. COLLECTING MARKETING INFORMATION: THE ROLE OF

MARKETING RESEARCH

Assignment 1

Marketing a New Product

Toni Pruden, Marketing Vice President of Ajax Chemical Company, first learned of the new product called *Whisker-Off* when she was invited to lunch by the product's inventor and holder of the patent rights. Exclusive rights for production and marketing of the new discovery were offered to Ajax for a royalty based upon a percentage of Whisker-Off sales.

Whisker-Off is a pink foam in an aerosol can (closely resembling that of shaving cream) that dissolves a man's beard in thirty seconds. All the purchaser has to do is to apply the cream, wait thirty seconds, and wash it off. No razor, blades, or other shaving implements are necessary. The product is similar to one used by women for their legs. A month's supply of Whisker-Off should retail for approximately the same price as the total expenditures for one month's supply of blades, shaving cream, and after-shave lotion. Whisker-Off contains a built-in after-shave lotion.

Pruden requested an immediate product test in three cities on the East Coast, in the Midwest, and on the West Coast. Consumer acceptance was favorable and appeared to increase with length of product exposure. Pruden then requested her marketing research department to began a subscription to the Neilsen research service to obtain information on retail sales in food and drug stores before considering a national launch for the proposed new product.

Directions Based upon discussion in this chapter, relate information needs of the Ajax Chemical Company and the stages in the management process for Pruden. Specify the types of information collected (and suggest other that could have been collected)for each stage in the process.

Assignment 2

Utilize secondary sources to collect the following information. In each instance, show the source used in obtaining the information.

a. total expenditures for food in Columbus, Ohio last year

_____

Source: _____

_____

b. Ford Motor Company earnings last quarter

_____

Source: _____

c. total U.S. oil imports for a recent month

_____

Source: _____

_____

d. number of households earning more than $25,000 in Los Angeles

_____

Source: _____

_____

e. average starting salaries for business school graduates last year

_____

Source: _____

_____

f. population change for Alaska: 1970-1980

_____

Source: _____

_____

Name _____   Course & Section _____

Instructor _____   Time _____

Chapter 9.   PRODUCT STRATEGY

Assignment 1

The ability to classify hundreds of thousands of consumer goods into a small
number of categories results considerable knowledge of appropriate decisions
concerning the remaining variables of the marketing mix.   In the space below,
identify each of the consumer goods categories and describe the impact of such
classification on the remaining marketing mix variables.

CONSUMER GOOD CATEGORY	CHANNEL LENGTH	PRICE	NUMBER OF RETAIL OUTLETS	PROMOTION
1. _____				
2. _____				
3. _____				

Assignment 2

Distinguish between the diffusion process and the adoption process.

_____

_____

_____

_____

_____

_____

_____

Assignment 3

The relative time period involved for an individual to progress through each stage in the adoption process is determined by five factors. In the space below, identify each of these factors and illustrate how a marketer might utilize each factor in attempting to accelerating the adoption rate for a product or service.

a. _____

_____

_____

b. _____

_____

_____

c. _____

_____

_____

d. _____

_____

_____

e. _____

_____

_____

Assignment 4

A number of factors are involved in the broader marketing conception of the term *product*. In the space below, identify each factor or component and illustrate the importance of each by including an example of a product or service whose overall consumer image is affected by this component.

_____

_____

_____

_____

_____

_____

_____

_____

Name _____   Course & Section _____

Instructor _____   Time _____

Chapter 10. PRODUCT MANAGEMENT DECISIONS

Assignment 1

American Patent Company

Four years ago three young Washington attorneys formed a company with a unique function: promoting patent exchanges between corporations. Their specialty was searching through corporation files for idle patents and setting up licensing agreements with other companies interested in using the dormant patents. Last January, American Patent Company went out of the patent brokerage business. The reason: one of the attorneys had uncovered a patent that looked so promising that APC decided to market the product itself.

The product was a new and unusual plastic called Plyon. On first inspection, Plyon looks and behaves just like other plastics. It is a hard, transparent material that can be cut, ground, or molded into a variety of shapes. Place it in water or an aqueous solution, however, and it beco es soft and pliable. Allow it to dry, and it reverts to its former hard state. Plyon is described as inert and fully compatible with human tissue; it is permeable to water; it is highly elastic when wet, but remains strong and holds its shape.

The attorneys are particularly interested in the product's possibilities as a denture liner, a large market target since more than 600,000 new dentures are reportedly sold each year. Dentures lined with Plyon offer two major advantages over ordinary dental plates: greater comfort and vastly increased adhesion. The new plastic does away with the need for pastes, pads, and other devices to keep plates in place. The attorneys feel that they can contract production of the liner plastic at a price of $3.75 for a 2-ounce tube, enough to line three dentures.

Directions. Utilize the steps in the new-product development process to outline a program for deciding whether the product should be marketed by APC.

_____

_____

_____

_____

_____

_____

_____

_____

_____

_____

_____

_____

_____

_____

_____

_____

_____

_____

_____

_____

_____

_____

Assignment 2

Distinguish among the following. Include an example of each.

a. Brands, Brand Names, and Trademarks

b. Generic Brands and Generic Products

c. National Brands and Private Brands

d. Family Brands and Individual Brands

Chapter 11.   INDUSTRIAL PRODUCTS

Assignment 1

Many of the small and medium-sized machine shops serving Detroit's automobile industry experienced a disastrous year in 1980. Relate this situation to specific characteristics of the industrial goods market described in this chapter.

Assignment 2

Classify the following products into the appropriate industrial goods category. Briefly explain your choices for each product.

a.   calculators: _____

b.   land   _____

c.   light bulbs   _____

d.   cotton   _____

e.   paper towels   _____

f. polyester   _____

g. tires   _____

Assignment 3

Identify the major differences likely to exist between a marketing program
designed for consumer goods and a program for industrial products.

_____

_____

_____

_____

_____

_____

_____

_____

_____

_____

_____

_____

_____

_____

_____

_____

_____

_____

_____

_____

_____

_____

_____

Name _____   Course & Section _____

Instructor _____   Time _____

Chapter 12.   SERVICES

Assignment 1

In the space below, outline a marketing mix for a suntanning salon.
Justify your decisions.

Assignment 2

Refer to U.S. Government statistics in your library to determine the employment statistics showing the relative distribution of the labor force among the agricultural, manufacturing, and service industries. Relate your findings to the Colin Clark hypothesis outlined in the chapter.

Assignment 3

In the space below, draw a goods-service continuum. Include at least four examples not mentioned in the text at the appropriate point on the continuum.

Categorize your four examples utilizing the bases described in Figure 12.2.

Name _____   Course & Section _____

Instructor _____   Time _____

Chapter 14. MANAGING THE PRICING FUNCTION

Assignment 1

Locate an example of a price quotation and attach it to the box below.

Relate the above quotation to the appropriate material in this chapter.

Assignment 2

Indicate the most appropriate new-pricing strategy for each of the following products. Defend your answer in each instance.

a. <u>tickets for new professional sports franchise in Baltimore</u>

b. <u>Amana combination microwave/convection oven</u>

c. <u>vitamin-enriched toothpaste</u>

d. <u>designer track shoes</u>

e. mail-order market books <u>How to Pick Up Girls!</u> and <u>How to Pick Up Guys!</u>

Name _____   Course & Section _____ _____

Instructor _____   Time _____

Chapter 15. CHANNEL STRATEGY

Assignment 1

A number of factors influence the choice of the most appropriate marketing
channel or channels to utilize in marketing consumer and industrial goods.
Included are factors as varied as: size of the product line; perishability;
geographic location of the market target; need for control over the
marketing channel; need for promotion to channel members; customer service
needs; unit value; technical complexity; order size; product resources; and
customer type.

Directions. Categorize these factors based upon whether they represent
characteristics of (1) the consumer; (2) the product; (3) the manufacturer;
or (4) an environmental factor. Then give an example of precisely how each
factor affects channel choice.

_____

_____

_____

_____

_____

_____

_____

_____

_____

_____

_____

_____

_____

_____

_____

_____

_____

_____

_____

_____

_____

_____

Assignment 2

In the space below, identify the three degrees of intensity of marketing coverage. Then indicate the typical marketing mix characteristics associated with each by writing the appropriate descriptions in the boxes to the right.

INTENSITY OF MARKET COVERAGE	TYPE OF CONSUMER GOOD	TYPE OF INDUSTRIAL GOOD	PRICE TENDS TO BE:	CHANNEL LENGTH	BURDEN OF PROMOTION
1. _____					
2. _____					
3. _____					

Assignment 3

Three types of vertical marketing systems are listed below. For each type, identify the likely channel captain and give an example of a channel captain.

1. Corporate

2. Administered

3. Contractual

    a. Wholesaler Sponsored Voluntary Chain

    b. Retail Cooperative

    c. Franchise System

Name _____   Course & Section _____

Instructor _____   Time _____

Chapter 16.   WHOLESALING

Assignment 1

Although more than 350,000 wholesaling establishments are currently operating
in the United States, it is possible to reduce this number to meaningful size
by a classification system based upon two characteristics. In the space
below, identify these two characteristics. Next, list the major categories
of wholesaling middlemen in each class. Finally, provide an example of a
type of wholesale intermediary for each category.

a. _____

   1. _____

      Example: _____

   2. _____

      Example: _____

   3. _____

      Example: _____

b. _____

   1. _____

      Example: _____

   2. _____

      Example: _____

Assignment 2

During the past 50 years, the relative importance of different types of wholesaling middlemen has changed considerably. The three major types of wholesaling middlemen are listed below. Indicate the change in their percentages of total sales at the wholesale level since 1929 in the box to the right with the appropriate response from the list below:

Large Increase:	greater than 8% growth in overall share of total
Small Increase:	growth in overall market share of less than 8%
Small Decrease:	decline in overall market share of less than 8%
Large decrease	decline in overall market share of more than 8%

TYPE	CHANGE SINCE 1929
MERCHANT WHOLESALER	
MANUFACTURERS' SALES OFFICES AND BRANCHES	
AGENTS AND BROKERS	

Assignment 3

Complete the following table.

TYPE OF WHOLESALING MIDDLEMAN	OPERATING EXPENSE RATIO		
	HIGH (over 10%)	MEDIUM (5-10%)	LOW (under 5%)
Full-function merchant wholesaler			
Cash-and-carry wholesaler			
Truck wholesaler			
Drop Shipper			
Broker			
Manufacturers' agent			

316

Name _____   Course & Section _____

Instructor _____   Time _____

Chapter 17. RETAILING

Assignment 1

The matrix of consumer behavior below utilizes a classification of both
retailers and products as consumer, shopping, or specialty to produce nine
cells. For each cell, insert the name of a local product-retailer combination.

	STORES		
GOODS	Convenience	Shopping	Specialty
Convenience			
Shopping			
Specialty			

Assignment 2

Chapter 17 classifies the nation's two million retailing operations by utilizing five characteristics or bases. List each of the five bases below and indicate by inserting two local examples precisely how the characteristics are employed in categorizing retailers.

a. _____

b. _____

c. _____

d. _____

e. _____

Chapter 18. MANAGEMENT OF PHYSICAL DISTRIBUTION

Assignment 1

Determine the economic order quantity for the following situation:

A firm estimates its sales for the coming year will be 18,000 units with inventory carrying costs at 18 percent. The cost for placing orders is estimated to be $6.50 per order. Cost per unit estimates are $10.50

Assignment 2

A firm has calculated the cost of placing orders at $5.10 per order. The annual cost of carrying the product in inventory is estimated to be 25 percent. Cost per unit estimates for the next twelve months are $14.90. Annual usage rates are estimated to be 5,900.

Calculate the economic order quantity.

The matrix below lists six factors used in comparing alternative modes of transporation. For each of the ten products listed in Column 1, indicate the importance of each factor by ranking it from 1 (most important) to 5 (least important). Based upon your evaluation of each of the six factors, indicate the most appropriate transport mode in the final column.

Product	Speed	Dependability in Meeting Schedules	Cost	Shipment Frequency	Availability in Different Locations	Flexibility in Handling Products	MOST APPROPRIATE TRANSPORT MODE
1. Tonka Toys							
2. coal							
3. newly-built army tanks							
4. hats							
5. natural gas							
6. electronic components							
7. jewelry							
8. plywood							
9. apples							
10. furniture							

Name _____   Course & Section _____

Instructor _____   Time _____

Chapter 19. PROMOTION: A CONCEPTUAL FOUNDATION

Assignment 1

In recent years, Dallas-based Dr. Peper has utilized an advertising
campaign designed around the theme "Be a Pepper!" In the space below,
make specific recommendations for assessing the effectiveness of the
campaign.

Assignment 2

Develop a hypothetical promotional budget for the following products and
firms. Use percentage allocations to the various promotion variables;
e.g., 50 percent to personal selling, 40 percent to advertising, 10 percent
to public relations. Defend your proposed budgets.

a. manufacturer of hot tubs, spas, and saunas

b. New York Life Insurance Company

c. American Airlines

d. U-Haul Truck and Trailer Rentals

e. Philadelphia Phillies Baseball Club

Name _____   Course & Section _____

Instructor _____   Time _____

Chapter 20.   PROMOTIONAL STRATEGY: ADVERTISING, SALES PROMOTION, PUBLIC
RELATIONS, AND PUBLICITY

Assignment 1

Design an advertising campaign for your college or university in which the
emphasis is on attracting non-traditional students (those outside the 18-to-
22 age bracket).

Assignment 2

In the space below, indicate with a check those advertising media most appropriate for the firm listed at the left. Place two checks in the relevant boxes to indicate media to receive strong emphasis.

FIRM	MEDIA				
	Magazines	Newspapers	Television	Radio	Outdoor
Mobil					
General, Motors					
Sears, Roebuck					
AT&T					
Pepsi Cola					
Holiday Inn					
American Tobacco					

Assignment 3

Outdoor advertising represents a controversial medium with considerable regulation and a somewhat negative image as a so-called "contributor to visual pollution." Develop a positive argument for the existence of outdoor advertising.

Name _____   Course & Section _____

Instructor _____ ____ ____   Time _____

Chapter 21. PROMOTIONAL STRATEGY: PERSONAL SELLING AND SALES MANAGEMENT

Assignment 1

The text discusses a number of steps in the sales process. Identify each
step in the process and utilize each step in developing a sales presentation
for a liability and property damage insurance program for apartment
dwellers.

Assignment 2

Develop a prospecting plan for a sales presentation for custom-made hairpieces for men.

Name _____   Course & Section _____

Instructor _____   Time _____

Chapter 22.   INTERNATIONAL MARKETING

<u>Assignment 1</u>

Develop pro and con arguments for restricting Japanese auto imports.

a.   <u>Arguments in Favor of Japanese Auto Import Restrictions:</u>

b.   <u>Arguments Against Restricting Japanese Auto Imports:</u>

Assignment 2

Identify each of the levels of involvement in international marketing. Illustrate each level with an appropriate example of a product or firm.

a. _____

    Example: _____

b. _____

    Example _____

c. _____

    Example _____

d. _____

    Example _____

e. _____

    Example _____

Assignment 3

List five examples (each from a different industry) of products marketed by foreign companies in the United States. Assess the relative importance of each listed product in its particular market.

Chapter 23. MARKETING IN NONPROFIT SETTINGS

Assignment 1

Prepare a brief analysis of the marketing strategies used by a major
candidate for President, governor, or senator in the 1980 general
election. How did they budget their promotional expenditures? Allocate
their campaign time? Develop issues?

Assignment 2

Prepare a brief, step-by-step plan to market your college or university to prospective students. Consider all elements of the marketing mix.

Name _____ Course & Section _____

Instructor _____ Time _____

Chapter 24. MARKETING AND SOCIETY

Assignment 1

Many people are calling for a reduction in environmental regulations on energy-producing industries. Relate this to the text discussions concerning the evolution of public issues facing marketers.

<u>Assignment 2</u>

Assume that you are a sales manager for a small manufacturing firm.
You would like to develop a statement on ethical conduct for your
sales force. How would you word that statement?

Name _____   Course & Section _____

Instructor _____   Time _____

Chapter 25. EVALUATION AND CONTROL

Assignment 1

Calculate the return on investment (ROI) for a firm that has invested
$500,000 in order to generate $1 million in sales and $50,000 in profits.
Show your calculations.

Assignment 2

Assume that a firm has earned $3 million (after taxes) on $30 million in
sales. The firm has $20 million in assets, including an inventory of $5
million. Stockholders' equity is $10 million.

a. What is the rate of return on common equity?

b. What is the rate of return on total assets?

c. What is the profit margin on sales?

d. What is the inventory turnover rate?

<u>Assignment 3</u>

Identify the steps involved in conducting a marketing audit.

Critically evaluate the available alternatives concerning the individuals who will actually conduct the audit.

What special problems would be faced by nonprofit organizations in conducting a marketing audit? How might they be minimized?

ANSWERS TO FINAL PRACTICE TEST QUESTIONS

Chapter 1.
  Multiple Choice: 1. (C); 2. (D); 3. (E); 4. (E); 5. (A);
                            6. (B); 7. (B); 8. (A); 9. (C); 10. (B).
  True-False: 1. (T); 2. (F); 3. (F); 4. (F); 5. (F);
                            6. (F); 7. (F); 8. (T); 9. (F); 10. (T).

Chapter 2.
  Multiple Choice: 1. (E); 2. (A); 3. (B); 4. (B); 5. (E);
                            6. (E); 7. (C); 8. (E); 9. (B); 10. (D).
  True-False: 1. (F); 2. (T); 3. (F); 4. (T); 5. (T);
                            6. (T); 7. (F); 8. (T); 9. (F); 10. (F).

Chapter 3.
  Multiple Choice: 1. (D); 2. (A); 3. (A); 4. (B); 5. (A);
                            6. (B); 7. (B); 8. (B); 9. (A); 10. (C).
  True-False: 1. (F); 2. (T); 3. (F); 4. (T); 5. (F);
                            6. (T); 7. (F); 8. (F); 9. (T); 10. (F).

Chapter 4.
  Multiple Choice: 1. (E); 2. (D); 3. (D); 4. (E); 5. (D);
                            6. (E); 7. (C); 8. (E); 9. (E); 10. (D).
  True-False: 1. (F); 2. (F); 3. (F); 4. (F); 5. (F);
                            6. (T); 7. (F); 8. (F); 9. (T); 10. (T).

Chapter 5.
  Multiple Choice: 1. (E); 2. (B); 3. (E); 4. (B); 5. (C);
                            6. (B); 7. (A); 8. (E); 9. (C); 10. (B).
  True-False: 1. (F); 2. (F); 3. (T); 4. (F); 5. (T);
                            6. (F); 7. (T); 8. (F); 9. (T); 10. (T).

Chapter 6.
  Multiple Choice: 1. (E); 2. (E); 3. (E); 4. (D); 5. (D);
                            6. (D); 7. (D); 8. (D); 9. (D); 10. (E).
  True-False: 1. (T); 2. (T); 3. (F); 4. (T); 5. (T).
                            6. (T); 7. (T); 8. (T); 9. (F); 10. (T).

Chapter 7.
  Multiple Choice: 1. (B); 2. (D); 3. (E); 4. (D); 5. (E);
                            6. (B); 7. (E); 8. (C); 9. (A); 10. (D).
  True-False: 1. (F); 2. (T); 3. (F); 4. (T); 5. (F);
                            6. (F); 7. (F); 8. (T); 9. (T); 10. (F).

Chapter 8.
  Multiple Choice: 1. (E); 2. (B); 3. (D); 4. (D); 5. (C);
                            6. (D); 7. (E); 8. (E); 9. (B); 10. (C).
  True-False: 1. (T); 2. (F); 3. (T); 4. (T); 5. (F);
                            6. (T); 7. (T); 8. (F); 9. (T); 10. (T).

Chapter 9.
    Multiple Choice: 1. (C); 2. (A); 3. (E); 4. (E); 5. (B);
                       6. (B); 7. (A); 8. (A); 9. (E); 10. (C).
    True-False: 1. (F); 2. (T); 3. (F); 4. (F); 5. (F);
                       6. (F); 7. (F); 8. (T); 9. (F); 10. (F).

Chapter 10.
    Multiple Choice: 1. (D); 2. (B); 3. (D); 4. (E); 5. (E);
                       6. (C); 7. (E); 8. (A); 9. (E); 10. (E).
    True-False: 1. (T); 2. (F); 3. (T); 4. (T); 5. (T);
                       6. (T); 7. (T); 8. (F); 9. (T); 10. (T).

Chapter 11.
    Multiple Choice: 1. (B); 2. (E); 3. (B); 4. (A); 5. (E);
                       6. (A); 7. (C); 8. (C); 9. (A); 10. (D).
    True-False: 1. (F); 2. (T); 3. (T); 4. (F); 5. (F);
                       6. (F); 7. (F); 8. (F); 9. (T); 10. (T).

Chapter 12.
    Multiple Choice: 1. (E); 2. (B); 3. (E); 4. (D); 5. (A);
                       6. (B); 7. (D); 8. (C); 9. (E); 10. (E);
    True-False: 1. (T); 2. (T); 3. (T); 4. (T); 5. (F);
                       6. (F); 7. (F); 8. (T); 9. (T); 10. (T).

Chapter 13.
    Multiple Choice: 1. (E); 2. (D); 3. (B); 4. (D); 5. (D);
                       6. (B); 7. (A); 8. (A); 9. (E); 10. (E).
    True-False: 1. (T); 2. (T); 3. (F); 4. (F); 5. (F);
                       6. (T); 7. (T); 8. (T); 9. (T); 10. (T).

Chapter 14.
    Multiple Choice: 1. (E); 2. (D); 3. (E); 4. (D); 5. (B);
                       6. (A); 7. (C); 8. (B); 9. (E); 10. (A).
    True-False: 1. (F); 2. (T); 3. (F); 4. (T); 5. (T);
                       6. (T); 7. (F); 8. (T); 9. (T); 10. (F).

Chapter 15.
    Multiple Choice: 1. (E); 2. (C); 3. (A); 4. (E); 5. (B);
                       6. (D); 7. (C); 8. (A); 9. (A); 10. (C).
    True-False: 1. (F); 2. (F); 3. (T); 4. (F); 5. (T);
                       6. (F); 7. (T); 8. (T); 9. (F); 10. (T).

Chapter 16.
    Multiple Choice: 1. (B); 2. (D); 3. (C); 4. (A); 5. (B);
                       6. (A); 7. (E); 8. (A); 9. (C); 10. (E).
    True-False: 1. (T); 2. (T); 3. (F); 4. (T); 5. (F);
                       6. (T); 7. (T); 8. (T); 9. (F); 10. (F).

ANSWERS TO FINAL PRACTICE TEST QUESTIONS

Chapter 17.
    Multiple Choice: 1. (C); 2. (D); 3. (E); 4. (B); 5. (D);
                           6. (D); 7. (B); 8. (E); 9. (E); 10. (D).
    True-False: 1. (F); 2. (F); 3. (T); 4. (F); 5. (F);
                           6. (F); 7. (F); 8. (T); 9. (F); 10. (T).

Chapter 18.
    Multiple Choice: 1. (B); 2. (E); 3. (D); 4. (B); 5. (A);
                           6. (C); 7. (A); 8. (D); 9. (D); 10. (D).
    True-False: 1. (T); 2. (F); 3. (T); 4. (F); 5. (F);
                           6. (T); 7. (T); 8. (T); 9. (F); 10. (T).

Chapter 19.
    Multiple Choice: 1. (B); 2. (B); 3. (D); 4. (E); 5. (B);
                           6. (B); 7. (E); 8. (D); 9. (C); 10. (B);
    True-False: 1. (T); 2. (F); 3. (F); 4. (T); 5. (F);
                           6. (T); 7. (T); 8. (F); 9. (T); 10. (T).

Chapter 20.
    Multiple Choice: 1. (D); 2. (A); 3. (C); 4. (A); 5. (E);
                           6. (C); 7. (A); 8. (B); 9. (D); 10. (B).
    True-False: 1. (T); 2. (F); 3. (T); 4. (T); 5. (F);
                           6. (F); 7. (T); 8. (F); 9. (T); 10. (T).

Chapter 21.
    Multiple Choice: 1. (E); 2. (E); 3. (B); 4. (E); 5. (A);
                           6. (C); 7. (D); 8. (A); 9. (B); 10. (D).
    True-False: 1. (T); 2. (F); 3. (T); 4. (F); 5. (F);
                           6. (T); 7. (T); 8. (F); 9. (F); 10. (F).

Chapter 22.
    Multiple Choice: 1. (E); 2. (B); 3. (C); 4. (E); 5. (A);
                           6. (A); 7. (C); 8. (E); 9. (B); 10. (E).
    True-False: 1. (F); 2. (T); 3. (T); 4. (F); 5. (T);
                           6. (F); 7. (F); 8. (T); 9. (F); 10. (T).

Chapter 23.
    Multiple Choice: 1. (E); 2. (B); 3. (B); 4. (E); 5. (A);
                           6. (E); 7. (C); 8. (B); 9. (C); 10. (D).
    True-False: 1. (F); 2. (T); 3. (F); 4. (T); 5. (F);
                           6. (F); 7. (T); 8. (T); 9. (F); 10. (F).

Chapter 24.
    Multiple Choice: 1. (E); 2. (A); 3. (B); 4. (D); 5. (B);
                           6. (B); 7. (D); 8. (C); 9. (E); 10. (B).
    True-False: 1. (F); 2. (F); 3. (T); 4. (F); 5. (F);
                           6. (F); 7. (F); 8. (F); 9. (F); 10. (F).

Chapter 25.
Multiple Choice: 1. (E); 2. (A); 3. (D); 4. (E); 5. (B);
                    6. (A); 7. (B); 8. (D); 9. (D); 10. (C).
True-False: 1. (T); 2. (F); 3. (T); 4. (T); 5. (F);
                    6. (T); 7. (T); 8. (F); 9. (F); 10. (T).